GWYNEDD

Oyster catchers on the coast of the Penhros Nature Reserve

THE NEW COUNTY SERIES

GWYNEDD

Ian Skidmore

ROBERT HALE · LONDON

© *Ian Skidmore 1986*
First published in Great Britain 1986

ISBN 0 7090 2638 2

Robert Hale Limited
Clerkenwell House
Clerkenwell Green
London EC1R 0HT

British Library Cataloguing in Publication Data

Skidmore, Ian
    Gwynedd.—(The New county series; v. 1)
    1. Gwynedd—History
    I. Title   II. Series
    942.9'2   DA740.G89

ISBN 0-7090-2638-2

Typeset in Palatino by
Derek Doyle & Associates, Mold, Clwyd
Printed in Great Britain by
St. Edmundsbury Press, Bury St. Edmunds, Suffolk
and bound by WBC Bookbinders Limited

• CONTENTS •

• ILLUSTRATIONS •

Plates

Line illustrations

Maps

Picture Credits

Roger Worsley: 1-3, 5-15, 17-40; RAF Valley: 4; Ed Povey: 16;
Ken Williams: 41, 52-4; Gwynedd Archives: 42-8, 55; George
Hedges: 49; Wales Tourist Board: 50-1; and map on page 54
reproduced by permission of the Director, British Geological
Survey (NERC).

• ACKNOWLEDGEMENTS •

My thanks are due to Dr Margaret Wood, the eminent geologist, whose pioneer work in pre-dating Anglesey's birth and fascinating field courses gives 'tongues to the very rocks'.

To my ever-patient wife, Celia, for editing, anglicizing, inspiring and, most of all, typing this book.

To my broadcasting colleague Roger Worsley, for the stunning photographs.

To Bryn Parry, a prince among archivists, and his staff, including Kathleen Hughes, who generously shared the Gwynedd archive.

And to everyone who reads the result.

• INTRODUCTION •

Few Welsh counties are as lovely as Gwynedd; none exceeds it in the writers and painters it has attracted since it was first 'discovered' by the painter Turner in the eighteenth century.

On the Great Orme at Llandudno you can stand on the turf where Matthew Arnold stood and conceived his essay on the Study of Celtic Literature with its sonorous opening paragraph: 'Over the mouth of the Conway and its sands is the eternal softness and mild light of the west; the low line of mystic Anglesey and precipitous Penmaenmawr, and the great group of Carnedd Llewelyn and Carnedd Dafydd and their brethren fading away, hill behind hill, in an aerial haze, make the horizon; between the foot of Penmaenmawr and the bending coast of Anglesey, the sea, a silver stream, disappears one knows not whither.'

At the foot of the Orme below the point where Arnold stood is Gogarth Abbey, a hotel now but once the home of Alice Liddell for whom Lewis Carroll created a Wonderland. The sands of Deganwy below the abbey are said to have been the ones that Carroll had in mind when the subjects under discussion included cabbages and kings. The sands are washed by the waters of the estuary in which Julius Caesar fished for the pearls he used to stud a votive shield for a Roman triumph. On the far bank is Conwy Castle, which Hotspur defended, Glyndwr captured and Turner painted. Dr Johnson and Daniel Defoe, Richard II and Coleridge all took the road that wound round the great cliff of Penmaenmawr. Beyond them lay Snowdonia, where lived Merlin and Taliesin and Maelgwyn, the British prince who was the original of Lancelot, and the Sir Percival who became transformed into Parsifal.

In another legend Prince Madoc, the son of Owain, the ruler of Gwynedd in the twelfth century, discovered America. But one of the reasons for the richness of Welsh history is that much of it is written to suit a particular need or political climate. The truth

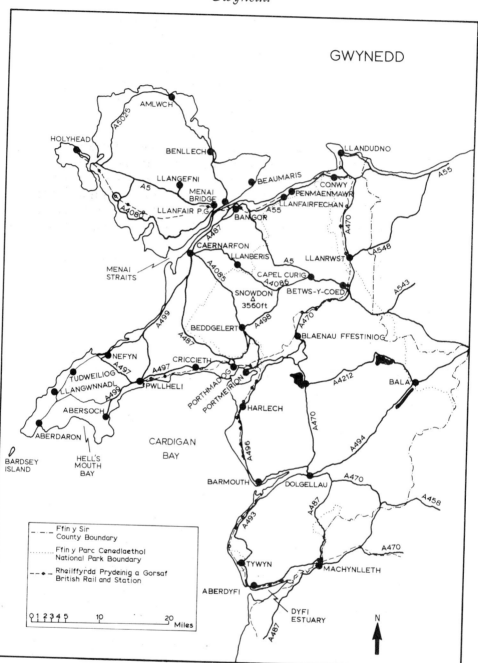

GWYNEDD

AMLWCH

HOLYHEAD

BENLLECH

LLANDUDNO

LLANGEFNI

BEAUMARIS

CONWY

PENMAENMAWR

MENAI BRIDGE

LLANFAIRFECHAN

LLANFAIR P.G.

BANGOR

CAERNARFON

LLANBERIS

LLANRWST

MENAI STRAITS

CAPEL CURIG

SNOWDON △ 3560ft

BETWS-Y-COED

BEDDGELERT

BLAENAU FFESTINIOG

NEFYN

CRICCIETH

TUDWEILIOG

LLANGWNNADL

PWLLHELI

PORTHMADOG

PORTMEIRION

BALA

ABERSOCH

HARLECH

ABERDARON

CARDIGAN BAY

BARDSEY ISLAND

HELL'S MOUTH BAY

BARMOUTH

DOLGELLAU

TYWYN

MACHYNLLETH

ABERDYFI

DYFI ESTUARY

N

Ffin y Sir
County Boundary

Ffin y Parc Cenedlaethol
National Park Boundary

Rheilffyrdd Prydeinig a Gorsaf
British Rail and Station

0 1 2 3 4 5   10   20 Miles

Crown copyright reserved

seems to be that the first recorded public mention of Madoc's voyage came as late as 1583, when a publicist produced a pamphlet promoting the British colonization of America. Yet the legend will not go away. According to Richard Hakluyt the younger, writing in 1584: 'Madoc ap Owen Gwyneth, weary of civil wars, had made his two voyages out of Wales and discovered and planted Longe Countrie which he found in the Mayne Ocean south westward of Ireland in 1170.'

Claims have been made that the Mandan tribe of Indians, who lived on the banks of the Missouri, were the descendants of Madoc's followers, and it is tempting to feel that there is some corner of a foreign field that is forever Gwynedd. For although Sir Thomas Herbert, the Restoration historian, had Madoc sailing from Abergele, and a later seventeenth-century historian placed his port of embarkation at Milford Haven in South Wales, at least one tradition places the launching of the first trans-Atlantic crossing firmly in Gwynedd.

Holyhead was the western frontier of the Roman Empire. The first author to write about Gwynedd was Tacitus. It is said that 'Tir n'an Og', the Blessed Isle of the Celts and the Enchanted Isles of the Hellenic cultures, was based on descriptions of the shores of Menai by Phoenician traders. Aberffraw, a fishing village on Anglesey, was once the capital of a Welsh kingdom whose heir was the same Prince Madoc who, if legend be believed, discovered America.

The poet laureate John Masefield was a cadet on the Merchant Navy schoolship *Conwy*. Betjeman wrote a delightful poem about the straits whilst staying at Plas Newydd, the home of the marquesses of Anglesey, said, with justice, to be the most comfortable stately home in Britain, where another guest, Rex Whistler, has left a remarkable mural. Plas Newydd was the home of the first marquess, Wellington's cavalry commander, who had his leg shot off at Waterloo. 'Begod,' he said, 'there goes me leg.' 'Begod,' said Wellington, 'so it do.' One descendant might not have pleased 'Peg Leg'. He was called 'the Dancing Marquess', and he toured the theatres of Europe with his Butterfly Dance. He spent a million pounds on personal jewellery and when finally he bankrupted the estate it took a month to sell his wardrobe.

Against stiff competition Wordsworth wrote the worst poem ever about Snowdon, Shelley wrote about Porthmadog, and Carlyle and Coleridge put their iambic oar in. But the literary invasion of North Wales was started by Gray's poem 'The Bard'.

The French Revolution chipped the gilt off the Grand Tour for aristocrats, who clearly did not believe the marble busts they would bring home would compensate for the flesh and blood heads they would leave behind them in Paris. So they came to North Wales, which, with its rugged beauty and foreign language, had all of the pleasures of abroad with few of the attendant disadvantages.

References to Gwynedd are scattered throughout literature. You can even find a chapter about a holiday in Llandudno in *The Card*, where Arnold Bennett has his hero Denry make a 'killing' taking trippers on lifeboat trips.

Gwynedd stretches from Llandudno in the north to the Berwyn Mountains in the east, down to Aberdyfi in the south. It is the centre of the Celtic Crescent, the heartland of the nation where the language and customs are predominantly Welsh. It has nearly three hundred miles of coastline, with an almost continuous sweep of silver-backed sands from Criccieth to Aberdyfi. Gwynedd comprises 956,055 acres (386,910 hectares) and had a population in 1982 – the County Council can supply no more recent figures – of 231,900. But that is only in winter. It is estimated that in summer well over a million people walk in the mountains of Wales *every week*. Most walk and climb in Snowdonia, which covers 840 square miles, and most of Snowdonia is in Gwynedd – which would be bigger if it were flatter. The range of mountains runs almost continuously from the Ormes in Llandudno to the majestic Arans which shelter Bala, down to Cader Idris and the Lleyn and Yr Eifl, 'the fork prongs', corrupted into English as 'the Rivals'.

Once this whole area was forest land but the deciduous trees which it comprised remain only as green echoes of the past. Now most of the forests are conifers planted by the Forestry Commission; strange, sinister cathedrals where few birds sing. This is the kingdom of the sheep, plump and succulent in the rich pastures of the valley bottoms, tough and defensively thick-fleeced on the harsher mountain slopes. In the long perspective of Gwynedd, towns are innovations. The A5 marches for long miles through satisfyingly empty valleys, round the hem of wind-buffeted crags and still, occasionally, as at Betws-y-Coed, 'the chapel in the woods', through the remnants of the early forests. It is a land of singing rivers, of streams full of tiny, tasty trout, of great lakes that are the mirrors of majestic mountains. Snowdonia is a national park, and within its boundaries there are sixteen nature reserves. But it is also the source of much of Gwynedd's riches, both mineral and animal. The greater part of the population live in the comparatively narrow strip between the mountains and the sea, traditionally the home of fishermen and farmers, though many had to go into the mountain quarries and mines, and now the source of its major income comes from the tourist industry.

Life was tough even for tourists when I first came to Gwynedd half a century ago. On the Lleyn where we stayed there was only one concession to twentieth-century notions of comfort. In the winter, in the farmhouses, the seats for the *Tŷ Bach*, the garden lavatory, were set in front of the fire in the kitchen to keep them warm.

I was a schoolboy then, paroled temporarily from the brick prison of a housing estate. We had driven down the A5, recently fitted with the eyes of a million cats, to a gypsy caravan in a field drowsy with bees. We had started in harsh, industrial daylight, but the evening was softer and from Betws-y-Coed onwards there had been trees and wild water. By the time we arrived I was drunk with sleep but I remember how it was the next morning. Fowls clucked fussily in Welsh and, for the first time, I heard the soft imprecations of a farmer urging his livestock. It took a long time until breakfast that long-gone morning but I can still taste the crisp bacon butties, smell the bread-and-butter scent of the hawthorn, see the butterflies with bright blue wings strafing the grass.

I remember how impatiently I waited for the first trip to the beach. All I had known until then were resort beaches with acres of deckchairs, side-shows and candy floss. That first day we walked down a cliff path, whipped by gorse bushes, bothered by butterflies, until we reached the golden sands of Lleyn.

I knew Gwynedd then under her maiden names, Merioneth, Caernarvon, Anglesey, and I was worried when in 1974 under local government reorganization the three counties were joined in Whitehall Wedlock, though less disastrously than most because they became again the kingdom of Gwynedd. But marriage has not altered her. She retains her haunting beauty, her charm and the spice of danger loving her brings. For her moods are unpredictable. Men have died at the caprice of her seas and the sullen whims of her mountains. Yet she is still the loveliest, the most feminine, of all the British counties. Blatant in summer, flaunting her sands like petticoats. Secretive in winter, blowsy with winds and the bawdry of fishing inns. She is endlessly captivating.

That first day on the Lleyn the bay stretched before us in loops of aquamarine suspended from the fingers of rock that imprisoned the horizon. What I took to be bathers in shiny black rubber caps turned out to be a colony of seals no further than paddling depth from 24-carat sands. They looked towards us with amiable curiosity as we made our way down the cliff path. There were no whelk stalls on the beach; no Punch and Judys; no puss-in-booted seaside admirals bullying you to take trips round the bay in boats that smelled of kippers. There was no one else. Just us and crab-filled rock pools and caves, and in a fold in the cliffs what instantly became and has remained my favourite place on earth. A stream from the meadowland above the beach toboggans down the cliff face and dives headlong into a pool at its foot. The pool is a basin worn from the rock over the millennia, and it is deep now like a salad bowl. When the stream is full, the water brims over into a second pool which, like the first, is hidden from the beach by a curtain of cliff round which the stream flows down the beach to the sea.

I was King Edward I in bathing drawers. Shortshanks. Building castles all down the banks of that stream, moated from its water by a canal system of a complexity that would have baffled the Venetians. Lost on every tide, reconstructed at its ebb. Tireless. A little Leonardo da Vinci. The Duke of Seawater's canal system was better by far than the one Bridgewater furrowed down the spine of Lancashire.

I came to live in Gwynedd the moment I decently could. But until 1984 I was afraid to go back to that beach at Llangwnnadl on the Lleyn in case it had changed. I preferred to remember it rather than reconstruct it from a landscape of caravan sites and neo-Wimpey bungalows that cover most fifty-year-old memories of seaside holidays. I was afraid the real Llangwnnadl might have ceased to exist in stone and slate and only lived on as a Brigadoon of the Brain. I would never have gone back had it not been for this book.

Sam Johnson's friend, the captivating Mrs Thrale, had inherited an estate at Llangwnnadl, and I retraced the steps of that admirable man on the Welsh journey he made to inspect it. He clearly hated Wales, and his bad temper was spectacular. Mine matched it as we approached Nefyn and I picked up the spoor of boutique. 'Gone to the dogs,' I warned my wife. But it hadn't. We drove on to the Lion at Tudweiliog where my father had gone for his daily nourishment of ale and argument. 'Road house, I'll bet,' I prophesied darkly. But it wasn't and we went in to as warm a welcome as ever we have had anywhere.

And finally to Llangwnnadl, which has not greatly changed either. There are no glow-worms in the hedges now. Their lights have been long blown out all over the countryside. But the hedgerows are so extravagant with wild flowers there should be one called Spendthrift. There is a car-park at the head of the cliff path where the rabbits used to be. But it's an unobtrusive car-park, and the hawthorns hide it behind their skirts. There are more caravans now but they are decently hawthorn-hidden too. The village shop is self-service, but you can still buy anything from stamps to sunburn cream, Windolene to wine. They will even lend you a corkscrew.

The butterflies still make blue clouds against the white skies of wild flowers. But, thank God, the plumbing is better.

THE SEA

For the seas have I been
        accustomed
I will walk by sea
        and river
Along the strand with my
        circled net.

           Maredudd ap Rhys (*c.* 1430-60)

• CHAPTER 1 •

The sea came first. Embedded in the highest crags of Snowdonia are the fossilized remains of marine creatures. The waters round Gwynedd are still rich in food, and generous, though less so in the polluted twentieth century than they have been in the past. Julius Caesar, it is said, fished for pearls in the mussel beds of the Conwy where, even today, as far up-river as Llanrwst mussel-fishers, part-timers now, still seek their fortune – or anyway the price of a pint of beer. They fish for the pearls in the fresh-water mussels called *cregyn y dilyw*, the deluge shells. In earlier times these reached great size and had a fine lustre. There is one completely unsubstantiated tradition that the biggest of the pearls in the Crown of Britain is from Conwy and was presented to Elizabeth I by Sir John Wynne, a local landowner.

The silver coinage of Gwynedd was the herring. A survey in one of the earliest Welsh Port Books, *A Survey of Creeks and Havens*, in 1565, reported of Aberdyfi: '... being a haven and having no habitacian, but only three houses whereunto there is no resort; save only in the time of the herringe fishinge at which tyme of fishing there is a wonderful great resort of ffyshers assembled from all places within this Realme ...'

Until recent times the shoals of herring coming to the coastal waters to spawn were vast, some as much as seven miles in length. I have friends, deep-sea sailors, who when they were younger arranged their voyages to be home when the herring shoaled so they could help with the family catch. The cheap and nutritious herring was part of Gwynedd's staple diet. The best were those that came from Nefyn, on the Lleyn Peninsula, where the boats were out in all weathers from September to January and would return after each trip loaded to the gunwales with herrings with 'bellies like inn-keepers and backs like farmers'. In the 1920s, when the industry flourished, they sold at about 2d per fish.

There have been fishermen in Gwynedd since the days of the cave-dwellers. Ynys Gorad, an island in the Menai Straits, derives

23

its name from the Latin of the Roman Legions, '*gurges*' meaning
deep water.

During the nineteenth century new systems of trawling
opened. First Caernarfon Bay, then Red Wharf and Conwy.
Trawler fleets from Liverpool, even from Dublin, fished off the
county's coast for sole, turbot and plaice. There was a
considerable herring fishery from the Lavan Sands to Holyhead,
and vast quantities of Arklow oysters were laid down to supply
the Liverpool and Chester markets.

Gwynedd seamen were at home not only in coastal waters.
Ships from the county played an important part in the great
emigration which began in Wales roughly at the time of the
French Revolution, when farmers fled from the tyranny of
English landlords and the crippling expense of tithes and church
rates to the promised lands of America and Australia. Thousands
of Welsh families emigrated from the great port cities of
Liverpool, Cardiff and Bristol. Others began their journey nearer
home, at Porthmadog and Menai Bridge on Anglesey. They were
all sailing towards the same dream: good land and prosperity.
Some found neither. Wrote one: 'When I heard Mr Bebb sighing
in Wales and groaning that we were suffering such oppression,
living on hopeless and sunless farms, boasting about the great
fortune that he had made for us and the paradise that was to be
had this side of the Atlantic, who would not have expected
something from him. I have not seen him proving any of his
claims ....'

It was not the prosperity or poverty of the United States which
worried some emigrants. It was the speed with which their fellows
threw off their culture, their very Welshness, and became
Americanized. A young Congregationalist minister from Bala, the
Reverend Michael C. Jones, was dismayed when he settled in
Cincinatti in 1849 at the speed with which his Welsh flock was
losing its identity and with it, he earnestly believed, its high moral
tone. He determined to establish an exclusively Welsh colony
where the language, culture, faith and what he saw as the native
righteousness could be kept alive.

Fifteen years later Jones led his flock to Patagonia, in South
America, and founded a colony which survives to this day and
has many links with Gwynedd. Every year at the National
Eisteddfod a day is set aside to welcome Welshmen from overseas.
There is always a strong contingent from Patagonia, and most of
them, it seems, have their roots in Gwynedd. But though the
language, the culture and the memories survive, the Congregationalist minister's plan was not a complete success. Only three

shiploads of Welsh Americans went to Patagonia, where their troubles were sufficient to put off other settlers. By the bitterest of ironies, in the Falklands Campaign of 1982 a BBC Wales TV crew making a film about the Welsh colony in Patagonia was besieged in a hotel room by the angry descendants of the Welsh settlers and had to be rescued by the Argentine army.

It was not only farmers who emigrated. Men from every trade made the hazardous crossing. A young man I know regularly visits relations in Wales, Wisconsin, a thriving town which is approached under a sign which says "*Croeso i Gymru'* – 'Welcome to Wales'. His grandfather's emigration involved a heart-rending story. When he arrived in Wisconsin, he met a Welsh farmer's beautiful daughter whom he courted for fifteen years. Sadly his father died and the young immigrant had to return to look after the home farm, sending his younger brother back in his place. Within two years, to his elder brother's chagrin, he had married the farmer's daughter. It is their descendants my young friend visits.

The troubles of the emigrants began the moment they set foot aboard frail, barely sea-worthy sailing ships which were to take them to the new Promised Land.

Amongst the first emigrants from Gwynedd was the Anglesey poet Goronwy Owen. From his wretched cabin on the convict ship *Trial*, on which he had bought a passage on 12 December 1757, he wrote to his friend, the scholar Richard Morris, one of four polymath Anglesey brothers:

The seamen are a frightfully vile bunch of men. God be my keeper, every one of them has taken to himself a strumpet from among the she-thieves, and do no work except whoring wantonly in every corner of the ship. Five or six of them have already contracted the pox (dare I mention it) from the women, and there is no doctor here save myself and my copy of Dr Shaw's book, and it is with its help that I tend them a little with what medicines are to be had in the chest which is here. I fear sometimes for myself lest I should get it from being amongst them. I baptised one child and buried him later and a thief and a she-thief besides. It was today that I buried the woman. Do you remember that my wife was to have one of the she-thieves to serve her whilst at sea? One of them is here in the cabin but it is to serve this captain's penis, and not to wait upon my wife. There was never seen a worse beast of a man than the master. For the past fortnight he has compelled us to drink stinking water or else choke (for there is no drop of small ale aboard) and to watch him drinking his wines and beer with his strumpet, smacking his devilish lips to whet our appetite and saying, 'It is very good'. What, say you, will become of us before journey's end? But I do have an unopened barrel of porter and a little rum. I half fear he will one day so anger me by killing my children or some trick, for he has a hundred mean tricks, that I shall run my sword under his short ribs.

Even the shortest sea journey was a nightmare. An Anglesey squire, William Bulkeley, noted in his diary in 1735 a hair-raising account of what to him was an ordinary passage from Dublin to Holyhead. It took twenty-six hours to cover roughly seventy sea miles.

Shipbuilding was once a major industry in Gwynedd. Until the building of roads in the late eighteenth century the cheapest, safest and most efficient way to freight cargoes was by water. The shallow draft coasters which carried these cargoes, hugging the coast and sailing far up the estuary, were all made in the county. There were boatbuilders in Conwy in the first Elizabethan age. Shipwrights worked over the centuries on Anglesey and at Bangor, Caernarfon, Barmouth, Nefyn and other parts of the Lleyn. Between 1776 and 1824 nine sloops and a brigantine were built on the Dwyfor, another eight sloops at Criccieth, three at Tywyn, just north of Aberdyfi. At Barmouth, on the Mawddach Estuary, two hundred ships were built; at Pwllheli, between 1759 and 1824, another 250 vessels were laid down.

The largest shipbuilding industry was at Porthmadog in the nineteenth century. It began with the development of a small pier on a strip of beach at the mouth of the River Glaslyn. It had been called 'Y Tywyn' (seashore) but when the pier was finished it was re-named after its developer, William Alexander Madocks, entrepreneur and friend of the poet Shelley.

Porthmadog owed its existence to Madocks' greatest work, the building of a mile-long cob which drained over three thousand acres of marsh and sand and, in diverting the Glaslyn and the Dwyryd rivers, excavated a commodious and well-sheltered harbour at a place extending from Garth Pen y Glogwyn to Ynys y Towyn. In return for being allowed to collect a toll from all shipping which used it, Madocks built the pier, which opened in 1825.

The first of more than 250 vessels to be built there was *The Two Brothers*, a 65-tonner, and for nearly a century Porthmadog-built vessels carried slate from the Ffestiniog quarries to Liverpool for trans-shipment to Australia. But as local skills grew, larger ships were laid down, and soon Porthmadog-registered boats were sailing with slate and emigrants, Gwynedd's principal exports, to the US of A. By the end of the nineteenth century Porthmadog-built ships were familiar sights all over the world.

Though some of the ships were owned by quarry proprietors and local gentry, others were financed by the community. Farmers, quarrymen, shopkeepers and small businessmen of all kinds had shares in the ships that were built at Porthmadog. As the demand for shipping grew, especially to the Baltic ports and to Australia during the Gold Rush of 1851, so did the business of the new port. In 1856 a hundred carpenters, joiners and smiths were fully employed. Within ten years the figures had nearly doubled. Unfortunately the largest customer for the biggest Welsh export, slate, was Germany. In 1866 North Wales exported a quarter of a million pounds worth. From Porthmadog it went to Hamburg and then by train all over Europe, but trade ended abruptly with the outbreak of war in 1914. Porthmadog's maritime heyday was over. It had lasted eighty-nine years.

Boats are still built in Gwynedd, of course, but usually for the leisure trade. Some yards, such as Dickies in Bangor, specialize in ocean-going craft. Not long ago they built a magnificent luxury yacht for a pop-star millionaire, but orders are usually at less ambitious levels.

Almost certainly unique is the Traditional Boat Shop, run on the quayside at Port Dinorwic – or *y Felinheli* as it is in Welsh – by Glyn Lancaster Jones. Former naval architect Mr Jones, whose ancestors painted the insignia on the Holyhead mail coach, specializes in building scaled-down paddle steamers, perfect steam-drive four-seaters, which can occasionally be seen at their trials in the straits. It chimes happily with local history. In 1830 the first paddle steamer sailed past Port Dinorwic. It was a pleasure yacht, the *Menai*, rather larger than Mr Jones's vessels, and it belonged to the Assheton-Smiths of Vaynol, quarry-owners and among the richest families in Gwynedd.

The boat-yard also produces a curious ocean craft, a rowing skiff with a sliding seat, which, it is claimed in America where the sport originated, is the rowing man's answer to jogging. Mr Jones is one of the few pracititioners in the area so far, but he publicizes the sport with great style. He once attended a formal cocktail party at the Royal Welsh Yacht Club in Caernarfon wearing white shorts, rolled shirtsleeves and a bow tie, having sculled from Port Dinorwic in under an hour.

Elsewhere in maritime Gwynedd prospects for the future seem

bright. Holyhead is the only non-tidal port between Newlyn in Cornwall and Girvan in Ayrshire. Boats can land fish and take on ice twenty-four hours a day. The Holyhead Quay Fishing Association has pointed out that fishing and allied trades already provide ninety full-time and 130 part-time jobs in the area. At the time of writing they were having some success urging the borough council to build a new quay at the port. This would provide many more jobs in an area of high unemployment.

In 1985 Holyhead's fishing industry received a boost from the EEC in the form of a grant of £19,627 to local fishmerman J.E. Webb, who had already received a similar grant from the Sea Fish Industry Authority to help pay for a new Ceynuss fishing vessel, *Gwenfaen*, a 38-footer with a 127-horsepower engine, which employs two other fishermen besides Mr Webb. These grants greatly strengthened the position of Holyhead fishermen at meetings with the Welsh Development Agency called to discuss recent studies of the potential for the Holyhead fishing industry. A fisherman told the meeting: 'A couple of years ago there were no fishing boats using Holyhead at all but today there are twenty-five of them, landing an average of thirty-one tonnes a day.'

Wales receives only a small share of the grants available from the EEC for the fishing industry, but, according to Mr Rhodri Morgan, head of the EEC office in Wales, this situation is entirely explained by the lack of applications received from the Welsh fishing fleet. It seems that Mr Webb's successful application has shown the way.

At present (1986) the fishing fleet nucleus is the seven beamers, between sixty and eighty feet, owned by Wilson's of Holyhead. They fish the scallop grounds around the Isle of Man, in the north Irish Sea and in Cardigan Bay. Their catch is processed by a Wilson subsidiary, North Wales Sea Foods, Holyhead.

Wilson's, which came into the business after World War II, now has a near monopoly of marketing in the North Wales lobster trade. The company has about twenty holding tanks at Rhydwyn, near Holyhead, and tanks and premises in the Outer Hebrides, where it is also a major buyer. The company has a large export trade to France, Holland, Germany, Spain, South Africa, the USA and the Middle and Far East. Products sold include scallops, peeled prawns, crabmeat, lobsters and crab claws. The group employs around 170 people in the Anglesey district.

Queenies can be caught all year round, but the king scallop fishery is closed for conservation between 1 June and 31 October in the north-east Irish Sea/Morecambe Bay area and between 1

July and 31 October in Cardigan Bay. The scallopers average one hundred to two hundred bags a day.

The other major fishery in Anglesey is for dogfish, worked by a fleet of small 'liners' based in Holyhead and other smaller harbours around the Anglesey coast, such as Amlwch and Cemaes Bay. This is a fairly new fishery which developed after local men saw good-quality 'dogs' being caught by local anglers. The Holyhead 'liner' fleet, in the thirty- to forty-foot range, is now eight to ten strong, and there are others in the smaller ports. The fishery has attracted several Cornish liners, mainly from Newlyn and Padstow. In 1985 there were four Cornish boats at Holyhead and one at Port Penrhyn, Bangor, with more expected. This follows the pattern of the last two years. The fishery runs throughout the year, and some of the Cornish boats spend the winter at Holyhead.

An important factor in the development of the dog-fishery was the arrival of Holyhead Fish Processors, a company specializing in handling dogs, which account for ninety-eight per cent of its throughput. New outlets for the dogfish are developing in France and Italy. The company bought four hundred tons of dogs in its first year, and this total has risen substantially since. The firm has moved into bigger premises with a seven-thousand-ton cold store.

Caernarfon has a fleet of ten trawlers in the thirty- to fifty-foot range, fishing mainly for white fish. The work is difficult, especially in winter, because of the exposed grounds in Caernarfon Bay, and the fleet is slowly declining. Two boats left the fleet recently. Plaice, whiting and roker are the main species. The fish is marketed through a small co-op, Caernarfon Trawlers Ltd, which sends the fish to Grimsby and, occasionally, Fleetwood. One boat scalloping from the port is the forty-foot *Celtic Pride*, and another boat, *Rogue River*, is prawning at Oban.

Port Penrhyn, Bangor, is base for three trawlers, two local doggers and, currently, one Cornish dogger, *Golden Hope of Pentroc*, from Padstow. The small processor Seafresh Ltd, formerly Celtic Fisheries, handles most of the local catch. Some smoking and breading are carried out, and most of the fish is sent to Billingsgate. Seafresh is hoping for an influx of Cornish doggers when the season gets fully under way.

There are only three trawlers working at Conwy, and the scalloper *Silver Seagull*. Fish is mainly sent overland to Lowestoft and Fleetwood, the boats pooling resources to arrange transport.

The remainder of the North Wales industry consists mainly of potting – much of it part-time – especially around the Lleyn Peninsula. There is also a small shrimp fishery along the North

Wales coast from ports such as Rhos-on-Sea and Rhyl.

The Conwy mussel fishery, which once supported thirty families, persists to this day. Against all the hazards of wind and tide a dozen men still earn a living from the mussel beds at the estuary mouth, though some, it is true, supplement their earnings with casual work on building sites. Mussel men work in teams of two and are usually related. It is easier to find a partner within the family. Ken Rimmer Hughes shares a launch with his cousin Derek Smith, a partnership which began thirty years ago. Smith occasionally works ashore but Hughes has known no other life than musselling since he left school at fourteen; he is now fifty-nine.

The life is a hard one. The mussel men go out on the tide some time between 4 and 5 a.m. They must find their beds by probing with long rakes twenty feet below the keel of the boat. They must also find the beds again on their return trip the next day by an accurate lining-up of landmarks. It is a precise business. A few yards of error and the bed is lost. Often a man raking on one side of a boat will bring up mussels by the score though his partner raking from the other side of the dinghy will draw nothing. At low tide, in oilskins and waders, the mussel men search by hand in the kelp for the mussels the rakes have missed. Once landed, the mussels must by law go through a forty-eight-hour purification process at the Ministry of Agriculture and Fisheries plant in Conwy. Only then can the men market them, in competition now from newer beds in the Menai Straits and at Morecambe and Boston, Lincolnshire. Pollution is not the only problem confronting the mussel men; there is also the 'natural' reduction of shellfish through gales, overfishing, strong tides and the disturbance of the river at Conwy, caused first by a succession of bridge-building and now by the construction of a road tunnel planned to run beneath the river bed.

In 1985 the Nature Conservancy Council succeeded in getting the Menai Strait designated as Britain's first Marine Nature Reserve. It is an endless source of fascinating study, twenty miles long, and through it water from Liverpool Bay is fed to the Irish Sea. The strait is, in fact, two deep gorges which separate Anglesey from mainland Gwynedd. The gorges are linked with a third scar made by glacial action.

They are dangerous waters. There is an eighty-four-minute difference in the tide table at either end, and in the central reaches there is an eight-knot tidal flow.

There is giant conger in the Strait, coral, sponges and shoals of bass, and in late summer families of seals can be seen off

Llanddwyn Island. In Brynsiencyn many of the smaller marine inhabitants of this stretch of water can be studied at a marine zoo. The Nature Conservancy Council have plans for a larger and more ambitious project farther along the coast at Menai Bridge but it may be some years before this is achieved.

• CHAPTER 2 •

For centuries, until the building of the A5, the sea was the most reliable highway into Gwynedd. The most reliable but not always the safest. There are more than a thousand charted wrecks on the bed of Liverpool Bay. Most of them lie in its surf-edged *décolletage* where it hangs in a deep curve stretching from the rocky shoulders of the Orme, on Gwynedd's border at Llandudno, to the Holy Mountain on Anglesey, where the legions halted their long march from Rome.

Roman rafts and galleys lie in the bay, and medieval barges, one still carrying its freight of slate roof tiles. Off Holyhead is the wreck of the first yacht to be seen in British waters, that in which Charles II raced his brother the Duke of York at Thames regattas. There are steamers and paddle boats; the world's first steam-driven submarine is somewhere off the Great Orme. Clippers, emigrant ships, cargo boats and treasure too.

In his book *In Search of Spanish Treasure*, the pioneer marine archaeologist Sidney Wignall recalls his first dive onto the *Royal Charter* which sank within hailing distance of Moelfre, an Anglesey fishing village, in 1859.

The *Charter* was one of the victims of the Great Storm of 25 October in which, round the coast of Britain, 133 ships sank, a further 90 were damaged and 800 lives were lost. The casualties of the *Royal Charter* accounted for more than half that number. October on the Gwynedd coast is always a month of fearsome gales. A hundred years later to the day there was to be another ship, the MV *Hindlea*, in peril in an Anglesey gale, though in that case the heroism of the RNLI crews from Moelfre and Holyhead saved the lives of the eight-man crew. In 1859 there was no RNLI, no way to save the auxiliary steam clipper *Royal Charter* as she was driven before a Force 12 gale, with winds gusting at more than a hundred miles per hour, onto the rocks off Moelfre. It was weather beyond imagination. The sea-level in the bay rose four feet. Liverpool Observatory recorded its highest ever wind force, twenty-eight pounds to the square foot, and the Meteorological Office described it as 'a complete horizontal hurricane'.

Outside Holyhead harbour, where she was moored on her round-the-kingdom public relations tour, Brunel's iron paddle steamer, *The Great Eastern*, was soon in danger. Inside the harbour ships sank at their moorings. Huddled in their cabins the 371 passengers of the *Royal Charter* either prayed or counted their gold. There was a lot of gold to count. The passengers were mostly miners returning to Liverpool from the Australian goldfields. In her holds the *Charter* was carrying a registered cargo of bullion, coin and gold dust which, in 1859, was valued at £322,440.

The voyage had been a pleasant one. They had made good time, and soon the *Charter* would be sailing up the Mersey, but as she passed the north-east coast of Anglesey the Great Gale hit her and drove her onto a lee shore, breaking her back and pounding her to broken sticks. More than four hundred people, passengers and crew, lost their lives. But many landsmen made their fortunes. A platoon of marines had to be marched to the village to turn back looters who were rifling the pockets of the dead, even pulling the rings from their fingers. Charles Dickens, sent from London as the *Times* special correspondent, was sickened by what he saw. His moving account can be found in his despatch in *The Uncommercial Traveller*.

Official salvage workers brought ashore £300,000 in bullion and coin but no official attempt had ever been made to find the private gold hoards of the passengers.

In 1958 Wignall and a colleague, Eric Reynolds, dived on the wreck. In the sand, jammed between an iron frame and a huge, jagged plate, Wignall saw a yellow ingot. Both men thought they had found a bar of copper. They struggled to free it without success until the air ran out in their cylinders and they had to surface. In the last moments Wignall chipped a fragment off the ingot which he subsequently discovered was gold. At the time of the dive the nearest source for compressed air for North Wales divers was the British Oxygen Company one hundred miles away in Cheshire, which twenty-six years ago entailed a wearisome journey along a second-class road. Back at the diving site, on their return with new tanks, the two divers discovered a full gale was blowing. When at last they were able to dive, Wignall and Reynolds found the configuration of the wreck had changed in the storm and their bullion was buried under a huge mound of sand. Some months later, when he was cleaning his diving knife, Wignall found a speck of gold trapped in the saw edge. It assayed at 23 carat.

In his book Wignall writes: 'My measurements, based on the

hypothesis that two-thirds of the ingot was buried, suggested that it must have weighed 70 lbs.' In 1981, before the phenomenal rise in the price of gold, he estimated the value of the ingot at £300,000. Writing in that year he said, 'The ingot still presumably lies on the wreck in about 15 feet of water no more than 20 yards from the rocks at the water's edge.'

The prophecy proved uncannily accurate. In July 1985, as this book was being prepared, Richard Simpson, writing in the *Daily Post*, revealed that divers had at last discovered the riches of the *Royal Charter*. The team had worked on the wreck for seven weeks before they started bringing up treasure, slowly working towards the ship's strong-room. Sovereigns in mint condition, a gold nugget, a gold ring and reportedly a gold bar were brought from the ship. Divers also found more than one hundred items from the ship, including silver tureens, silver ladles, silver forks, leather boots, a leather jacket and two pistols, cocked and ready to fire. The incredible discovery, worth possibly many millions, astonished the diving team and the local community. The eleven-man diving team from Liverpool believed the wreck contained up to 48,000 gold sovereigns as well as gold bars, lying in twenty-five feet of water and covered by thirty feet of sand.

Simpson reported:

> They are using a compressor to suck up sand to reveal the wreck, and are now bringing in more equipment to help with the archaeological project because of its success to date. Team leader Joe McCormack and project researcher Bernie McDonald yesterday kept quiet about exactly how much gold they have taken from the wreck. They showed five gold sovereigns, minted between 1852 and 1859 in Australia, a gold nugget and a gold ring. The sovereigns are worth between £200 and £500, but they believe the wreck contains rare sovereigns which could be worth up to £5,000 each. 'We are showing a sample of what we have found. We want to make sure the rare sovereigns are still in the wreck and to do so we are bringing in extra equipment,' said Mr McCormack.
>
> Mr McDonald also revealed that he believed a large gold nugget as well as whole and broken gold bars are hidden in the wreck. The local community council, who have welcomed the dive, were last night holding an emergency meeting about its implications. The diving company, Best Speed Limited, who have been given valuable co-operation by the community, have promised some of the find from the wreck to the village. The divers are now mounting a round-the-clock guard on the wreck over which they have been given sole rights.

HMS *Thetis* is no longer on the bed of the bay, though she sank there on her first sea trials in July 1939. No one knows where she lies. The submarine, the tomb of ninety-nine of her complement of 103 men, was raised and sent for refit to Birkenhead. A year later, renamed HMS *Thunderball*, she sailed off to war under lieutenant-Commander Bernard Crouch, DSO and bar. She sank two U-boats and five supply ships. In 1943 she vanished.

One submarine does still lie somewhere off the Great Orme. In the summer of 1984 naval divers believed they had found it, and plans were made to raise it. Salvaged, it would probably be worth as much to a maritime museum as all the gold in the *Royal Charter*, because it is the world's first steam-driven submersible, the *Resurgam*, the invention of the Reverend George William Garrett.

Garrett was the son of a poor Manchester vicar, who was put to Rossall School at the expense of the great Victorian philanthropist Baroness Burdett Coutts. He was a prodigy of scholarship. At Trinity College, Dublin, he passed his first-year examination within a week of joining the class. At the age of seventeen he was appointed an assistant master at the Manchester Mechanics Institute. In his spare time he won proficiency certificates in Science, Art, Physical Geography, Geology, Higher Mathematics and Higher Chemistry. While studying for his BA at the South Kensington Museum, in the fashion of the day he read theology and was ordained by the Bishop of Manchester. He became a competent navigator by making a voyage round the world. And he had a secret dream. He wanted to invent the first workable submarine.

In the nineteenth century far-sighted naval chiefs all over the world realized that underwater warships were the key to naval supremacy. A fortune awaited the inventor of such a craft. The Russian Government offered £144,000, the British £50,000.

Garrett first invented an air-purifying apparatus which he fitted into an airtight case. He demonstrated his faith in it by being shut in it under water for several hours. As a by-product he invented a primitive diving suit which he called Pneumatophore. Next the Reverend took out patents and, with J.T. Cochran, a shipbuilder of Duke Street, Birkenhead, formed the Garrett Submarine Navigation and Pneumatophore Company Limited to 'work certain inventions, consisting of a breathing apparatus, submarine torpedo boat, diving dress and Pneumatophore'. The company had a capital of £10,000.

The first submarine the company built at Birkenhead was only $4\frac{1}{2}$ tons in weight. She was taken on secret trials in the Mersey. A tugboat man who watched them remembered them some years later. He recalled: 'His favourite run was from the Grain Warehouse to the entrance of Egerton Dock. The submarine's movements were slow and you could tell where she was by the ripples she made on the surface. Now and then you would see her dome-shaped helmet come to the surface.' A contemporary newspaper reported: '... a torpedo boat invented by the Rev. G.W. Garrett which has the power of sinking and remaining under water for many hours and thus can easily enter any blockaded port unperceived. The air is maintained at its normal composition by a chemical apparatus invented by Mr Garrett.'

The success of the prototype encouraged the Reverend Mr Garrett to greater things. His second submarine, the twelve foot long *Resurgam*, was powered by a steam boiler eleven feet long and five feet high. Her pointed brow and stern were made of solid steel. When she was launched, shortly after Garrett's twenty-seventh birthday, from the Alfred Dock, Birkenhead, on Wednesday 10 December 1879, it was only one year after Garrett had designed the first scale model, and the *Resurgam* had taken only three weeks to build.

Her three-man crew consisted of Garrett, Captain Jackson, a master mariner, and George Price, an engineer. Conditions for the crew were appalling. If the hull flooded, it could be pumped dry only by hand. To reach the pump the crewman would have to inch past the scorching boiler. On the surface the pilot had to stand on the boiler with his head stuck out of the conning tower. Inside her hull the temperature remained constant at 110° Fahrenheit.

The success of the prototype had generated interest in the Admiralty and the first trial in the Mersey so impressed naval observers – Garrett claimed he could submerge under power for five hours at a speed of three knots – that they offered to arrange official sea trials off Portsmouth in 1880.

A further inducement to carry on with the project came from Thorsten Nordenfeldt, the Norwegian inventor of the machine-gun. Garrett was using a modified engine based on the Lamm design. Nordenfeldt was also planning to build submarines, and he offered to take Garrett into partnership if the Portsmouth trials were a success. The profits on the machine-gun would provide Garrett with much needed capital. He also needed the Norwegian contacts with the war ministries of major European countries. At 10.30 on a dark and foggy night *Resurgam* was lowered into the water from the dockside at Liverpool and the adventure began.

The bad weather conditions made the cruise on the surface hazardous in the extreme, and Captain Jackson was permanently on watch on the deck of the submarine as they cruised down river until they were clear of the other ships. Let Garrett take up the tale in his own words:

> We reached the Rock Lighthouse without accident of any sort and entered the Rock Channel. I took the helm in the conning tower but as soon as we were in the Channel Captain Jackson came inside, when we shut ourselves in and fairly started on our way.
>
> We passed down the Rock Channel and safely making Spencer's Spit, we turned into the Horse Channel which we cleared in due course and were then out to sea. We laid our course for the North West Lightship and went very slow, intending to make some experiments in Victoria Deep as soon as daylight should come.
>
> When the morning of Thursday came there was very thick fog which prevented our making all the experiments we wished and necessitated our proceeding very carefully. The fog did not lift all day so we moved about, testing various parts of our interior machinery until Friday morning when the sun rose beautifully and clear.
>
> We had now been at sea about 36 hours, a great deal of the time under water and we felt desirous of making some port, as sleeping on board was not attended with such comfort as we wished.'

Engineer Price was to recall that they surfaced almost under the bowls of a fully rigged sailing ship, homeward bound to Liverpool. To the amazement of the skipper, Garrett lifted the conning-tower hatch, hailed him and told him they had spent the last three hours under his keel. 'Where are you bound?' the skipper asked. 'In passage from Liverpool to Portsmouth,' he was told. The skipper stared for a moment at Garrett's head, then his glare raked the tiny *Resurgam* from stem to stern. 'How many crew?' he asked. 'Three,' replied Garrett. And the skipper declared history's first verdict on the submarine service. 'Well,' he said, 'you are three of the biggest fools I have ever met.'

Garrett's log continues:

'At this time we found the North West Lightship close at hand, bearing about North, so we determined to put into the River Voryd as there is good anchorage there and she will dry out on every tide which is convenient as we were going to make a series of experiments. The boat answered splendidly in the sea way. The seas pass easily over her and cause hardly any motion. Nor do they interfere in any important degree with her steering.'

Safely ashore at Rhyl, there was a dispute with Cochran, the shipbuilder. The trials had been successful and he argued that at this stage they should be cautious. He wanted the *Resurgam* winched ashore and taken by road to Portsmouth. He felt it would be unwise, with a fortune within their grasp, to run the risk of losing her at sea. But the Reverend Mr Garrett insisted she should go by sea. He suggested an escort, and Price was sent back to Birkenhead to bring back Garrett's steam yacht, *Elfin*, which, it was decided, would take her in tow for the rest of the passage.

Engineer Price was critical of Garrett's impatience when he steamed into Rhyl. Common sense dictated that the *Elfin* should undertake the difficult, narrow passage out of Rhyl in daylight. But Garrett was clearly anxious to get to Portsmouth. He was young and impetuous and, for all he knew, other submarine inventors might be hard on his heels. His impatience was to cost him a fortune.

At 10 p.m. on Tuesday 24 February 1880, the *Resurgam* was towed out of Rhyl harbour to the cheers of the fishing community. All that night they hugged the coast and by the next day they were nearing the Great Orme. But the weather was worsening rapidly. The barometer plunged and by 8 p.m. they were being buffeted by a full west-north-west gale. Engineer Price remembered:

'Whilst off the Great Orme's head the captain of the *Elfin* signalled to the *Resurgam* that they were in difficulties and unable to feed their boilers. They sent a boat across and we all three went over to the yacht, taking the submarine in tow. Garrett and Jackson went below whilst I went to the engine room to repair the pumps. During that time the gale sprang up and prevented us from returning to the submarine. We towed her until 10 o'clock the following morning when she broke her hawser and we consequently lost her ...'

The weather was so bad that no search could be made. Indeed, it was only with difficulty the *Elfin* made the Dee Estuary, where she dropped anchor off Mostyn. Later that night there was more drama. The *Elfin* parted her chains, and her crew came on deck to find they were being swept out to sea. They fired Verey lights, and a steamer, the *Iron King*, came to her rescue. Unfortunately, in doing so, she rammed the *Elfin*, and her crew had barely time to get on board the rescue ship before the *Elfin* sank.

Undaunted, Garrett hired a special train as soon as he was put ashore and returned to Liverpool to recruit a salvage crew. Unhappily the sea was now so rough that no boats could leave the Mersey and the whole adventure ended in failure. Nevertheless, Garrett had given sufficient proof of his ability for Nordenfeldt to take him into partnership. Garrett's modified engine was used in two submarines, one for Turkey and the other for Russia. In gratitude the Turks made Garrett a Bey, but neither submarine was to prove itself. It was almost as though the maritime gods had cursed this new vessel which was to bring such disaster to the seas over which they ruled. The engine in the submarine the Turks bought proved unsatisfactory, and the Russian submarine was lost under tow, eventually breaking up on Jutland.

Garrett's adventures continued. In 1890 he emigrated to the United States where he became a soldier, fighting for the Americans in Cuba in the Spanish-American War. But he died peacefully in his bed in New York on 26 February 1902. He was only fifty.

A man after Garrett's heart was John Rees of Machynlleth who in 1867 announced that he intended to walk across the Menai Straits without losing his equilibrium and 'he would besides go through several other rather extraordinary manoeuvres'.

Watched by thousands from the hillsides above the Straits and deafened by their applause, Mr Rees, in a stiff oilskin suit, sat down in the shallows, took two tiny oars from a pocket and rowed himself in a sitting position across the Straits to the Anglesey shore where it was said the cheers made windows rattle a mile away. He returned across the water lounging nonchalantly on the waves and for an encore walked the last several yards before he touched bottom and waded ashore.

Mr Rees explained: 'The apparatus of which I am the patenter and inventor consists of an air and waterproof dress which envelops the whole person without impeding the limbs. It contains eleven air and waterproof compartments, each completely independent of the other and under perfect control of the occupant. When partially inflated it places the wearer in a perpendicular position which attitude can be easily maintained in the roughest sea in wildest storm. When fully inflated – a proceeding only recommended when the storm has abated – it permits the assumption of a sitting position in which the individual may, with the aid of the accompanying paddle or even his own hands, propel himself in any direction at the rate of two or three miles an hour with perfect safety.'

The suit had pockets that would hold several days' provisions. Mr Rees also unveiled a pneumatic apparatus that covered an entire ship. Like the waterproof dress it worked perfectly, and one wonders why neither was ever heard of again.

Off the Gwynedd coast are wrecks of many emigrant ships that sailed out of Liverpool and sank before they had left the Great Orme behind them. Typical of these was the 1,300-ton *Ocean Monarch* which on 28 August 1848 steamed out of the Mersey bound for Boston and the promised land of America with three hundred emigrants aboard.

The morning had been uneventful but at noon a steward brought the captain some startling information. A passenger had lit a fire in the aft ventilator. By the time the captain got aft, smoke was pouring from a store-room through an open door into the main after cabin. Soon the whole of the after end of the ship was ablaze and passengers were crowding forward. As some edged along the bowsprit, others, panicking, pushed them off into the sea, where they drowned, only to be followed by more passengers pushed off in their turn.

The SS *New World* hove to and, seeing terrified passengers huddled on the *Ocean Monarch* afraid to jump, an American seaman, Frederick Jerome, tied a rope round his waist and swam to their aid. Grabbing a line from the *Monarch*, he raised himself, hand over hand, until he reached the blazing deck. The records do not say how many Jerome saved by tying his rope round their waists and lowering them from the deck into the sea, but he stayed at his work of mercy until the flames became too much for him and, with only minutes to spare before the *Monarch* sank, he too jumped into the sea. In recognition of his bravery he was made a freeman of the city of New York, and Queen Victoria sent him 'a gift'.

The seas off Gwynedd have produced many heroes, not least of them coxswain Dick Evans, the hero of two spectacular rescues, one in October 1959, the other in November 1966, for which, on both occasions, he won the RNLI's highest award for gallantry, the Lifeboat VC. Cox'n Evans' rescues are known all over the world but there were other less well-known lifeboat heroes.

William Owen was one. In 1909 he was coxswain of the steam lifeboat *Duke of Northumberland* based in Holyhead harbour. A sailor since boyhood, Owen knew of no more frightening stretch of water than the 'Race' where the seven-mile-an-hour current is lashed by gales and the sea becomes a cauldron of spume and wild water. And he had never known it as deadly as it was when the lifeboat was launched on the morning of 22 February. The west-south-westerly gale was gusting at more than eighty miles per hour. Outside the harbour the seas were awesome. Owen had been a lifeboatman for forty-three years, the last twenty as a coxswain. His son had already been lost at sea on a life-saving mission. He recalled: 'I was in the sailing lifeboat that time and she passed us. We were just slipping our mooring when I saw her pass in the night and I heard my lad's last hail. From that time to the present I have never seen him nor his body for he was never found. All I can suppose is that the boat carried too much sail and was driven under. There were five men in the boat and all were

A typical Gwynedd panorama of sea, mountain and sky. Rhinog Fawr, Llethr and Arenhig from Ynysagin, Lleyn Peninsula

Amlwch Harbour built as a commercial port, used later as a Marina but now returning to commerce with fishing boats and marine traffic to an off-shore oil terminal; perhaps even ore from the Parys Mountain it was built to serve

The filigree of the railway bridge across the Mawddach Estuary,
recently saved from dereliction by British Rail

No rivalry between rescue organizations in Gwynedd. A Wessex helicopter from C Flight, 22 Squadron RAF Valley, on exercise with the crew of Hoylake lifeboat in Liverpool Bay

lost ...'

The *Duke* was the marvel of her day. She had screws; her propulsion came from water forced through tubes in her hull. It took only minutes to build up a head of steam. There had been services, thirty years past, which might have ended differently had the *Duke* been on the station. In one week two ships had been lost before the pulling and sailing boats could reach them.

That February day the *Duke* had already been out on one service to the steamer *Bencroy* out of Liverpool. Out of control, the heavy seas were carrying her onto the breakwater when the lifeboat came alongside and lowered her to safety. Less than an hour later the *Duke* was launched for a second time. A tiny coaster, the *Harold*, had fired distress rockets. Another Liverpool vessel with a crew of nine, she was hopelessly under-powered and she, too, was being carried to destruction on the rocks.

The weather had worsened disastrously in the brief hour since the last service. There was a howling, bitterly cold gale, and the crew were drenched and smothered by huge seas. They were hardly making any way at all. Even under the *Duke*'s power it took them nearly two hours to get out of the harbour and round the breakwater. At any time the deck crew could have been swept over the side while, battened below decks, the engineers, should the *Duke* capsize, would have been trapped.

When the *Duke* hit the Race, it was like being tossed into a foaming cauldron. The roar of wind and sea was deafening. She was thrown about like an empty rum keg. If she ever reached the *Harold*, there was every chance she would be smashed against her side by the pitching sea.

Owen ordered drogues out to steady the *Duke* on her course. Though they did steady her, they reduced her power, drawing her back onto the rocks. Signalling for the drogue to be brought inboard and for more power from the engine room, he made a breakneck dash for the *Harold*. Once alongside, Owen had to take the *Duke* right round her hull looking for a place to board her. He found it on the starboard hand. As they were borne by on a huge wave, he hailed the skipper and told him to pay out a string rope so they could tie up alongside. The rope was thrown and caught, but no sooner was it made fast than it snapped and the *Northumberland* was swept away on a heavy swell. When they were carried back by the next swell, Owen hailed the skipper for the second time. 'Another rope. And from the same place.' He paused. 'We can do nothing without one. If you don't give us one you will be utterly lost.'

A second rope was thrown and made fast on the lifeboat, and a

bosun's chair was improvised. One by one, seven crewmen came
swinging across to the safety of the *Duke of Northumberland*.
The eighth was just preparing to follow when an immense sea
broke over the lifeboat from the north hand. Owen felt the deck
lifting under his feet as the *Duke* was carried on the wave. They
must be carried over the *Harold*'s deck, he thought, and drowned
or smashed to pulp against her broad side. Between them the two
vessels carried thirteen fenders but they would have been no use
against such an impact.

A second mountain of water struck the lifeboat. At first it
carried them head-on towards the *Harold* but then it slackened
and they felt themselves sailing past her stern. The two vessels
were almost touching. For the skipper and the remaining men it
was the final chance. There would be no opportunity now of
rigging a bosun's chair. Their only chance was to leap from the
deck. They launched themselves at the moment the *Duke* was
swept broadside along the starboard hand and landed on her deck.

The rescue won for William Owen the RNLI's gold medal, the
lifeboatman's VC, to be worn with the silver medal he already
held. It was presented to him by King George V, at that time – 4
May 1908 – still Prince of Wales and President of the RNLI, in a
ceremony at Marlborough House. The citation described his
action as one of 'exceptional merit attended by grave risk to all on
board the lifeboat which would certainly have ended disastrously
had it not been for the gallant and extremely skilful management
of the lifeboat by Coxswain Owen'.

The Prince of Wales was interested in the engineering of the
steam lifeboat, and Owen did his best to explain the principles. He
also told the Prince that, within twelve hours, the seas had
reduced the abandoned coaster to matchwood. In a burst of
confidence he added: 'It seemed as if the Almighty had just hurled
us up to the broadside to get those last two sailors off the wreck.
For I believe that God has always given a big hand with me
whenever I put to sea to save men's lives.'

The first Irish Packet station was established in Holyhead in 1656
to carry mails from the British Court to the armies in Ireland. At
first the mails were carried in Navy ships but in the eighteenth
century private sailing cutters such as the Cork-built forty-two-
ton *Henrietta* took over. In 1820 two paddle steamers, the
Ivanhoe and the *Talbot*, ushered in the steam era, cutting the
sailing time between Britain and Ireland to six hours.

In 1834 the Admiralty once again took over the mails,
introducing another paddle steamer, the *Cuckoo*. Thirteen years

later, during the sort of economy drive which was to become familiar to service chiefs in the next century, the run was returned to civilian hands. The mail service was divided between the City of Dublin Steam Packet Company and the North Western Railway Company until the Steam Packet Company won the exclusive contract, leaving the Railway Company to concentrate on passenger traffic.

By this time the Steam Packet vessel the SS *Prince Arthur* was making the crossing in $4\frac{3}{4}$ hours, and the fleet included four more ships, the *Ulster*, *Leinster*, *Munster* and *Connaught*. The LNWR's passengers used the steamers *Anglia*, *Scotia* and *Hibernia*. But, thanks to patrolling U-boats, the fleets of both companies were cut in half in World War I.

For the LNWR it was merely the continuation of a run of appalling luck. On 17 April 1863 the company's paddle steamer *Telegraph* ran aground near South Stack. On 8 September 1875 two of its ships, the *Edith* and the *Duchess of Sutherland*, collided at the end of Holyhead breakwater. A month later the LNWR paddle steamer *Earl Spencer* collided with a Llanelli steamer, the *Merlin*, which sank near the breakwater. On 31 October 1883, the company's steamer *Holyhead* struck a German barque, and both were sunk. On 4 January 1887 the paddle steamer *Banshee* ran aground off Porth Tywyn, and the steamer *Eleanor* which was sent to tow her off was herself grounded on the same bank. A year later, almost to the day, the *Earl Spencer* was in trouble again when she went aground beyond Holyhead breakwater. In 1900 it was the *Eleanor*'s turn again. She rammed another of the company's vessels, the *Connemara*, which in turn, on 20 March 1910, rammed and sank a cargo steamer off the Skerries. For the *Connemara* it was third time unlucky. On 3 November 1916 she was rammed and sunk by a collier. This run of bad luck continued when the Admiralty requisitioned four ships from the jinxed line. By 1917 all had been sunk, two by mines and two by torpedoes.

The *Hibernia*, renamed the *Tara*, set up a naval record by patrolling sixty thousand miles in a year in the North Channel between Scotland and Ireland. But her fame was to rest on a more spectacular exploit.

In 1916, part of the North Egyptian Coastal Patrol based on Alexandria, she was torpedoed in the port of Sollum. The U-boat commander who sank her took the ninety-two survivors on board but he refused to land them under a flag of truce in a British port. Instead he handed them over to cut-throat Sennussi tribesmen. The crew – some men were in their seventies – were then force-marched hundreds of miles across the Desert in Libya.

They were rescued at last by the Duke of Westminster and a
column of armoured Rolls-Royces he had fitted out and
commanded in the desert war.

Off the Skerries lies the wreckage of Charles II's yacht the
Mary, which in the 1670s carried military mail and courtiers from
Holyhead to Kingstown, as Dun Laoghaire was then known. On
11 July 1971 it was discovered by accident by divers from the
Chorley and Merseyside branches of the British Sub-Aqua Club.
The club had been diving for lobsters when a change in the
weather drove them onto new ground. On their first dive they
found four bronze cannon. It was the first anyone had heard of
the *Mary* since a day in March 1675 when John Anderton wrote
to the Rt. Hon. Joseph Williamson, Principal Secretary of State at
the Crown Office in Chester:

> That the *Mary* yacht is certainly shipwrecked I have it from the
> mouths of two gentlemen that escaped from aboard her who relate
> thus: On Thursday the 25th instant about 2 o'clock in the morning
> in foggy weather the ship launched upon a rock to the N.W. of the
> Skerrys that lie to the Eastward of the Bay of Holyhead. The seamen
> and the passengers were for the most part snug under decks. The first
> touch raised the seamen who cried all was well but immediately the
> ship struck upon another rock and there sank. The Skerrys is a small
> isle – an appendage to Anglesey about a league from the shore. The
> rock on which the ship struck was so near land that when the sea
> made the ship roll the mast touched land.
>
> The Earl of Meath and about 34 more perished in the ship whereof
> the master, Captain Birslow, the Boatswain and two more sailors were
> of this number. The Master and 23 mariners with 15 passengers got
> safe upon the island. Amongst the 15 passengers was the Earl of
> Ardgloss and Lord Ardee, son of the Earl of Meath and now his
> father's successor to the family estate.
>
> The Master bravely went back along the mast to lead the Earl of
> Meath to safety. He lost his own life in the attempt. It was 12 noon on
> Thursday on the 25th instant before the mast gave way. The
> preserved were on the island from Thursday morning until Saturday
> afternoon and had relief by a flask of gun powder by which they
> struck fire with a steel and of the wreck boards of the ship made a fire.
> Now they roasted some mutton but had no bread nor any liquid but
> salt water till providence cast ashore a small cask of whiskey which
> they divided proportionate among themselves ...

The survivors were at last rescued by a Wicklow vessel which
landed them at Beaumaris three days after their ship had sunk.

Perhaps the most pitiful of all the sea disasters on the Gwynedd coast was that of *Rothsay Castle*. When she was launched in 1812, she had been one of the first steam-driven vessels. When she went aground on the Lavan Sands nineteen years later, carrying trippers from Liverpool to Anglesey, she was barely seaworthy. Her single 50 h.p. engine was worn out; she had one lifeboat but no oars, and her only signal gun was an obsolete fowling piece.

The major contributory fact in the tragedy, in which ninety passengers were lost, was the delay in leaving Liverpool. By the time the *Rothsay Castle* cast off, the tide had turned, slowing her down so much that she reached Dutchman's Bank at the mouth of the Menai Straits at dead low water. The voyage had taken twelve hours in heavy weather. The captain, a former Navy lieutenant called Atkinson, was drunk. The passengers were so frightened by the heavy seas that they sent deputation after deputation to the captain's cabin to beg him to turn back for Liverpool. Atkinson was contemptuous. He told the deputation: 'I think there is a damn deal of fear aboard. And very little danger. If we were to turn back now with passengers it would never do.'

At midnight, with the tide running against her and a head of steam so low she could hardly keep a course, the *Rothsay Castle* struck the Bank. 'It's only sand,' the captain reassured his passengers. 'She will soon run off.' But she did not. She pounded into the sandbank fifty times before the captain gave the order to go astern. And every time she hit, passengers were flung into the sea. An eye-witness recalled: 'The females in particular uttered the most piercing shrieks; some locked themselves in each other's arms, while others, losing all self command, tore their caps and bonnets in the wilderness of their despair. The women and children collected in a huddle together and kept embracing each other, uttering all the time the most dismal lamentations. When tired with crying they leaned against each other with their heads inclined like inanimate bodies.'

Yet incredibly in at least one instance Victorian proprieties were rigidly observed. Miss Mary Whittaker had been dragged onto a makeshift raft by a male passenger who had six companions. Without oars every wave carried them farther from the land. A whispered argument broke out amongst the men. One was pushed towards Miss Whittaker. He came reluctantly and blushing. He confessed that the argument was over the propriety of asking her to take off her skirt so that they could use it as a sail. She agreed and the group were among the twenty-three survivors, though the *Rothsay Castle* finally broke up less than half a mile from the pilot station at Penmon Point. A single rocket fired, a light shown and a rescue flotilla could have reached her in ten minutes.

Holyhead was the centre of an ambitious plan to smuggle arms and ships from Britain to help the Southern cause in the American Civil War. In October 1861 a Confederate arms-buyer, Colonel Edward Anderson, met an agent from the South, James D. Bulloch, in a Holyhead inn to await the arrival of the Clyde steamer *Fingal*. In breach of the British Proclamation of Neutrality which Yankee lobbyists had forced through Parliament, the *Fingal*'s holds were crammed with fourteen thousand Enfield rifles, five hundred revolvers, two $4\frac{1}{2}$-inch breech loaders, bayonets and quantities of ammunition and medical supplies.

The escapade nearly ended in disaster. As she rounded the Holyhead breakwater in thick fog, the *Fingal* struck the bows of an Austrian coal-carrier, the *Siccard*. The coal-carrier sank at once and all her crew were drowned. The three Americans were now concerned to reach the *Fingal* before the customs men who would have been alerted to the sinking. At the harbour they hired a punt and were soon aboard the *Fingal*. Bulloch ordered the skipper to weigh anchor. She had cleared the point of the breakwater and was steaming down channel before anyone in the port, including the Yankee consul who believed he had them under surveillance, even knew there had been a sinking.

Bulloch was a resourceful man. Posing in Liverpool as the agent of a private shipping line with millions of dollars worth of credit, he commissioned two boats using the basic design of a British gunboat, though disguised as a merchantmen. The first, the *Florida*, harried shipping for two years before she was captured. The second, the *Alabama*, proved more difficult to smuggle out of British waters. Bulloch learned that Yankee agents had broken his cover and that a Union ship-of-the-line, the *Tuscora*, was steaming from Gibraltar to intercept the ship which had been commissioned under the Spanish name of *Enrica*.

To allay the suspicions of the Yankee agents, Bulloch took a party of Liverpool businessmen and their wives for a sail in Liverpool Bay. The agent who saw the *Alabama* steam down the Mersey, gay with bunting, failed to notice the tug that was following her. The *Alabama* sailed along the Gwynedd coast until in the late afternoon Bulloch announced that he was going to keep the *Alabama* out for night trials. 'We will sail to the Mersey Bar,' he said. 'There is a tug waiting to take us ashore.'

Bulloch led the party aboard the tug. But he had left instructions for the *Alabama* to lie at anchor off the Anglesey fishing village of Moelfre. When he had landed his guests,

Bulloch set sail again and by nightfall he was alongside the Confederate ship. At 1 a.m. she set sail in a south-westerly gale. Just in time. The next morning the *Tuscora* sailed into Moelfre Bay.

The *Alabama* was fitted out with armaments at a secret base at Terceira in the Azores and spent the next two years at sea. She was sunk in the Battle of Cherbourg.

The Robbers of the Rocks of Crigyll plied their bloody trade looting wrecked ships in the eighteenth century at the mouth of the River Crigyll, roughly on the site of what is now the Anglesey resort of Rhosneigr. By day the robbers were respectable members of the community. They included wealthy landowners, farmers, tailors, a weaver, a fuller, housewives, even children. On one occasion a group of Calvinistic Methodists was discovered by an elder looting a wreck. The robbers were not wreckers themselves. They had no need to be. That part of the coast is strewn with rocks, and there was no shortage of unaided wrecks.

It proved almost impossible to convict the gang, who practised their trade for over thirty years. On one occasion in 1741 four robbers were arraigned to appear before William Chapple, the Chief Justice of Anglesey. Unfortunately he was away. His place was taken by a notorious drunken judge, Thomas Martyn, and the men were freed. Squire Bulkeley explained to his diary: 'Martyn the Judge being every day drunk deferred all the business to the last, when they were hurried over in a very unbecoming manner.'

Only one mariner ever succeeded in getting justice. He was William Chilcott, whose ship the *Charming Jenny* was pounded on a Crigyll rock. His cargo of wine, gin and furniture bobbed in the sea. His wife who was aboard filled her pockets with valuables and money and scrambled to the beach, which was filled with shouting men. As her husband watched helplessly, one of them grabbed Mrs Chilcott and held her head under water until she drowned. Later, when her body was examined, it was found that a finger had been broken in ripping off her gold wedding ring; the silver buckles had been torn from her shoes, her gold watch taken and the clothes ripped from her body. Dazed with horror, Chilcott watched carts being galloped down the beach, where men fought over casks of gin, smashing them open with axes. It was several months before he could persuade the island's magistrates to bring a prosecution. Even when warrants were issued, they were seldom executed. When eventually the magistrates met, a fight broke out between them and in the confusion an order was

signed freeing the robbers. On that occasion one of the
magistrates, William Lewis, seemed about to fight an attorney but
he thought better of it and ordered his servant to beat the attorney
on his behalf.

As a final resort Chilcott sought a writ to have the men tried in
Shrewsbury. Even so it was 14 March 1755 before two of the
robbers were sentenced to death 'for the felony of stealing from
the *Charming Jenny*'. Only one was hanged.

The story of the robbers is more than balanced by the number
of people saved from wrecks on the Anglesey coast.

On 26 March 1823 the packet boat *Alert* got into difficulties
east of the Skerries when the wind dropped and she was carried
on an ebb tide onto the West Mouse rocks. In the wreck which
ensued, one hundred passengers lost their lives.

Watching from the cliffs at Llanfairynghornwy was a
Caernarfon girl, Frances Williams, and her new husband, the
Reverend John, the vicar of the parish. They had just returned
from their honeymoon when disaster struck the packet boat.
Frances was fascinated by the sea: as a teenager she had drawn
the first practical chart of the Menai Straits; now she saw a chance
to give even more aid to mariners.

There had been unco-ordinated attempts by local boatmen to
pick up survivors from the wreck of the *Alert*. With her husband
Frances Williams began to plan an organized rescue service with
sea watches posted in rough weather. She raised funds, selling her
sketches and collecting subscriptions from the local gentry. When
at last there was enough to buy a boat, the Reverend Mr Williams
became the cox and took part in every rescue in which the boat
was involved. By the time the Anglesey Lifeboat Service was
taken over by the newly formed RNLI in 1856, the Williamses
and their crew had saved four hundred lives.

Many of the Gwynedd gentry were so closely connected with
smugglers that one was able to ask the other for a favour. Though
things sometimes went awry.

Between Abersoch and Llanbedrog on the Lleyn Peninsula
there was a house called Castel March. In the seventeenth century
it was the home of Sir William Jones, the local squire and Justice
of the Peace, who was on excellent terms with a gang of smugglers
who used to run their cargoes ashore under Llanbedrog head. The
squire was a jovial, easy-going man who enjoyed simple pleasures
like hunting the hare in the Llanbedrog hills and getting drunk
with his cronies at Pwllheli market. The only fly in the warm
amber of his days was a butler who bullied him abominably.
Though he was sacked many times, the servant ignored the

dismissals and continued to plague his master. In desperation the squire begged the skipper of the smugglers' sloop to kidnap the bullying butler. A price was agreed and some nights later the smugglers let themselves into Castell March, seized, bound and gagged the servant and dragged him off to ship him to some foreign coast and there abandon him. But the butler proved so amiable a companion, so inventive a criminal, that instead he was sworn in as a member of the gang. In the year that followed he took command.

The vessel was away for a year or two pursuing a successful career of piracy before it returned to Llanbedrog. This time it was the squire's turn to be bound, gagged and kidnapped. When morning broke, he lay trussed on the deck of the sloop watching the vanishing coast of Lleyn. This time the butler had power of life and death over him. Many years passed and a good deal of sea water under the prow before Sir William was exchanged for a heavy ransom. When he was freed, he removed instantly to Caernarfon, where he spent the remainder of his days in the shadow of the castle. And no doubt always looking over his shoulder in case the butler did it again.

THE LAND

Living paradise of flowers,
Land of Honey, land of violets
And blossoms, land rich in crops,
Land of nut bushes and dear
Land of the hills.

                              Machreth

• CHAPTER 3 •

Gwynedd was born some 4,600 million years ago, a spinning cloud of dust and gas. As the earth heated with the emission of radioactive minerals, the lighter material in the spinning nebula was forced to the surface, driven by convection currents. Like the scum on a cauldron of boiling jam, the accretion of the first continents began.

Over the millions of years to follow, as convection currents became more numerous, whatever crust had formed was split time after time and the wandering continents knew no rest. Today the continents are still on the move. One hundred and twenty million years ago North Wales was attached to part of North America. As convection currents, in what is now the mid-Atlantic, began to rise, North Wales and parts of Europe split from America and have been moving apart by up to one-and-a-half inches (four centimetres) a year since that time. As we head towards Russia, so the roots of the continent drag against the hotter, more plastic mantle beneath the crust. Gwynedd more than most places felt the effect of this in the summer of 1984. Earthquakes shook her shores as the continent beneath flexed its muscles against the continuous pull of the dragging continent.

Meteorites tell the story of the earliest time. Rocks from west Greenland have been dated at 3,700 million years; slightly older rocks are thought to exist in part of the Canadian shield. As time goes on, we are likely to find even older rocks.

The Palaeozoic era began 570 million years ago, followed by the Mesozoic and then Cenozoic, each decreasing progressively in length. We live today in the Cenozoic era. Each era is further subdivided into geological periods. Of the period up to 600 million years ago, the Pre-Cambrian era, which covers eight-ninths of the Earth's history, little is known and its history is difficult to unravel.

Until 1967 some of the rocks of Anglesey and Lleyn were said to be Pre-Cambrian because of their ancient, deformed

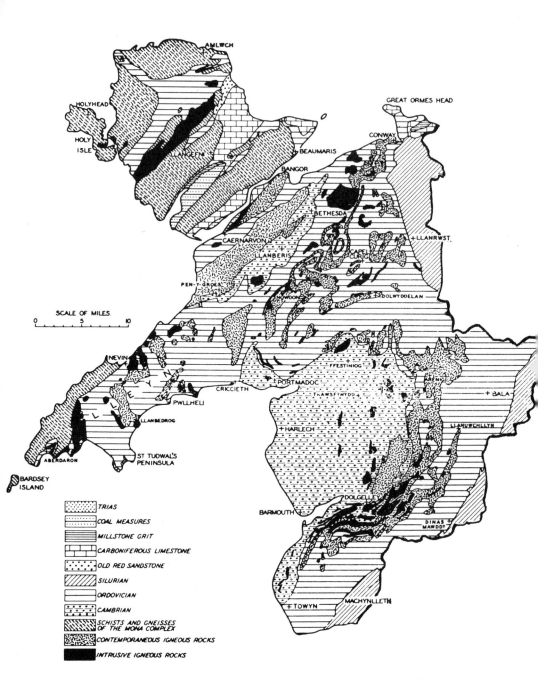

AMLWCH

HOLYHEAD

HOLY
ISLE

LLANFERN

BEAUMARIS

GREAT ORMES HEAD

CONWAY

BANGOR

BETHESDA

LLANRWST

CAERNARVON

LLANBERIS

CAPEL
CURIG

PEN-Y-GROES

DOLWYDDELAN

SCALE OF MILES
0   5   10

NEVIN

FFESTINIOG

ARENI

BALA

CRICCIETH

PORTMADOC

TRAWSFYNYDD

PWLLHELI

LLANBEDROG

HARLECH

LLANUWCHLLYN

ST TUDWAL'S
PENINSULA

ABERDARON

BARDSEY
ISLAND

DOLGELLEY

BARMOUTH

DINAS
MAWDDY

	TRIAS
	COAL MEASURES
	MILLSTONE GRIT
	CARBONIFEROUS LIMESTONE
	OLD RED SANDSTONE
	SILURIAN
	ORDOVICIAN
	CAMBRIAN
	SCHISTS AND GNEISSES OF THE MONA COMPLEX
	CONTEMPORANEOUS IGNEOUS ROCKS
	INTRUSIVE IGNEOUS ROCKS

TOWYN

MACHYNLLETH

Simplified outline of the 'solid' geology of Gwynedd

appearance and lack of fossils, which appear in abundance only in the Palaeozoic era. It is thought that before about 600 million years ago the atmosphere was not conducive to the type of life we see today.

It was in this context, on a field course, that rocks at Cemaes Bay, on Anglesey, were examined which did not entirely fit their previous description. The rocks were said to be Pre-Cambrian but could not be dated. The Caledonian Orogeny – a great earth-building period – some 450 million years ago had altered the rocks of Anglesey and imprinted that age upon them. As luck would have it, a small area of rocks had remained unaltered as the underlying sediment, a mud-like deposit, now called the gwna melange, and some carbon-rich rock, a graphite schist, had underlain some fossil-rich limestone. The underlying rocks had acted as a lubricant when earth movements took place which crushed and folded other rocks within a distance of a mile or so. These rocks remained fairly unaltered and were floated in various directions until they reached their present position.

The fossils in these Pre-Cambrian sedimentary limestones were all algal. Present-day equivalents are termed stromatolites. Stromatolites grow today in inter-tidal areas within the tropics. The fossils occur in fossilized reefs along the Cemaes coastline, and at least four reef structures have been recognized. In the area between each reef would have been lagoons. Between the reefs are masses of rock filled with broken reef fragments and uni- and multicellular creatures called vesicularites. On close examination of the stromatolites, various types were found, some with branching columnar structures, which can be found growing today, but some which looked like upturned ice-cream cones with other cones, like parasitic volcanoes, growing out from the sides. These were subsequently identified as Conophyton, a particular type of stromatolite with a narrow time range found only in the late Pre-Cambrian period.

Comparing these with specimens from Canada and Australia and in particular with reports from Russia, their age was given as between 600 and 900 million years. Since that discovery at Cemaes Bay, geologists' interest has been re-awakened and many more workers have examined the area in an effort to unravel the history of the late Pre-Cambrian and early Cambrian period. As a result there is rethinking on where the boundary between the Pre-Cambrian and Palaeozoic eras should be fixed and to which era these rocks belong.

It is thought that during the Palaeozoic era the great thicknesses of rock in central and north Wales were deposited in a north-east/south-west basin which was sinking rapidly as the crust below the area was dragged down by descending currents. On the Padarn ridge near Llanberis the earliest rocks are frequently volcanic and above this exhibit shallow-water sedimentary sequences, but as the sagging crust gained momentum, the basin deepened and was filled by thousands of feet of purple and blue-grey mudstone from which much of the famous slate is derived. Above these slates are fine silt stones showing that the basin was shallower by the end of Cambrian times.

After this period of relative quiescence, the Ordovician period arrived, heralded by the development of a series of volcanic centres which extends from Nant Ffrancon through the Carneddau. The volcanoes, many of which occurred on the sea bed, poured out lava and ash and were frequently explosive, rather similar to the Mount St Helen's Volcano in Washington State. These ashes and lavas are particularly well displayed in the Devil's Kitchen, and some lava surfaces even exhibit ripple marks on their upper surfaces where the sea washed gently over them.

The volcanic episode terminated with extensive ash eruptions in the Capel Curig area. Following this period, volcanic calm prevailed with only sporadic minor eruptions. Associated with this eruptive period was an uplift and doming of the area around Snowdon and consequent faulting in the rocks. All this activity waned as the sedimentary environment of the Upper Ordovician became one of shallower seas and the rocks began to acquire the features of the succeeding Silurian system.

At Dulas and Lligwy, on Anglesey, the rocks exhibit some cracks and other muddy surfaces with worm burrows. Following Devonian times the area was transgressed by clear, tropical seas, and highly fossiliferous limestones were deposited. Locally at Penmon and Benllech these rocks have been quarried for stone which was used to build Caernarfon and Beaumaris castles, as well as Bangor Normal College in more recent times. These limestones at one time would have been continuous with those seen on Puffin Island and the Ormes but at present are separated from Anglesey by the Irish Sea.

By Upper Carboniferous time North Wales had moved from the southern hemisphere and was straddling the equator. The coal fossils today have very similar appearance to those found in the present-day equatorial forests. The forests which provided our present seams were on an unstable, forested, swampy area, first above sea-level, then below. The processes were repeated many times. The coal seams represent thousands of years of forest

The stone finger of Llithfaen. Prehistoric relics of this kind abound in Gwynedd

Tre'r Ceiri hill fort on Yr Eifl above Llanaelhaern on the Lleyn was once a huge stronghold. And then someone told the villagers there was gold there . . .

A 2,000-year industrial handspan. In the foreground Penmon Quarry which provided the stone for the Conwy and Britannia Bridges. In the background Penmaenmawr, the site of a Stone Age axe factory whose products were found all over Britain

Workers at Penyrorsedd slate quarry had to make this 360-foot vertical climb up rotting wooden ladders at the end of every shift. And when they reached the top they had a five-mile mountain walk to reach their homes in Talysarn

cover, found now on what the miners call the seat earth, which was the original soil, and each seam overlain by sandstones which represent the material swept in by the sea as it transgressed over the forest.

Red sandstone beds, also present on the straits opposite Caernarfon, represent the youngest solid rocks found on Anglesey. Since they are above the coal measures, they probably represent deposits formed in desert areas as the position of North Wales had moved northwards and was in a position similar to that of today's Sahara desert. The redness indicates aerial deposition and could explain why the rocks of the Mesozoic era are missing from North Wales. Britain continued to move northward, probably at only a few inches a year, until the Tertiary period some 65 million years ago.

Those oscillations at the end of the Carboniferous era represent the Earth again flexing its muscles as it did in the Lower Palaeozoic prior to the Caledonian Orogeny. The final thrust which uplifted the land is termed the Hercynian Orogeny and was responsible for pushing up the Armorican mountains of Brittany and the Harz mountains in Germany. Most rocks in Britain received impetus from the south which caused east-west folding of many mountains. Because the ancient rocks of North Wales had been packed and hardened by the earlier Caledonian Orogeny, it was relatively protected by the disturbances, and only gentle folding and uplift took place. There was, however, much fracturing and further movement along old Caledonian faults.

The Hercynian movements brought to an end the period of subsidence and deposition experienced in the Upper Palaeozoic. The whole of North Wales was uplifted to form part of a huge continent, a much enlarged 'St George's Land', the shores of which lay many miles to the south and east.

Very little is known of events during Tertiary times, and the time gap is in the order of 180 million years. During mid-Tertiary, when the Alps and Himalayas were uplifted in the most recent orogeny, slight movement occurred again along the major Gwynedd faults, and some dykes were emplaced from basic magmas deep in the crust. These can be seen in several places but are by no means as numerous as those intruded during the Caledonian Orogeny. This Tertiary activity heralded the splitting of the continent and the formation of the ever-widening Atlantic Ocean. This implies that Britain was then much farther north than the desert latitude it experienced some 100 million years beforehand.

As the Atlantic split widened, Britain has moved progressively eastward, and the 'push' from the ever-widening ocean floor probably accounts for the earthquakes experienced in North Wales in 1984. It was again the major faults, created in Caledonian times some 450 million years ago, which moved and shook the Lleyn and Anglesey.

At the end of the Tertiary era the climate cooled and the Pleistocene ice covered most of Britain. The Merioneth ice which covered most of North Wales was at least two thousand feet thick and was centred to the east of Snowdonia. Only the highest peaks protruded through the ice, and these were subjected to the action of freeze and thaw. The underlying landscape was carved as the ice, armed with all the loose debris from the valleys and the loosened blocks from the peaks, ground its way slowly down the valleys, creating the magnificent scenery for which the mountains of Gwynedd are now so well known.

Apart from a small enclave on the western side of the Conwy valley around Conwy, Silurian strata are confined to Clwyd. However, at one time they must have overlain the Ordovician rocks across Snowdonia but have since been eroded. The fact that these rocks show no sign of vulcanicity indicates that there was a period of quiescence. In Anglesey the only Silurian strata are found on top of the Ordovician rocks on Parys mountain.

Following the deposition of Silurian rocks, earth movements, which had continuously affected the Welsh basin, increased in intensity, the rocks became elevated, folded and faulted and rose to form a great mountain range. The movements were known as the Caledonian Orogeny. Following this uplift the geological history of Snowdonia is little known until the recent events of the Pleistocene ice age. However, on Anglesey, the record is better as sedimentation occurred and has been preserved, possibly because the area was quickly eroded after Ordovician times.

The Upper Palaeozoic era on Anglesey was heralded by the red rocks of the Devonian period which are mostly fine-grained muds and sands which were exposed much of the time to aerial activity.

The rocks of Gwynedd are rich in minerals. The Queen's wedding ring is made from gold mined in the county, and I was once offered a cottage in Bala with its own gold mine in the garden for 1s. 6d. a week. Gold mining has become yet another tourist attraction. In 1985 a local paper reported: 'Holidaymakers are buying pans at £7.75 made for panning gold by a firm in Birmingham and sold by a store in Dolgellau. The town is only a couple of miles from the famous St David's gold mines which supplied the gold for the royal weddings rings. Mrs Molly Evans, who works at the hardware store selling them, said: "A few came back after doing some panning and showed us some little bottles with gold in them, but they would not say where they found it." '

At the present time the worked mineral deposits of the Lleyn are confined to quarrying for setts at Trevor which are exported worldwide. The manganese ores were worked until World War I and were shipped mainly from Pwllheli. A small industry was once sited on the semi-precious jasper deposit near Aberdaron on the Lleyn but this, like the similar jasper of Llanddwyn Island, is now merely a collector's item for budding geologists and gem-polishers.

The mineralization of the Lower Palaeozoic rocks of North Wales, including the Dolgellau gold belt, is attributed, like the Anglesey copper, to deep-seated Ordovician igneous intrusions which released metal-rich waters and steam into any surrounding rocks which could act as a suitable host. Oolitic (egg-shaped bodies) and pisolitic (pea-size oolites) iron ores are found in marine sediments on the Gwynedd mainland as well as on Anglesey. They yield hematite, pyrite and siderite iron ores, together with nodules of sponge fragments in lenticles in the sediments. The best-known ore bodies occur at Betws Garmon, Cader Idris, St Tudwal's peninsula, Tremadog, Trefriw and Llandegai, near Bangor, as well as in Anglesey around Llanfaes.

Manganese ores also occurring as oolites and pisolites are found in the Lleyn and in the mountains south of Betws-y-Coed. These too originated as manganese solutions migrating from volcanic sources. Because the rocks are broken by faulting, thrusting and shearing, the economic exploitation of the ore is correspondingly difficult.

The Anglesey coalfield, which has probably the same origin as the Flint-Denbigh field, stretches the six miles from Ceint, near Llangefni, to the coast beneath the Malltraeth marshes. There were fourteen seams and one twenty-seven-foot oil shale deposit in a 1500 foot coal measure deposit overlain by seven hundred feet of red sandstone.

Minerals have been mined in Gwynedd since pre-historic times. Lead, zinc, copper, gold and iron have all been worked in their turn. In many mines galleries hewn by the Romans can still be seen today.

Lead and zinc ore were mined at Llanergan on the Lleyn Peninsula and in the Conwy Valley, notably round Llanwrst, where ore was last mined as recently as 1963. The Trecastell mine at Henryd, near Conwy, reached its capacity of 6,448 tons of lead between 1892 and 1913. At Betws-y-Coed 2,548 tons of zinc ore were raised between 1869 and 1904.

Though the Mawddach Valley gold mines were first worked by the Romans, they subsequently fell into disuse and were not re-opened until 1844. There have been three 'gold rushes'. The first was in 1853, the second in 1862 and the last in 1887. Though mining continued on a large scale until World War I and has continued sporadically to this day, the peak production was in 1904, when 19,655 ounces of gold were recovered. In all between 1861 and 1938, 279, 027 tons of ore produced 126,340 ounces of gold.

Another sheet of ice in the Irish Sea moved south-westwards and met the Merioneth ice along the Menai Straits. Within only a few miles of Snowdon one can find the erratics carried from Scotland and the Lake District and dropped on the present shores of Anglesey where, twice daily, the tides wash away the loose deposits left over ten thousand years ago. Eventually the main ice retreated to isolated centres, leaving Snowdonia as a snow-covered peak with glaciers in the valleys. By ten thousand years ago the ice had retreated to the highest cwms and finally disappeared.

The meltwater streams and decaying ice redistributed the debris collected from the highlands and deposited it in valleys and on the lowlands, especially on Anglesey where the drumlin swarms nestle like eggs in a basket above the eroded ancient rocks of the Mona complex. Most rocks are plastered by thick deposits of this till, and these can be seen rising majestically, as twenty-to-thirty-foot-high cliffs, along the Straits between Beaumaris and Penmon.

Today the Isle of Anglesey is a mecca for professional geologists intent upon unravelling its complicated origins as well as for the hoards of students who hammer away at its long-held secrets. Snowdonia and Lleyn are equally interesting, but here the human impact is mainly from the heavy-booted feet of climbers, walkers, tourists and winter sports enthusiasts. The seas are teeming not only with fish but with the sails of numerous yachts and dinghies. The sewers pour out effluent into the surrounding seas, and caravans clutter crazily in the beauty spots. The mine and quarry tips crowd our landscape, and the smelters, chemical works and power stations all contribute to the air we breathe and the sea we bathe in. Gwynedd had been evolving for 4,600 million years. Its surface has changed little in the last ten thousand years. Will it remain recognizable in the next thousand years?

There were three copper mines in the Great Orme at Llandudno and a cluster in Snowdonia. The ruin of the Britannia mine crushing-mill on the banks of Llyn Lydaw can still be seen but all trace has vanished of the Llanberis copper mine. In Llandudno the engine house of the Ty Gwyn mine stood where the Empire Hotel now stands in Ty Gwyn road.

But it is the copper mines on Anglesey which come most readily to mind in any discussion of the mineral deposits of Gwynedd. It was the rich vein of copper which made Anglesey the target for Roman invasion. In those far off times, when the island held the last Druidical college in Europe, the copper was used to fashion weapons for the British underground fighters on the mainland.

The ore came from Mynydd Tryglwyn in north-east Anglesey. In 1406 the mountain was renamed to honour Robert Parys the younger, who had been appointed by Henry IV to collect fines from the 2,121 islanders who supported Owain Glyndwr. The mountain was his reward. The King did not know he was giving away a mineral resource which would have turned him from one of the poorest kings in Europe into unquestionably the richest. It was not until the seventeenth century that mining began again on the mountain, and the eighteenth before it was pursued with any degree of enthusiasm.

The cause was war, as is so often the case in matters of industrial prosperity. Copper was in high demand for sheathing the keels of fighting ships.

In 1766 Alexander Fraser, a renegade Highlander and a member of the House of Lovat who had fled Scotland after killing a piper, was employed by Sir Nicholas Bayley, the owner, to mine land he owned on Parys. Fraser found ore on the mountain but the difficulties of mining it persuaded Sir Nicholas to lease the mineral rights to a Cheshire mining consortium. On 2 March 1768 a rich vein of copper was found by a Derbyshire miner, Jonathan Roose. The date was celebrated for many years by Anglesey miners, and the shaft in which the ore was found was christened 'The Golden Venture'. On Roose's tombstone in Amlwch churchyard the epitaph reads:

He first yon mountain's wondrous riches found
First drew its minerals
Blushing from the ground.
He heard the miners'
First exulting shout
Then toil'd near 50 years
To guide its treasures out.

A local miner who was with Roose when he found the ore, Roland Puw, was given a bottle of brandy and a rent-free cottage for life.

The conditions under which the miners worked – women as well as men – were far from ideal. In the nineteenth century they were not paid for their first month's work. They had to exist on a small subsistence allowance, providing their own chisels and spades, hammers, candles, powder and fuses, bought at shops owned and run at a handsome profit by the mining companies. The wages on Anglesey were only half those paid to Cornish miners. During the late eighteenth century, when the mines were at their most productive, the workers were paid in coins minted by the mine-owners themselves. These were copper tokens, today much prized by collectors, which were introduced in 1787 at a time when there were no banks on the island. They had the advantage of being made from copper mined from the mountain and provided the mine-owners with yet another profitable market. It was not until 1817 that they were declared illegal.

The nineteenth century saw the decline in the copper industry, and the mines were closed in 1920. In the 1970s a Canadian mining firm, Cominco, did test drilling on the mountain, which is jointly owned by the Marquess of Anglesey and Sir Arundel Neave. Nothing came of the investigation but in 1984 another Canadian firm, Imperial Metals Co-operative, leased land on the mountain and commenced operations. The company said they were looking not for copper alone but for lead, silver and gold, and they announced plans for a £25 million mine of five shafts which would give employment to 150 people. The first shaft has already been bored, and the first ore samples have been brought to the surface. The engineers plan to go to a depth of thirteen hundred feet.

Penmaenmawr was a stone axe factory in 2000 BC. Its products have been found as far away as Wiltshire, Hampshire and Cambridgeshire. The granite quarried from the mountain has the reputation of being the most durable and hard in Britain. In more recent times it has been used in both tunnels under the Mersey and will be used for lining the road tunnel under the River Conwy. Many of Liverpool's great buildings are built with the stone. Its streets are paved with it, as are those of towns and cities all over north-west England.

This flourishing quarry industry was started in 1830 by a Cheshire man, Philip Whiteway of Runcorn. He was impressed by the quality of the pebbles from the shore at Penmaenmawr which were brought back as ballast from North Wales by coastal ships and used for paving the cobbled streets of Lancashire. He took a lease and started quarrying the mountain. At its peak the quarry employed a thousand men. The quarries are now run by Kingston Minerals, which has recently invested £4 million to transform the old quarry into one of the most modern in Britain. A new crushing and screening plant has been installed at twelve

The Penrhyn Slate Quarry at Bethesda in the nineteenth century. Once
the biggest slate quarry in Europe, it supplied writing slates to every
British school

hundred feet on the mountain top where the ninety-six-acre
quarry is situated. Four conveyor belts send fifteen hundred tons
of rock an hour down a 1-in-3 gradient to storage silos.

The most famous building material produced in Gwynedd is
slate, quarried in remote mountain areas, often in appalling
conditions. The eighteenth century was the most profitable for
the slate quarry owners. Until that time the quarries had been
small family businesses, but as demand grew, landowners smelled
the scent of profits. They refused to renew the self-employed
quarrymen's leases and began to merge their workers into their
own larger operations. These followed two methods: slate mining,
largely confined to the Blaenau Ffestiniog district, and open-site
quarrying which predominates over the rest of Gwynedd. These
open sites consist of a series of terraces sixty feet or more high.
Each terrace is given a name. At the Dinorwig Quarry, which in
the nineteenth century had terraces two thousand feet above
sea-level and employed three thousand men, there was Jubilee
Terrace, one named after Princess Mary and another rather
puzzlingly called Abyssinia.

The slates themselves were given regal names at the suggestion
of Lady Penrhyn, the wife of one of the biggest and, even against
some stiff competition, one of the most unpleasant of the

nineteenth-century quarry-owners. She suggested that the slates should be called by the degrees of the aristocracy. To this day a twenty-four by twelve-inch slate is a Duchess, a twenty by ten-inch a Countess and the sixteen by eight-inch a Lady.

This prompted a guest at Penrhyn Castle, Mr Justice Laycester, to write a poem:

> There's a man who makes Peeresses here by the hundred,
> By a stroke of a hammer, without the king's aid,
> A Lady or Countess or Duchess is made.
> And where'er they are seen, in a palace or shop,
> Their rank they preserve, they are still at the top.
> This Countess or Lady though crowds may be present
> Submits to be dressed by the hands of a peasant.
> And you'll see when her Grace is but once in his clutches
> With how little respect he will handle a Duchess.

In fact, few aristocrats ventured to the quarries, where workers' conditions were appalling in the eighteenth century, disgraceful in the nineteenth and dreadful in the twentieth. I have a friend, a former quarryman who served as a fighting soldier in almost every campaign in World War II, who on the fortieth anniversary of VE day told me: 'I've always been grateful for the war. It got me out of the quarries.'

Quarrymen lived all week in damp dormitories on the mountain, carrying a week's food in a pillowcase when they trudged up the mountain to work just as dawn broke on Monday morning, returning to their villages on Friday evening for a brief weekend. Which probably explains why the single street village in which I live once had sixteen public houses.

They were admirable men. In their rat-infested, tumbledown quarters they held *eisteddfodau* and athletic events, whilst below them the owners and their ladies sailed through the Menai Straits in their magnificent steam yachts or strolled through such marvels of bad taste as the mock Gothic castle of Penrhyn with its slate four-poster bed and rooms like crematoria.

The money that was wasted on such tasteless toys grew like mimic mountains in the nineteenth century with the increased demand for roofing slates. It was a demand which came not only from Britain but from Europe and North America. Slate ports were built at Penrhyn, outside Bangor, and at Port Dinorwic. Horse-drawn trams were used at first to bring the slate from quarry to ship side. They proved unsatisfactory, and between 1840 and 1842 a railway was completed which ran along the shore of Lake Padarn through the valley to a point in the hills above the port.

Dinorwig Quarry is closed now but its buildings have become a fascinating museum of the trade. The lakeside rail trip is deservedly popular with tourists. At Penrhyn Castle you can see the original rolling stock of the quarry railways, beautifully restored and gleaming. But in the quarry hospital there is a grim reminder of the reality of slate-mining life. It is an artificial arm made for a quarryman so that he could raise his hat to the quarry master.

The other method of producing slate was carried on in huge caverns where men worked in pitch darkness hewing their 'bargains', the name that is given, with unconscious irony, to each man's stretch of rock. Typical of them is the network of caverns at Llechwedd. These are now another tourist attraction which has welcomed $2\frac{1}{2}$ million visitors since the caverns were developed in 1972. It is an awe-inspiring outing to take a seat on what was the miners' underground railway through the slate caverns, peopled now with a tableau of Victorian miners, or to take the alternative ride on Britain's steepest passenger railway, down a 1-in-1.8 gradient, into the Deep Mine.

When the mine first opened as a tourist attraction, a party of men who had worked there were taken round. The caverns were floodlit, and for the first time they were able to see the height from the cavern floor to the face they had been working. It was too much for one of the party. He fainted.

Though there is still a market for slate – indeed, it is growing apace – some of the uses to which the quarry caverns have been put would have surprised the old miners.

In 1940, at the lowest ebb of World War II, when London was being blitzed nightly, Winston Churchill became worried about the safety of Britain's great collection of art treasures and ordered their evacuation to a place of safety. Sir Kenneth Clarke, the art historian and at that time the Director of the National Gallery, had known the Welsh mountains since childhood. He advised taking the paintings to the caverns of Manod quarry on the outskirts of Blaenau Ffestiniog. Inside the mountain a cluster of brick shelters was built and fitted with sophisticated ventilation and heating systems. The men who built them had no idea of the purpose for which these 'air-raid shelters' were to be used. It was not until the war ended that they discovered that for five years the mountain had protected some of the world's greatest works of art. They included the fabulous collection of the King's pictures, priceless antiques from the royal palaces, masterpieces from the collections of the Tate and the National galleries. There were nineteen Rembrandts, several van Dycks, da Vincis, Titians and Gainsboroughs. And, according to one story, the Crown Jewels of Great Britain. They had been brought in lorries disguised as chocolate delivery trucks. Not without difficulty. The cave entrance had to be widened for an equestrian portrait of Charles I by van Dyck. At Blaenau the pictures were put under the care of the quarry manager, Charles Vaughan. It was his daily job to walk down the galleries where the great masters hung, unseen by anyone but him and the occasional high officer of State. Whenever it rained, night or day, he had to rush to the cavern in case it flooded. According to his daughter, the responsibility shortened his life by several years. He must have been more relieved than most when the war ended and the treasures were returned to London.

But the story does not end there. Whoever negotiated the lease of the cavern clearly took a gloomy view of the likely duration of the war. The lease was for forty years. Even when it expired in 1981, the Ministry still refused to hand it back, on the rather sinister grounds 'that it might be needed for another war'. The brick gallery was kept in a constant state of readiness for this alarming contingency. For forty years two brothers were employed full time to make a daily visit to the cavern, to keep the ventilator fans running and the heating and humidity constant, although since 1945 there has been nothing in the gallery to protect.

Not surprisingly, when there was a public disclosure of the government's attitude, rumour had a field day. According to one report, the gallery was being kept as a nuclear shelter for the Royal Family. More thoughtful people pointed out that, even given the much publicized athletic prowess of the princes, it was difficult to imagine them covering the two hundred miles from Buckingham Palace to Manod in the four minutes allowed for nuclear warnings. Very well, quoth rumour, it's going to be used by a War Cabinet. Alas, the picture of the Prime Minister's fencibles panting up the road proved even more risible.

The speculation was ended when in 1966 the High Court ruled that the Ministry must give up its little grey hole in the west. A local family named Williams had bought the quarry. They assumed they would take possession of it when the lease the government held expired in 1981. But the Property Services Agency – part of the Department of the Environment – would not give it up. After polite negotiations failed, the Williamses fought a two-year battle which cost them £120,000 before they succeeded in winning back the quarry. Mr Eifion Williams explained: 'We wanted it for slate production and once we'd gone to law there was no going back. We never thought when we bought it the government wouldn't give it up when their lease expired. It's a gamble. You can never tell with a quarry what the slate is going to be like.'

In celebration the Williamses opened the caverns to the public so that local people, for the first time, could visit the underground art gallery. An eerie experience it was. Behind steel and timber doors in the mountain lies a tunnel four hundred yards long which opens into a honeycomb of caverns eerily lit and a thousand feet below the mountain top. The caverns are the height of cathedrals, and dwarfed on the rock floor of the biggest, which is two hundred feet high, are the four brick shelters. On the walls inside were the labels which identified the artists whose pictures once hung there. But dust was beginning to gather over the clean spaces which the pictures had occupied. In one cavern a scaffolding tower stretched into the darkness. It was erected after Mr Vaughan discovered that a rise in temperature and a fall in humidity, caused by the air-conditioning in the brick shelters, had cracked the cavern roof. There were fears that a general collapse might follow. Happily it didn't.

THE HISTORY

To a Wales made one, contented and fair,
To a prince throned, laden nobly with gifts,
To the Lord of Dinorwig's bright citadel land,
To the country of Dafydds where Welsh freely flows.
                    Dafydd Benfras (d. 1257)

• CHAPTER 4 •

Iberians swept out of Asia in pre-historic times in three great waves. The first went eastward to create China and Japan; from the second came the colonists of the Nile basin; the third came to Europe.

Common to all three was the worship of ancestors. Thus the obelisk of Egypt is nothing more than a sophisticated version of the menhir, the stone finger which points heavenwards from meadowland all over Gwynedd. The massive pyramids of the Nile Valley, the Shinto temples of Japan, the burial chambers of the Chinese Bronze Age Shang Dynasty at Anyang and the cromlechs of Gwynedd share a common purpose, express an identical view: the belief in the immortality of the soul.

This was the philosophy of a gentle people, dark, long-headed, small in stature, unwarlike and no match for the next great folk movement. This came not from the fertile valley of an Asian Garden of Eden. The new wanderers were forged by harsher conditions in Siberia. They were the Celts, divided into the Goidels (the Gaels) and the Brythons (the Britons).

The Gaels populated the areas now called the Scottish Highlands, Ireland and the Isle of Man; the Britons settled in what became England, only to be forced out of their settlements first by the Romans in AD 59 and then by successive waves of invaders, beginning with the Irish led by King Cormac Macairt in 240. His warriors invaded Gwynedd through Anglesey and the Lleyn Peninsula, 'Lleyn' being a corruption of 'Leinster'.

In their turn the Irish were ousted by the man who was to found a dynasty of kings of Gwynedd which lasted down the centuries until Plantagenet times. His name was Cunedda and he lived with his followers, until he was ousted by the Picts, in what is now Strathclyde. Followed by his sons, his warriors and his womenfolk, Cunedda attacked the Gaels in a war which continued until, in 400, the Irish invaders were driven out of their last stronghold in Gwynedd. The final engagements were in

Anglesey. Cunedda's grandson Cadwallon 'Longhand' fought a series of battles culminating at Holyhead, where he slew the Irish chief Serigibi.

Gwynedd was Cunedda's first kingdom. His son Ceredig gave his name to Cardigan, now happily restored to its ancient name Ceredigion, although the name of another son, Mereion, was lost in the reorganization of counties when Merioneth became part of the new county of Gwynedd.

In 605 the Britons in North Wales were separated for ever from their kinsmen in Strathclyde when the latter were defeated by the newest invaders from Germany, the Angles and the Saxons.

From Chester the Britons were pushed further and further back into the mountains and to the Celtic heartland of Gwynedd. Some even fled beyond the seas to found a colony in 'Lesser Britain', Brittany. Mona, the latinized form of the British 'Mon', became Anglesea (Saxon 'Engles Eage' – the 'g' is pronounced 'y' – the Island of the Angles) when a colony of Angles settled there. The Saxons gave the Britons a new name too. Impertinently these new arrivals called the natives 'Weallas', 'the strangers'. The Britons, however, have continued to call themselves to this day 'Y Cymry', 'the companions'.

The Cymry were a brave race. Fearless warriors, sensitive artists, imaginative and handsome, they had one fatal weakness. Down the centuries writer after writer has drawn attention to this flaw. They lost battles not from cowardice. Ironically, for a race which labelled itself 'the companions', the Britons were forever squabbling amongst themselves. The three great Saxon tribes which straddled England fought to unite; the companions fought to stay apart. In Wales this readiness to betray each other for small tribal gains was of enormous advantage to the Normans and their descendants on the English throne.

Gildas, the historian, was an example. Dispossessed by the Picts in Strathclyde, his family fled to Anglesey where they were given shelter and land by Cunedda's family. He returned the hospitality years later by penning a venomous attack on the British.

At about this time Wales had been divided into three kingdoms, Deheuberath, Powys and Gwynedd. Each had its independent king, but the king of Gwynedd was 'Gwledig', the over-king to whom others paid tribute, and the supremacy remained in this family until 817, when Cynon Tyndaethwy's daughter Esyllt married Mervyn Vrych, the King of Powys, thus uniting North Wales. Their son Rhodri 'the Great' married Angharad, whose father Meurig ruled all of South Wales.

For the first and only time in its long history, Wales became one nation. It did not last, of course. On Rhodri's death, by the literally divisive law of inheritance in Celtic societies, Wales was split equally between his sons, and Rhodri's great work came to nothing. In 887 Anarawd became King of Gwynedd, and for the two hundred years that followed Gwynedd was in the thick of tribal squabbles.

Viking landings in Gwynedd began in the ninth century and continued sporadically for two hundred years. Norse Vikings came by sea from Dublin, Danes overland through north-east Wales from Chester. In 853, according to the *Brut y Tywysogion*, Mona was ravaged by the Black Pagans and in the tenth century conquered. The two thousand islanders were sold into slavery. Yet scarcely a century later, in 1087, a native chieftain, Gruffydd ap Cynan, grandson of Cadwalladr, used Orkney Vikings to support his claim to the Gwynedd throne.

The *Hanes Gruffydd ap Cynan* records that Gruffydd and his mercenaries slew one usurper, Cenwic, soon after they landed at Abermenai, now one of the loveliest, most tranquil nature reserves on the island. The second battle was in a valley called the Bloody Land (*gwaed erw*) where a second usurper, Trahaern, was defeated. Gruffydd was proclaimed King of Gwynedd. It was a short reign. He had unwisely appealed for aid to Hugh 'the Fat', Earl of Chester, and his henchman Robert of Rhuddlan. They saw immediately the chance of extending their realm. The *Brut y Tywysogion* records that in 1094 the King of Gwynedd was in shackles in the market-place in Chester. He was rescued by a young man named Cenwric who brought him back to Gwynedd. But within four years he was, once again, in exile. Hugh 'the Fat' and Robert invaded Gwynedd and Gruffydd fled to Ireland 'for fear of the treachery of their own men'. The victors were in turn forced to defend Anglesey against Magnus and a Saxon fleet, also hoping to occupy the island. When the Saxons met the Normans, they forgot the native enemy and fought each other. Earl Hugh was wounded. The Saxons sailed away and a year later Gruffydd returned from Ireland and made peace with the Normans.

It was from Gwynedd's capital at Aberffraw on a remote headland in Anglesey that Llywelyn ap Iorwerth 'the Great' set about re-uniting Wales in the thirteenth century. He sought first to consolidate his position with the English by marrying the daughter of King John. But in 1211, using the excuse of 'raids upon the English' by Llywelyn's followers and aided by other Welsh princes, John attacked and Llywelyn fled to Snowdonia. King John's forces suffered considerable hardship. At Deganwy, where they had laid siege to a Welsh castle, the large English army almost starved. A contemporary chronicler wrote: 'The army was in such great want of provisions that an egg sold for a penny half-penny and it was a delicious feast for them to get horse flesh.' Temporarily defeated, King John quit Wales but he was back later in the year, 'his mind being more cruel and his army larger'. This time the King swept through Gwynedd and put Bangor to the torch. Robert, Bishop of Bangor, was seized. Though he was ransomed for two hundred hawks, he died the next year, probably as the result of his ill treatment. Llywelyn sent his wife to make peace with her father, and after Llywelyn paid a ransom of twenty thousand cattle and forty steeds the King returned to England.

Wales was a one-man business. When Llywelyn 'the Great' died in the monastery of Aberconwy, having in his old age taken vows, Wales died with him. This moving tribute to him is in the *Annales Cambriae*: 'He ruled his enemies with sword and spear, gave peace to the monks, provided food and clothing for those who made themselves poor for Christ's sake, enlarged his boundaries by his wars, gave good justice to all according to their deserts and by the bonds of fear or love bound all men duly to him.'

His grandson, Llywelyn ap Gruffydd 'the Last', sought to put Wales together again, by war if necessary but above all by exercising his political skill. He consolidated his power base by a simple expedient. He offered his four brothers the choice of exile or imprisonment. Only one, Owen, chose imprisonment and spent the next twenty-two years in the tower of Dolbadarn Castle on the shore of Lake Padarn in Snowdonia. The other three brothers fled to England and in the fine old Celtic tradition planned to assassinate Llywelyn, who meanwhile established his right to rule the kingdom by buying it from the English for the equivalent of £12 million. To this day no one knows where he got the money. At the time he had an income of £4,000 a year. As part of the deal he agreed to accept Henry III as his overlord.

Llywelyn was not a gentle ruler. He slew and he burned. He built castles to enforce his rule and to compel the allegiance of lesser chieftains. He established towns. He employed, in fact, all the tactics of the Norman Marcher lord. Then Henry III died, to be succeeded by Edward I.

The quarrels began at once. Llywelyn may have seen in the confusion that followed Henry's death the moment to throw off the yoke of the English King. At all events he refused to attend Edward's coronation, ignored four commands to pay homage and stopped paying his annual tribute. In doing so he gravely misjudged Edward. The new King loved war and he did not care how much it cost him. French, Scots or Welsh, he would fight anyone.

Llywelyn struck first. In 1256 he recovered Deganwy Castle, subdued Ceredigion and conquered Powys. He entered South Wales but in doing so stirred a hornet's nest. Edward assembled the largest army that Wales had ever seen: 15,640 warriors marched behind him, one half of whom were Welsh. In the face of overwhelming odds Llywelyn surrendered. In return he was given Anglesey and Snowdonia to rule. It was mountain country that a seasoned campaigner like Edward would hardly have wished to fight over anyway.

The final act began in 1282, when Llywelyn and his brother David, with whom he was now reconciled, launched a second rebellion against the Crown. According to an account in the *Flores Historiorum*, Llywelyn and David 'at the dead hour of night' on Palm Sunday surrounded the castles of Rhuddlan and Flint, captured Lord Roger Clifford, loaded him with chains and took him to Snowdonia. In the campaign which followed, Edward built the first bridge over the Menai Straits, but as his soldiers crossed it they were set on by Llywelyn's men and roundly beaten. Emboldened by this victory, which he saw as the fulfilment of a prophecy by Merlin that he would be crowned Britain's king with Brutus' diadem, he left David to fight on in the mountains whilst he once again struck into South Wales. Adam of Usk recorded the final drama: 'Two English knights John Gifford and Edmund Mortimer surprised him unarmed on the banks of a stream [the River Irfon near Builth Wells]. He was decapitated, his head washed in a stream and carried to London.' With his last words Llywelyn begged in vain for a priest to give him absolution so that he could be given Christian burial. An anonymous letter in the Rolls Series of royal correspondence, addressed to King Edward, reads:

Lady Maud Longespere prayed us by letter that we would absolve Llywelyn, that he might be buried in consecrated ground and we sent word to her that we would do nothing if it could not be proved that he showed signs of true repentance before his death. And Edmund de Mortimer said to me that he had heard from his servants who were at the death that he asked for the priest before his death, but without due certainty we will do nothing.

Beside this, Sire, know that the very day he was killed a white monk sang mass to him and my Lord Roger de Mortimer had the vestments.

It is unlikely that Edward ordered Christian burial although it is said the headless body was taken to Abbey Cwm Hir. Nothing has been seen to this day of Llywelyn's regalia, which included a fragment of the True Cross.

Florence of Worcester recorded what happened after the head of Llywelyn was taken to Edward at Rhuddlan Castle: 'He at once sent it to his army stationed in Anglesey, and after the people of Anglesey were satiated with the spectacle he ordered it to be conveyed immediately to London. On the morrow of St Thomas the Apostle the Londoners went to meet it with trumpets and cornets and conducted it through all the streets of the city with a marvellous clang.' In mockery of the prophecy that Llywelyn would wear a crown in the streets of London, Edward ordered that before the head was shown it should be crowned with ivy.

No mercy was shown to Llywelyn's family. His brother David was hanged, drawn and quartered, the first man in legal history upon whom this barbarous punishment was carried out. David's son was sentenced to perpetual imprisonment. In 1305 he was still alive in a Bristol dungeon. Edward was not a forgiving man. In that year he ordered that an iron cage be made in which to keep the prisoner. The Welsh King's baby daughter, Gwenllian, was sentenced to perpetual imprisonment in a nunnery at Sempringham in Norfolk.

With the death of Llywelyn the dynasty of Cunedda, which had lasted for a thousand years, came to an end. In 1301 at Caernarfon Castle Edward had his namesake son proclaimed Prince of Wales. This was not the benevolent act of unity and peace-making Edward's apologists have claimed. He had inherited the Normans' love of royal precedent. As Prince of Wales the King's son could claim title to the mineral-rich kingdom of Gwynedd. It is a right which in some circles is hotly, sometimes violently, disputed to this day.

Perhaps the saddest thing about the death of Llywelyn was the speed with which his followers went over to Edward's Court. Not that they were the first of the Welsh *uchelwyr* (gentry) to change sides. That distinction belongs to the princely House of Powys, the ancestors of Owain Glyndwr, who surrendered their estates to Edward I in the early days of his occupation.

The denouement came in 1399 when there was enacted at Conwy a royal drama which was to inspire Shakespeare. In February of that year Richard II had forbidden Duke Henry of Lancaster to return to England to claim his inheritance on the death of his father, the King's uncle, John of Gaunt. Unwisely at this critical time, Richard chose to leave his kingdom to mount an expedition to Ireland. In his absence Henry of Lancaster landed. When Richard hurried back, landing at Milford Haven in Pembrokeshire, his cause was almost lost.

One of the most colourful accounts of this dramatic period can be found in a little-known contemporary work, *The Chronicle of Jean Creton*, which purports to be by a Frenchman, Jean le Creton, who was one of Richard's courtiers. But recent scholarship now places its authorship with Bishop Trevor, a turncoat of such acrobatic enthusiasm that in the space of five years he served Richard II, his usurper Henry IV and the rebel Welsh prince Owain Glyndwr. Whatever else this made Trevor, it put him in a unique position to describe Richard's final weeks as king.

The chronicle tells how, riding hard with five friends and thirteen men-at-arms and disguised as a monk, Richard completed the 135 miles from Milford Haven to Conwy in thirty-six hours. But no sooner had he left Milford than his cousin the Duke of Aumale, the High Constable of England, betrayed him and marched his troops into Henry's camp. When Richard heard that, the chronicler says, he fled to Beaumaris and from there to Caernarfon. But he did not stay long in either castle, for want of money, and soon returned to Conwy.

From Chirk, where he had established his headquarters, the Duke of Lancaster sent the Earl of Northumberland to Conwy to trick the King into surrender: 'He formed his men into two bodies under the rough and lofty cliffs of a rock (Penmaen-Rhos); they were fresh and eager, persecuting traitors that they were, to take the king.'

The Earl took boat for Conwy. He was brought before the King in the castle, and in the chapel, the ruins of which can be seen today, they celebrated Mass together. The Earl swore loyalty to the King; the King swore clemency to the Earl. And both of them determined to do down the other at the first opportunity. As the chronicler writes: 'One had bad intentions, the other worse.' The Earl then left the King to prepare, so he said, a reception at Rhuddlan Castle.

The king set out after him from Conwy and on his road to Rhuddlan he passed the very broad and great water and then rode on four miles till he mounted the Rock where the earl and his army were concealed on the descent (Penmaen-Rhos). When he beheld them he was greatly astonished saying, 'I am betrayed; what can this be? Lord in Heaven help me.' Then they were known by their banners that might be seen floating. 'I think,' said he, 'that it is the earl who hath drawn us upon his oath.' Then all were in bitter dread ... I must tell you how the king had come so near to them that it was much nearer to return to the town than descend the rock, which was washed by the main sea. We could not get away the other side, owing to the rock; so cost what it might, we were forced either to die or pass into the midst of the earl's people. He appeared armed in mail. Then did the king demean himself so sorrowfully that it was a pity to behold ...

The earl came and kneeled quite on the ground saying to the king, 'Be not displeased, my rightful lord, that I should come to seek you for your better security. For the country, as you know, is disturbed by war.' Then said the king, 'I could very well go without so many people as you have brought here. I think this is not what you promised me. You told me that you had been sent with only five others. This is very ill done considering the oath that you made. You do not seem to be sound in your loyalty, having this token post around this place. Depend upon it, I shall return to Conwy which I left this day.' Then said the earl: 'My Lord, you accuse me of dishonour, but I solemnly declare since I have you here, I will bring you to Duke Henry as directly as I may, for you must know that I made him such a promise these ten days past.'

Then he caused bread and wine to be brought, which he himself presented to the king, who, considering his power, durst not refuse what the earl chose to command. When this was over they remounted, went on straight to Rhuddlan and dined sumptuously in the strong castle there.

For Richard the beach below Penmaenmawr was the place where his reign ended. For the Welsh it was the place where the first stirrings of revolt began. They had been loyal to Richard, the son of the Black Prince who had fought at Crécy and Poitiers with Welsh archers. With the fall of his son, the stage was set for one of the bloodiest confrontations in the warlike history of Gwynedd. Properly led and diligently pressed, it might well have led to the overthrow of the House of Lancaster and the setting of a Welsh king on the throne of England.

Owain Glyndwr is the third of Gwynedd's great heroes. Yet like the Llywelyns before him he had little regard for the ordinary people whose prince he proclaimed himself to be. Sir John Wynne, writing the history of his family at Gwydir, near Llanrwst, in the early days of the seventeenth century, talked of the desolation Glyndwr brought: 'Green grass grewe on the market place of Llanrwst ... Deer fed in the churchyard of Llanrwst, as it was reported, for it was Owain Glyndwr's policy to bring all things to waste, that the English should not find strength

Before the coming of Telford's roads, carriages were manhandled over these crags. Penmaenmawr Crag in 1750. (J. Boydell)

nor resting place in the country.'

Two of the fiercest supporters of the Glyndwr rising were Gwilym ap Tudor and his brother Rhys, whose descendant Henry VIII was by an irony of history to bring about the Act of Union which anglicized Wales. It was these two men of Anglesey who, at Easter 1401, struck the first blow in Gwynedd for their cousin Glyndwr. They captured Conwy Castle while the garrison of fifteen men-at-arms was attending church on Good Friday. Since, according to the rules of war, no one was allowed to fight on Holy Days, only two guards had been left in the castle. Both men were strangled by a rebel disguised as a carpenter.

By the time the castle's governor, Sir John Massy of Puddington, Cheshire, and his men had raced back from church, the town was ablaze. The bridge at the town gate, the lodgings of the chamberlain and the King's justiciar, and the records of the town's exchequer were all destroyed. The Tudors held the castle until May, when, after prolonged parleys, they handed it back in circumstances which shocked even the worldly Adam of Usk: 'The Welsh surrendered the said castle, cowardly for themselves and treacherously for their comrades. For having bound twelve of their number who were very hateful to the Prince, by stealth as they slept after their night watches, they gave them up on condition of saving their own and others lives. And nine thus bound and yielded up to the Prince they straightaway saw them drawn, disembowelled, hanged, beheaded and quartered.'

Harry 'Hotspur', the eldest son of the Earl of Northumberland and one of the best soldiers of his own or any other day, was Chief Justice of North Wales, and Conwy was under his direct command, so Henry IV held him responsible. With characteristic bluntness Hotspur replied that, if the King would not pay his soldiers' wages, he could not expect them to defend his possessions.

A chamberlain at Caernarfon Castle warned that revolution was spreading throughout Gwynedd: 'It does seem to be true because of the way the Welsh are behaving, for they sell their cattle and buy horses and harness, saddles, bows and arrows. And reckless men of many countries leave their homes and thrifty governance and assemble in desolate places and wild and hold many meetings private and though we do not know their purpose the young people are difficult to govern.'

Hotspur met Owain's soldier's only once in battle. It was in Snowdonia. The Welshmen were pushed back to Llyn Peris, where they suffered a second defeat at the hands of John Chorlton, the King's officer in Powys. Nevertheless, in the years that followed, Glyndwr achieved complete ascendancy in North Wales. By 1404 Henry had given up hope of recovering the country and returned to England. Owain assumed the trappings of royalty. His Court at Harlech Castle was a brilliant one. There were his fighting generals, Rhys Gethin, who had captured the Earl of March after defeating his army, and Cadogan 'of the Battle Axe' who led tribes in the Rhondda and summoned them to battle by the sound of sharpening his axe. There were the administrators, able and cunning men who had deserted Richard II to follow Henry IV and now, when they thought Henry's race was run, had flocked to Glyndwr. There were bards, of course, like Iolo Goch, who sang:

> Here's the life I've sighed for long.
> Abashed is now the Saxon Throng
> And Britons have a British Lord
> Whose emblem is the conquering sword.
> There's none I know but knows him well
> The hero of the watery dell
> Owain of bloody spear in field
> Owain his country's strongest shield.

Dolwyddelan Castle below Moel Siabod, guarding the pass from Betws to Blaenau Ffestiniog, has been under siege for nearly 200 years now – from artists. Understandably it is one of the most painted scenes in North Wales

Lligwy village on Anglesey was lived in from the Iron Age probably
until Viking times. It has a defensive stone wall and such sophisticated amenities as central heating – a fire in the middle of the floor
with round-the-wall seating and a front step

Gwynedd is haunted with a sense of ancient past. On the slopes of
Rhobell Fawr is this medieval trackway which crosses the mountain

A sovereign bright in grandeur drest
Whose frown afrights the bravest breast.

Owain held a formal coronation at Dolgellau, where he signed an alliance between Wales and France and took his place on the world's stage. It was a glory which was to last until 1413, when, after a long siege at Harlech Castle, Glyndwr, his son Meredith and a small band of warriors disappeared from Harlech and from history.

It was not Owain but one of his lieutenants, Tudor ap Goronwy, one of the leaders in the capture of Conwy Castle, who founded the first Welsh dynasty to rule from the English throne. His descendant Owain ap Maredudd ap Tudor married Catherine de Valois, the widowed queen of Henry V. The historian Hall was vaguely shocked, though he clearly approved of her choice: 'Being young and lusty and following more her own appetite than friendly counsel and regarding more her private affection than her open honour, [she] took to husband privily a goodly gentleman and a beautiful person, garnished with many godly gifts both of nature and of grace called Owen Tudor.'

Sir John Wynne tells how Catherine, a Frenchwoman, could never understand that England and Wales were separate countries. She asked to see some of her husband's kin. He brought his cousins, 'men of goodly stature and personage, but wholly destitute of bringing up and schooling, for when the Queen had spoken to them in divers languages and they were not able to answer her, she said they were the goodliest dumb creatures that ever she saw.'

The marriage was a happy one. The couple had three sons and a daughter, but the moment the Queen died, the Establishment pounced. Owain was twice imprisoned, though both times he managed to escape, and finally he fought for his Lancastrian son Edmund, Earl of Richmond, in the Wars of the Roses, whose own son was to become the first Tudor king, Henry VII.

Owain Tudor was captured at the Battle of Mortimer's Cross and beheaded in Hereford. As he reached the block he told his executioner: 'Be tender to my head. It hath lain in the lap of a Queen.'

Though no one seems quite sure where the Battle of Bosworth was fought there can be no doubt of its glittering consequences. The father of the boy who was to be Henry VII was created Earl of Richmond by his stepbrother Henry VI. Although through his grandfather Owain Tudor he claimed descent from the Senescals to the Princes of Gwynedd it was through his mother Margaret of

Beaufort, 14 years old and widowed when he was born, that Henry inherited a claim on the throne of England. Henry spent the first 14 years of his life in Wales, at Pembroke Castle with his uncle Jasper, Earl of Pembroke, until politics forced him out of the country and he lived in France for the next fourteen years.

Fittingly for a Welsh king Henry's first army was of poets. During his exile Dafydd Llwyd of Machynlleth led the Welsh poets in a brilliant campaign of symbolic poems in support of the 'Seagull' as the poets called Henry. By the time he landed at Milford Haven in August 1485 the whole of Wales was behind him. His first powerful support came from the great magnate Sir Rhys ap Thomas of Dynevor, landowners from North Wales met Henry in mid-Wales with vast herds of cattle and he fought at Bosworth under the Red Dragon. Small wonder that when he climbed onto the throne he returned the help with gifts of high office.

After the Battle of Bosworth, in 1485, the Welsh gentry flocked to London for their rewards. So many were given offices at court that in their resentment the English coined a bitter joke. It described how there were so many Welshmen in Heaven that St Peter was driven distracted until he hit on the idea of sending an angel outside the pearly gates. The angel was told to shout the name of the Welshmen's favourite dish, toasted cheese. When the Welshmen rushed out of Heaven for their share, St Peter slammed the gates behind them.

In 1504 Henry VII granted a Charter of Liberties to Gwynedd and began the work of uniting Wales with England which his son, Henry VIII, completed with his Act of Union of England and Wales. For the first time Welsh MPs sat at Westminster. Nationalists who despise the links between the two countries ponder uneasily on the awkward truth that the first links were forged by our only Welsh monarchs. There can be no doubt of Henry VII's Welshness. Look on his death mask in the museum of Westminster Abbey. You can see the same face repeated endlessly in the streets of Llangefni, Anglesey's principal town, any market day. It is the archetypal face of the Gwynedd farmer.

The Gwynedd Welsh, who love a battle, were largely indifferent to both sides in the Civil War, though Wales, and especially Gwynedd, was Royalist. Conwy was a key garrison town and the link with King Charles I's forces in Ireland. Into the harbour there came ships containing munitions and weapons, collected in Ireland by the Earl of Ormonde. Dr John Williams, a Conwy man who became Archbishop of York, fortified the castle and town. But in 1645 the Royalist Colonel Sir John Owen was

Three bridges now disfigure this prospect of Conwy Castle and a tunnel is planned to cross the estuary underwater. In 1749 when J. Boydell made this engraving the only way across the estuary was by ferry-boat

appointed Constable of the Castle by Prince Rupert. This displeased the Archbishop. He had spent a great amount of his own money on fortification. In a letter the King had assured him the money 'should be repaid him before the custody thereof should be put in any hand but his own'. Out of pocket and temper, Williams changed sides and assisted General Mytton and his Parliamentary forces to capture the town in 1646. He participated with such enthusiasm that he was with the soldiers when they scaled the town walls and was wounded in the neck. Despite his efforts Conwy Castle was one of the last Royalist garrisons in England and Wales to hold out for the King.

During the Commonwealth an English linen-draper, Sir John Carter, was governor of the town. He married a Miss Holland who brought him an estate in Flintshire. 'I have got for myself the finest piece of Holland in the country,' he boasted.

The last castle in England and Wales to fall to the Protector was Harlech, which had withstood its first siege in 1646 when Sir Hugh Pennant defended it against Cromwell's Welsh brother-in-law, John Jones. The Constable, Colonel William Owen, had held it with only fifty men against General Mytton for a year before he was forced to surrender.

So firmly Royalist were the Gwynedd gentry that on Anglesey

a twenty-three-year-old Colonel Bulkeley, in August 1648, persuaded many of them to sign a Declaration of Intent. It promised 'the reinstating of our gracious sovereign to his rights, dominion and dignity'. It was even hoped that King Charles I would rule from Anglesey, where it was proposed he should live at Baron Hill, the house that the colonel's father had built on the Menai Straits for the entertainment of the King's brother Prince Henry who had died before he could visit it. This Royalist flourish was short lived. General Mytton crossed the straits, landing at Cadnant Gorge, and marched his fifteen hundred men against the Royalists in Beaumaris. The Cavaliers were driven back, some were locked in the parish church, and the brief hope of Beaumaris to be the capital of Britain died on the air. General Mytton stayed at the Old Bull's Head on the main street which, happily, is open to travellers to this day.

The history of Gwynedd is largely a history of battles, so it is fitting that the Regimental Museum of the Royal Welch Fusiliers should be housed in the Queen's Tower of Caernarfon Castle. The exhibits include the sixteen-pounder Russian gun captured by a fusilier captain at the Battle of the Alma on 20 September 1854.

Among the medals and the paintings, the weapons and the silver, perhaps the most poignant exhibit is a cigarette case which was owned by Major G.L. Compton Smith DSO, whose portrait hangs above. He left the case to the officers' mess when he was taken hostage by the Sinn Fein in Ireland and subsequently shot in 1921. Inside the case his brother officers found his last letter. It reads:

Dear Royal Welch Fusiliers,

I am to be shot in an hour's time. I should like you fellows to know that this sentence has been passed on me and that I intend to die like a Welch Fusilier with a laugh and forgiveness for those who are carrying out this deed.

I should like my death to lessen rather than increase the bitterness which exists between England and Ireland ...

THE FABLES, THE FAITH
AND THE SCHOLARS

Those men who love the crwch and the harp
Chynghanedd, song, the englyn's art
They love the best things God has given
To please his angel-hosts in heavens.

Seventeenth-century anonymous folk poem

• CHAPTER 5 •

The Welsh in Gwynedd paid their Roman overlords the supreme compliment of mythologizing them. Magnus Maximus, the Spanish mercenary soldier who aspired to be Emperor of Rome, is only a footnote in the history of Europe, but in the *Mabinogion* he wears the imperial purple. He becomes the folk hero Macsen who comes to Britain specifically to marry a Celtic princess, an historical character who is called variously Elen of the Hosts or Elen the Road Builder because of the highroads she built across Britain, perhaps Roman military roads made fabulous.

Celts have an enviable gift for writing their history as they go along and, if necessary, rewriting it to suit changed circumstance. It is doubtful if the fifteenth-century peasant saw Owain Glyndwr in the same chivalrous light as that in which we see him now, especially when the light that the peasant saw came from the flames of his crops. In the nineteenth century Glyndwr in the popular imagination was a Celtic crusader wrapped in animal skins and wielding a club, a far picture from the lawyer and royal servant he was in life.

In the eighteenth century, a Beddgelert innkeeper called Pritchard started a very successful cottage industry making myths for the gullible tourist. In this case it was Gelert, the greyhound, owned by Prince Llywelyn. According to the legend, Gelert was the gift of Prince John who was left to guard Llywelyn's palace and his infant son. When he returned, in the words of the nineteenth-century balladeer William Spencer

O'erturned his infant's bed he found
With bloodstained covert rent
And all around, the walls and ground
With recent blood besprent.
He called his child, no voice reply'd
He searched with terror wild
Blood, blood he found on every side

But nowhere found his child.
'Hell hound! my child's by thee devoured'
The frantic father cry'd
And to the hilt his vengeful sword
He plung'd in Gelert's side.

Alas, it was only when Llywelyn had taken his precipitate action that he discovered the baby Prince alive and well and living in his cot. At the foot of the cot was stretched the corpse of a wolf, killed by Gelert as he attacked the Prince.

Ah, what was then Llywelyn's pain
For now the truth was clear
His gallant hound the wolf had slain
To save Llywelyn's heir.

When the ballad was recited in the sitting-room of the Royal Goat, this final splendid stanza surely claimed a tear from every Victorian dog-worshipping eye:

Vain, vain was all Llywelyn's woe.
'Best of thy kind, adieu,
The frantic blow which laid you low
This head shall ever rue.'

Almost every country's mythology has a similar legend but the first printed mention in Wales came in the *Musical and Poetical Relics of the Welsh Bards* by Edward Jones, which was published in 1794, though the legend was poached from classical sources two hundred years earlier by Sir John Wynne of Gwydir, a member of Parliament who himself became the subject of a myth in which be became, literally, the first political 'wet'. So wicked was he, so the story goes, that his soul is imprisoned for ever in the pool at the foot of the Swallow Falls in Betws-y-Coed, to be purged and purified by the water.

Other animals found their place in mythology. The wild boar, the insignia of the Roman XX Legion, in Gwynedd became the ravening pig monster Twrch Trwyth of the fairy tale. It has been suggested that the Welsh Red Dragon is descended from the dragon standards of the Roman cohorts. They were red, three-dimensional streamers of light fabric, used by archers to gauge the strength and direction of the wind. These floating dragons had whistles fitted to them and no doubt made a deep impression on the tribesmen of the day.

The first dragon story in Wales concerns the luckless Vortigern, whose fort, Dinas Emrys, was in Nant Gwrtheyrn. Vortigern was the first of the Roman-British kings, the man who unwisely invited Saxon mercenaries into Britain to help keep order. According to legend, when he began to build his castle in the valley, there was subterranean shuddering and the foundations came tumbling down. The Court magicians advised Vortigern that the earth would be at peace only if it was sprinkled with the blood of the child of a pure virgin. Rather surprisingly, a child was found, apparently an immaculate conception by a Vestal Virgin, though in fact the son of a Roman consul. The child was Merlin, or possibly Ambrosius, the fables vary, and when he was confronted with the magicians they found him so wise that his life was spared. He told the King that the reason the earth shook beneath his castles was that two dragons were fighting, one red, representing the British, the other white and Saxon. He

> ... showed where the serpents fought
> The white that tore. The red from whence the prophet wrought
> The Britons sad decay then shortly to ensue.

Merlin became celebrated as a poet and mathematician and, according to one legend, built Stonehenge on Salisbury Plain. He was one of the three principal bards of Britain, an honour shared by another Gwynedd man, Taliesin.

Taliesin changed the fortune of the unluckiest young man in sixth-century Welsh history. His name was Elphin and he was the son of Gwynddno Goronhir, a sub-prince of Maelgwyn, King of Gwynedd. He had his first piece of bad luck when the kingdom in Cardigan Bay which he was to inherit from his father was drowned when Seithenyn, the man whose duty it was to guard the sea gates in the harbour wall, got drunk and forgot to close them – he was to go down in history as one of the great drunkards of Wales. As a consolation for his lost kingdom, Prince Elphin was given a famous salmon weir on the mouth of the River Dyfi on Gwynedd's border. It produced one hundred pounds of salmon every year until Elphin's servants put their nets across it. They did not pull in a single fish. The only harvest was a leather bottle which they found suspended from one of the piers. When they opened it, they found a small child who smiled happily upon them. It was the son of the witch Caridwen who wanted to be rid of him. When Elphin saw him, he christened him Taliesin – 'bright face' – and carried him off to his father. As they rode along, the baby began to sing 'A Song of Consolation' of which Elphin was in much need.

Taliesin was a bold child. When Elphin asked him where he had learned to sing, he replied, 'Though I am very little, I am very wise.' And when Elphin's father quite reasonably asked his son what use a boy treble was, it was Taliesin who replied, 'I will do him more good than the weir ever did.' The child, who is said to have had in him the 'three drops of inspiration', was true to his word. He saved Elphin's wife from a fate worse than death. But his great moment came when Elphin was imprisoned by King Maelgwyn.

When Taliesin entered Maelgwyn's Court, all the bards were struck dumb in his presence. He told the King: 'I was with the Lord in the Highest Sphere on the fall of Lucifer into the depths of hell.' Taliesin said he had been with Adam, Noah, Moses, Joshua and the prophets. 'I am the wonder whose origin is not known.' The King asked why he had come to Court, and Taliesin said 'to free Elphin'. As he spoke, the castle shook and Elphin was quickly set free. Taliesin then suggested that Elphin's mare should be set to race the King's twenty best horses. Elphin rode a broken-winded mare so the King was quick to strike the wager. Before the race began, Taliesin gave Elphin's jockey twenty-four twigs of holly, burned black, which would slow down the King's horses if they were struck in turn by a twig as they passed Elphin's mare. The jockey was also told to throw down his cap where his horse stumbled. Everything happened as Taliesin said it would, and when the race was over he told Elphin to dig where the jockey's cap had landed. He did and found a cauldron of gold. Said Taliesin: 'Elphin, behold a payment and reward unto thee for having taken me out of the weir and having succoured me from that time to this.'

He became the principal bard of Britain and a knight of Arthur's Round Table. When Arthur died, he returned to his estate on the banks of the Dyfi, where there is to this day a village called Taliesin.

Gwynedd, too, had a drowned kingdom. Helig-ap-Glanawg extended from the Great Orme at Llandudno to Puffin Island and the Lavan Sands on Anglesey. It was part of the kingdom of Helig which also included Abergele, Rhos and the Lleyn Peninsula. The inundation had been threatened for generations because of the crimes of Helig's ancestors. Night after night a ghastly voice was heard crying, '*Dial a ddaw, dial a ddaw*' ('Vengeance will come').

The calamity occurred, as calamities always do in fairy stories, while the Court of King Helig was enjoying a great feast. '*Dial a ddaw,'* came the cry. The courtiers ignored it. They sent a servant to the cellar for more wine and reproached the harpist who had ceased to play. As his hands reached for the strings, the servant came running back. 'The tide, the tide,' he called. It was too late. In a single tide, the entire kingdom was drowned.

In the parish of Dwygyfylchi, in the Sychnant Valley between Penmaenmawr and Conwy, is a hill called Trwyn-yr-Wylfa, the Point of Wailing, where, it is said, Helig and the survivors fled to save themselves.

The Roman-inspired fables were not the only ones rooted in history, as this account from a popular Victorian book, *Heroines of Welsh History* by T. Llewellyn Pritchard, shows:

Bronwen, who resided at Harlech Castle, anciently called from her Twr Bronwen (Bronwen's tower), was sought and obtained in marriage by Matholwch, king of Ireland. Being afterwards ill treated by him, and insulted by a blow on the face, she left the country to return to her paternal home; but on landing in Wales we are told that she looked back upon Ireland, which freshening the memory of the indignity she had suffered, broke her heart. Bran, to avenge his sister, invaded Ireland, and destroyed an immense number of the people of that country. The historical romance also states that a square grave was made for Bronwen on the banks of the river Alaw, and there she was buried. In 1813 a most interesting discovery was made, which serves to give great authenticity to our Welsh documents, as, in the present instance, the romance has evidently been founded on historical facts. A farmer living on the banks of the Alaw, in Anglesey, having occasion for some stones, supplied himself from a *carnedd* (cairn), which was close to the river, and having removed several he came to a cist of close flags covered over, on removing the lid he found within an urn of ill-baked earth, about a foot high, placed with its mouth downwards, full of ashes, and half-calcined fragments of human bones. Another circumstance may be added, that the very spot has always been called Ynys Bronwen, or the islet of Bronwen, which is a remarkable confirmation of the genuineness of the discovery. All the circumstances together seem to place the matter beyond a doubt that the remains were actually those of Bronwen. Publicity was first given to this discovery by Sir Richard Hoare, who received the account from his friend Fenton, the Pembrokeshire historian. The latter in his statement says, 'the report of this discovery soon went abroad, and came to the ears of the parson of the parish and another neighbouring clergyman, both fond of, and conversant with Welsh antiquities, who were immediately reminded of a passage in one of the early Welsh romances called the

Mabinogion, the same that is quoted in Dr Davies's Latin and Welsh Dictionary, as well as in Richards's under the word *petrual* (square). *Bedd petrual a wnaed i Fronwen ferch Llyr ar lan Alaw ac yno y claddwyd hi.* A square grave was made for Bronwen the daughter of Lear, on the banks of the Alaw, and there she was buried. 'Happening to be in Anglesey soon after this discovery,' says Fenton, 'I could not resist the temptation of paying a visit to so memorable a spot, though separated from it by a distance of eighteen miles. I found it, in all local respects, exactly as described to me by the clergyman above mentioned, and as characterised by the cited passage from the romance. The tumulus raised over the venerable deposit was of considerable circuit, elegantly rounded, but low, about a dozen paces from the river Alaw. The urn (of which a sketch is given in the Cambro Briton, vol. LI., p. 72) was preserved entire, with an exception of a small bit out of its lip, was ill-baked, very rude, and simple, having no other ornament than little pricked dots; in height from about a foot to fourteen inches.' In conclusion he remarks, 'never was there a more interesting discovery, as it greatly serves to give authenticity to our ancient British documents, even though they be introduced to minister to romance, as in the present instance, and fixes the probable date of the interment in question within a few years – a desideratum we despaired of being ever gratified with – a circumstance beautifully alluded to in the close of Mr Bowles's Barrow Poem.'

We have to add to the foregone details, from our own information, that the urn of Bronwen with its contents, became by purchase the property of the late Richard Llwyd, author of Beaumaris Bay. On visiting that patriotic poet, in the year 1829, we were favoured by him with a sight of that antique relic of buried ages, which minutely agreed with the account given by Fenton, even to 'the little pricked dots,' and the 'small bit broken out of the lip.' Mrs Llwyd, our host's lady, we learnt, was quite ignorant of the antiquarian treasure of which her husband was possessed, nor did he ever enlighten her on that subject; as he felt convinced, he said, that the terror of a visit from the ghost of Bronwen would keep her sleepless ever after, or induce her to insist on the re-internment or removal of her remains. Before his death Mr Llwyd presented the urn and its contents to the British Museum.

Twr Bronwen, it appears, was the most ancient name of this fortress. In after times it was called Caer Collwyn, from Collwyn ab Tango, one of the fifteen tribes of North Wales, and lord of Evionydd, Ardudwy, and part of Lleyn. His grandchildren flourished in the time of Griffith ab Cynan. According to Pennant he resided for some time in a square tower in the ancient fortress, the remains of which are very apparent; as are those of part of the old walls, which the more modern in certain places are seen to rest on.

Giraldus Cambrensis, who toured Wales and wrote the first of the Welsh topographical guides, was particularly fascinated by the fables of Anglesey:

As many things within this island are worthy of remark, I shall not think it superfluous to make mention of some of them. There is a stone here resembling a human thigh, which possesses this innate virtue, that whatever distance it may be carried, it returns, of its own accord, the following night, as has often been experienced by the inhabitants. [The stone was in the old parish church of Llanidan, Brynsiencyn.] Hugh, earl of Chester, in the reign of King Henry I, having by force occupied this island and the adjacent country, heard of the miraculous power of this stone, and, for the purpose of trial, ordered it to be fastened, with strong iron chains, to one of a larger size, and to be thrown into the sea. On the following morning, however, according to custom, it was found in its original position, on which account the earl issued a public edict, that no-one, from that time, should presume to move the stone from its place. A countryman, also, to try the powers of this stone, fastened it to his thigh, which immediately became putrid, and the stone returned to its original situation.

There is in the same island a stony hill, not very large or high, from one side of which, if you cry aloud, you will not be heard on the other; and it is called (by antiphrasis) the rock of hearers.

There is also in this island the church of St Tefredaucus, into which Hugh, earl of Shrewsbury, (who, together with the earl of Chester, had forcibly entered Anglesey), on a certain night put some dogs, which on the following morning were found mad, and he himself died within a month; for some pirates, from the Orcades, having entered the port of the island in their long vessels, the earl, apprised of their approach, boldly met them, rushing into the sea upon a spirited horse. The commander of the expedition, Magnus, standing on the prow of the foremost ship, aimed an arrow at him; and, although the earl was completely equipped in a coat of mail, and guarded in every part of his body except his eyes, the unlucky weapon struck his right eye, and, entering his brain, he fell a lifeless corpse into the sea. The victor, seeing him in this state, proudly and exultingly exclaimed, in the Danish tongue, 'Leit loup,' let him leap; and from this time the power of the English ceased in Anglesey. In our times, also, when Henry II was leading an army into North Wales, where he had experienced the ill fortune of war in a narrow, woody pass near Coleshulle, he sent a fleet into Anglesey, and began to plunder the aforesaid church, and other sacred places. But the divine vengeance pursued him, for the inhabitants rushed upon the invaders, few against many, unarmed against armed; and having slain great numbers, and taken many prisoners, gained a most complete and bloody victory. For, as our Topography of Ireland testifies, that the Welsh and Irish are more prone to anger and revenge than any other nations, the saints, likewise, of those countries appear to be of a more vindictive nature.

There is a small island, almost adjoining to Anglesey, which is inhabited by hermits, living by manual labour, and serving God [Puffin Island, off Penmon, near Beaumaris]. It is remarkable that when, by the influence of human passions, any discord arises among them, all their provisions are devoured and infected by a species of small mice, with which the island abounds; but when the discord ceases, they are no longer molested. This island is called in Welsh, Ynys Lenach, or the ecclesiastical island, because many bodies of saints are deposited there, and no woman is suffered to enter it.

We saw in Anglesey a dog, who accidentally had lost his tail, and whose whole progeny bore the same defect. It is wonderful that nature should, as it were, conform itself in this particular to the accident of the father. We saw also a knight, named Earthbald, born in Devonshire, whose father, denying the child with which his mother was pregnant, and from motives of jealousy accusing her of inconstancy, nature alone decided the controversy by the birth of the child, who, by a miracle, exhibited on his upper lip a scar, similar to one his father bore in consequence of a wound he had received from a lance in one of his military expeditions.

Thomas Pennant, six hundred years later, still found marvels. Barmouth was the birthplace of

> ... the noted astrologer and ill-favoured knave, Arise Evans, a character and species of imposter frequent in the reigns of Elizabeth and James I. His figure is preserved in the Antiquarian Repertory, and answers the description given of him by his great pupil, William Lilly, of having a broad forehead, beetle brows, thick shoulders, flat nose, full lips, a down look, black curling stiff hair, and splay foot. He was a deep student in the black art; and Lilly assures us, that he had most piercing judgment naturally upon a figure of theft, and many other questions, he met withal; was well versed in the nature of spirits; and had many times used the circular way of invocating ... His friend Evans, by means of the angel Salmon, brought to him a deed, which one of his customers had been wronged of, at the same time blowing

down part of the house of the person in whose custody it was: and again, now, to satisfy the curiosity of Lord Bothwell and Sir Kenelm Digby, who wanted to see a spirit, he liked to have lost his life, being carried over the Thames, and flung down near Battersea by the spirits, whom he had vexed at the time of invocation, for want of making a due fumigation. These ridiculous impostures were the fashionable credulity of the times; and the greatest men were the dupes of these pretenders to occult science.

Dolbadarn Castle on the shores of Lake Padarn was the home of two knights, William of Montgomery and Hector of Marchlyn Mawr, who fought a tournament for the hand of a lady. They agreed that the one who came to grief should present to the other a steed on which to convey the lady to church on her wedding day. Hector, doubtful of the issue, and the 'villain of the piece', consulted a witch and arranged with her that, if he was second best in the lists, the Devil was to provide him with a palfrey. Montgomery, the lady's choice, was the victor and, as Hector fell unhorsed, a milk-white palfrey galloped into the arena. The wedding day speedily arrived and the lady, attended by a host of armed knights, rode the palfrey. On her right was the bridegroom and on her left Hector. Just as the church was reached, the horse became restive, and the sight of a cross on the church gates caused it to start at full speed away from the throng, with the bride on its back. At once a hundred knights gave chase, but they were nowhere in the hunt, and soon only her lover, William of Montgomery, remained. Hours of hard riding at a tremendous pace ensued and just as the enchanted palfrey reached the steep side of Penmaenmawr, the bridegroom got alongside on his horse and clasped the lady round the waist. But it was too late, and with one loud cry both lovers and their horses disappeared into the sea.

On the road from Llanrwst to Trefriw is Carreg-y-Gwalch (the rock of the falcon) where, in the reign of Henry VII, a man called Jordan had a curious experience in a cave once inhabited by a medieval outlaw called Jenkyn. In Jenkyn's Cave Jordan saw a goat with its hooves on an iron-bound chest. When the goat saw Jordan, it threw a heap of gold into a crucible and told him if he drank the red hot liquid he would become a man of gold. He did. Literally. For the rest of his life he was afraid to leave his cottage in case someone stole him.

In the same area, between Betws-y-Coed and Cerrig-y-Drudion, there was an inn run by two sisters which catered for travellers to Ireland. It was a place of mystery. Visitors were frequently robbed but no one knew how it had happened. Their bedroom doors were always locked and there was no sign of forced entry.

Finally the mystery was solved by a half-pay officer, Huw Llwyd of Ffestiniog. He booked a room and pretended to fall asleep. In a little while a partition in the wall opened and two cats climbed through. They romped about the room and clawed his clothes at the foot of the bed. As one of the cats put its right paw in the pocket which contained Huw's purse, he struck it a blow with a sword. Both cats instantly disappeared. The next morning only one sister came to wish him goodbye. The other, he was told, was ill. But Huw insisted on saying goodbye to her and eventually he was shown to her room. Huw took her right hand, which was beneath the bedclothes. It was heavily bandaged.

Some months later there was a sequel to the tale. Huw was on his way to preach at Ffestiniog church when he saw the sisters coming towards him, clearly intent on revenge on the man who had discovered their power to change into cats. He foiled them by walking backwards all the way from his home to the church, and from the safety of the church porch he deprived the sisters of their power. From that day forward they were just as any other spinster sisters in the parish.

It is not surprising that by far the most enchanting of British counties should have earth-bound spirits who prefer it to paradise. Nor that so many of them should have chosen the romantic medieval walled town of Conwy to haunt.

Some years ago a local journalist, Margaret Williams, published an entertaining monograph on the subject. Her ghosts included a figure of a horseman silhouetted against a night sky between Conwy and the village of Gyffin, a mile away, and a homesick chambermaid from Anglesey who died in a Conwy inn pining for her home across the straits. She had begged to be buried on Anglesey; instead she was laid to rest in Conwy churchyard.

'After that,' wrote Miss Williams, 'nothing seemed to go right. The head waiter [at the hotel] entering the dining room with a laden tray, tripped over nothing at all and sent the dishes flying across the room. A housemaid looking away from her bucket for a moment found it had disappeared. Oil lamps refused to light. Hot water jugs broke into a thousand pieces.' So many strange things happened that trade fell off at an alarming rate. A chambermaid mentioned the dead girl's wish to be buried on Anglesey, so, desperate to restore his hotel's fortunes, the landlord had the girl's body exhumed and re-buried on the island. At once order returned to the hotel and so did the customers.

In Castle Street the premises of the Black Lion, now an antique shop, have a ghost who appears so often that the proprietress no

The delightful twelfth-century Llangelynnin Church is little more than a hermitage on the road from Tywyn and Barmouth. But many medieval features remain

St Beuno once built a monastery on the site of the cathedral-like parish church of Clynnog Fawr, which perhaps owes its magnificence to the revenue from a toll on split-eared cattle

When this Baptist chapel, Capel Mud, near Penygraigwen, was being built on Anglesey its congregation had to hire a 'bouncer' to prevent vandalism from local Methodists

Alas, modern vandals have completed their work at Capel Mud. A sad ending for a building which is part of the history of Nonconformism in Wales

longer takes any notice of him. She told Miss Williams: 'He's a nice old fellow. We've got used to him and take him for granted.' He is an elderly gentleman who sits before a fireplace, smiling to himself and nodding benignly. A second ghost at the former inn is less welcome. He is a fierce character who rocks beds and frightens the staff. One girl who saw him said: 'He was a tall man in a cloak but I couldn't see his features. He seemed to be drawing the life out of me and all I could think of was to pray.'

In Berry Street is a house bought by a young couple from London, whose small son told of meeting a nice gentleman in a room at the top of the house. The boy said the man had whiskers and shiny buttons and his name was Albert. Some time later the mother glimpsed a navy sleeve with a man's hand gripping the bannisters. On a third occasion, during rough weather, the boy pointed to a wall and said: 'There's Albert. He's waving to me.' The couple later learned that an old sea-going man had lived in the house, from the top rooms of which, in earlier times, the Conwy River could be seen, though now the view is blocked by buildings.

The Conwy mermaid appeared at low tide, stranded on a rock, and begged local fishermen to throw her back into the sea. The fishermen refused and the mermaid cursed the town. Pretty effectively. Conwy has been twiced sacked, by the Tudors and again by General Monk, and for many years it has suffered horrendous traffic jams every summer.

The most distinguished building in the town and one of the few to be spared the ravages of time and eager architects is Plas Mawr, built by an Elizabethan privateer, Robert Wynne. It is now, thankfully, preserved as the headquarters of the Royal Cambrian Society of Art. The curators, Mr and Mrs Leonard Mercer, support Miss Williams' stories of the hauntings of the house. Miss Williams has personal knowledge because her own family lived at Plas Mawr until 1877, when they moved to the Elizabethan house next door.

Policemen on the beat have seen figures walking through the wall of the mansion where once there was a door, and faces looking out to sea from the window of the lantern room at the top of the tower. Many years ago the wife and child of a deep-sea captain who owned the house climbed the narrow spiral stair to the lantern room to watch for the captain's ship. On the way down the mother, who was carrying the child, missed her footing and fell. The housekeeper who found her sent a servant for a doctor. He never returned. A second man was sent and he came back with Dick, the deputy of the man who usually attended the family. When Dick examined the mother and child, he said they were both dying. Hysterically the housekeeper ran out of the room, locking it behind her. The captain, when he came home some months later, opened the locked room, found the bodies of his wife and child and himself died of grief on the spot. The body of Dick was never found, and no one knows what happened to him. To this day the captain paces across the lantern room and will continue to do so, it is said, until the bones of the doctor are found and given Christian burial.

There are other stories about the house, all locally attested: wet footprints leading to a blank wall, the sounds of revelry, the smell of unwashed bodies, even the smell of spectral manure. Miss Williams' great-grandmother kept cows in an upper courtyard of the house and sold milk from her back door.

Leonard Mercer is fiercely protective of one wraith, a small girl in a blue crinoline, who appears all over the house, in rooms and corridors, and has been seen by staff and visitors so often that she has become part of the family. She is a mischievous spirit. Once recently a student who took a holiday job as a waitress at the mansion after several sightings of the little girl in blue handed in her notice. She said she was not frightened of the ghost. Indeed, once she had crept up behind her and said 'Boo', causing her to disappear. The trouble was that the little girl appeared so often and so unexpectedly that she was afraid of dropping a tea tray in confusion.

It might be thought that the coming of Christianity to Gwynedd would wipe away many of the myths. The opposite happened. Gwynedd was the home of one of the three Saintly Kindreds of Wales. Almost every village on Anglesey and the Lleyn has a personal, and often highly improbable, saint to watch over it. This part of the book might well have been headed 'Oh, my sainted haunts!' There are 365 saintly sites of worship in the county, and one thousand saints are said to be buried on Bardsey Island alone.

In the Age of Saints, between the fifth and seventh century, achieving sainthood in the Celtic Church was a bit like gold mining. One selected a site, frequently near a pagan well to make sure of getting a congregation, lived on it, prayed on it, fasted on it and established oneself as a Christian teacher. Sainthood followed by, as it were, automatic promotion. The system produced unlikely candidates, many of them descended from Cunedda. St Gwynhoedl, who is the patron of Llangwnnadl on the Lleyn, was the son of Prince Seithenyn, that Great Drunkard of Wales who carelessly let the sea submerge the kingdom of Gwaelod in Cardigan Bay.

The tradition of Christianity in Gwynedd is stronger than that of the rest of Britain. After its introduction by the Romans, Christianity survived through the time when, in England, it was being stamped out by the pagan gods of the Saxons. When in 622 the Saxons destroyed the monastery at Bangor Iscoed, one of the greatest religious communities in Britain, the monks who survived fled to Bardsey Island at the foot of the Lleyn Peninsula, where they founded the first religious community in North Wales.

It was not only the English monks who found refuge in Gwynedd. According to one story, St Patrick was shipwrecked on Anglesey. Another story goes further. It claims Patrick was born on Anglesey, at Din Lligwy. Captured by Irish pirates who were raiding the island, he was sold into slavery in Northern Ireland.

In the fifth century St Columba infuriated St Finian of Mouille by copying a Book of Psalms which Finian had just received from Rome after Finian had forbidden him to do so. The two saints appealed to Diarmaid, the High King of Tara, to arbitrate. The King found in favour of Finian with the dubious judgment: 'To every cow her young cow, that is her calf, and to every book its transcript.' This so angered St Columba that he declared war on the High King of Tara. In the battle of books which followed, three thousand men were killed and St Columba was excommunicated. He left Ireland for Scotland, contrite and vowing to convert as many souls as had perished by his fault. And from Scotland his monks came down the coast to Gwynedd and beyond.

Christianity came in other ways. In the case of St Ffraid, riding on a piece of turf across the sea.

Ffraid was born in Fochan, Armagh, the daughter of a petty chieftain. When her father tried to marry her off against her will, she begged the Lord to intercede. He obliged by making her eyes drop out. The legend says: 'When she was sure the prince would not have her, she cunningly took them up again, washed them and put them in their places, where they fitted as well as ever.' To prevent any further unpleasantness, Ffraid, who by the time she died in 523 had become known as the Virgin of Kildare, decided to leave Ireland. With her knife she cut turfs for herself and her handmaidens, on which they sailed across the Irish Sea to what is now Treaddur Bay on Anglesey. The remains of the chapel built on the spot where she landed are still to be seen in the sand dunes. There are several churches dedicated to her in north Wales, such as Llansanffraid in Conwy where she performed a miracle by throwing a handful of rushes into the River Conwy where they changed into fish. Other miracles attributed to this versatile lady include turning the mayor of London into a horse, butter into ashes, ashes into butter, extracting honey from a stone and giving her mother-in-law a new leg when one of her own was amputated.

St Seiriol, whose cell is at Penmon on Anglesey, was only a little less dramatic. He had a second hermitage at Penmaenmawr and, in order that he might walk dry footed from one to the other, he had a rock pathway built. According to the *Hanes Helig ab Glanawg* in the Caerwys MSS Collection, he was a formidable road-builder over any terrain: 'Sythence this great and lamentable inundation of Cantre Gwaelod [the kingdom of Helig] the way and passage being stopped in this strait in regard the sea was come in and did beat upon the rocks of Penmaenmawr, this holy man Seiriol, like a good hermit did cause a way to be broken and cut through the main rock, which is the only passage that is to pass through that strait. This way leadeth from Dwygyfylchi to Llanfairfechan and is the king's highway from Conwy to Beaumaris, Bangor and Caernarfon and the only passage that the king's post both to ride to and from Ireland.'

St Seiriol himself never rode when he could walk. Every week, according to another tradition, he walked to the centre of Anglesey, to Llanerchymedd, to meet St Cybi, who walked from his cell at Holyhead. Because St Cybi faced the east coming and the west going home, he had the sun on his face both ways and was splendidly sun-tanned. Seiriol, however, was walking west in the morning when the sun was behind him and in the evening walked east with his back to the setting sun. Which is why St Seiriol was known as the White Saint and St Cybi as the Yellow.

St Elian had a less happy travelling experience. The sixteenth-century bard Gwilym Gwyn tells how the saint and his family – it was not until the fifteenth century that priests in the Celtic Church gave up their right to marry – came from Rome to Anglesey, where Cadwallon Lawhir offered him land. Elian had a tame doe, and Cadwallon offered as much land as the doe could run round in a day. Unfortunately the doe was pulled down and killed by a greyhound. In a fury Elian cursed the inhabitants of Llanelian and condemned them to a life of poverty.

St Elian's curses were not taken lightly. His cursing well at Old Colwyn, believed to be the most potent of its kind in Wales, was in regular use up to 1829, when it was filled in. The last guardian was a woman who lived in a farm nearby and collected the handsome sum, for those days, of £300 a year. Her duties were to read a passage of the scripture over the well while the cursers dropped a pin in the water, crying the name of the man or woman to be cursed; then, as they cursed their victim, the guardian poured well water over their heads. The cursed was known as 'the offered', and there was a formula by which, on payment, he could get himself taken out of the well.

St Dwyn, the Welsh patron saint of lovers, also had a well on her island of Llanddwyn on Anglesey. And the well had a guardian who would interpret the meaning of the movement of two eels who lived in it. St Dwyn's phrase in the Saying of the Wise is 'There is none so lovable as the cheerful.' She cured pain, found lost cattle and prophesied. Until the Reformation her shrine on the island, a ruin now, was one of the richest in Wales. Nevertheless, it is difficult to see how she qualified for the job of patron saint of lovers. Her father, Brychan Brycheiniog, wanted to marry her to a rich neighbour, Maelon Dafodrill. Alas, Maelon sought for what is discreetly described in the Iolo MSS as 'inappropriate union'. St Dwyn spurned him and prayed that they both be made impotent. 'God appeared while she was asleep, gave her a delicious draught which entirely cured her of her love and she saw the same draught being given to Maelon who thereupon became frozen to a lump of ice.'

St Beuno was one of the most amiable of the Celtic saints, and his church at Clynnog is a handsome sixteenth-century building which stands at the gateway to the Lleyn. It was built on the site of a monastery which Beuno founded in the sixth century. A charming story is told of its foundation. Beuno had lived near Welshpool by the River Severn, but one day hearing huntsmen calling their hounds in English, he said to his disciples: 'My sons, put on your garments and your shoes and let us abandon this place, for the nation of the man with the strange language whose voice I have heard inciting his dogs will invade this place and it will be theirs.'

First Beuno and his monks went to Meiford, where they stayed with St Tysilio, then to Gwynedd, where Beuno was given by Cadwallon land on which to build a monastery, in return for the gift of a gold sceptre worth sixty cows. As Beuno was digging the foundations, a woman came up with a crying child in her arms. When Beuno asked why the child was crying she told him: 'You are enclosing land that belongs to his father and is properly his.' Enraged, Beuno called for his chariot and rode to the Court of Cadwallon at Caernarfon. The unknown monk who tells the story confirms: 'Beuno said to the king, "Why didst thou give me land when it was not thine to give and belonged to this child? Give me other land or else return to me the gold sceptre".' When

Cadwallon refused to do either, Beuno cursed him and left the
Court. A cousin of the King's followed him and offered him land
to which no one had claim but himself, and it is on this land at
Clynnog that the first church there was built. The stone over
which the deal was struck can be seen in St Beuno's chapel in the
church. It bears an incised cross, said to have been made by the
saint himself with two strokes of his thumb.

'Cyff Beuno', or St Beuno's chest, is preserved in a glass case
by the front door. It is ancient and cut from a single piece of
timber nearly four feet long and $1\frac{1}{4}$ feet thick. There is a slit in the
lid through which a curious form of offering was made. A nick
which appeared in the ears of some cattle is called 'St Beuno's
nick'. Until the eighteenth century it was the custom of local
farmers to bring such cattle to the church on Trinity Sunday.
They were sold by the priests, and the money they brought went
through the slit in St Beuno's chest. It has been suggested that the
nick was introduced to the district by cattle from France which
carried the inherited mark. In 1589 something of this may have
been in the mind of John Ansliss, a visitor to Clynnog, when he
wrote:

> People went on pylgrimage to offer unto idoles far and near, yea, and
> that they do offer in these days not only money (and that liberally)
> but also bullocks unto idoles. And having harde this of sundry
> persons while I was there upon Whitsuntide last I went to the place
> where it was reported that bullocks were offered ...
>
> ... and as the bullocks did enter through a little porche unto the
> charchyard the yonge man spoke aloud and said, 'The Halfe to God
> and to Beuno'.
>
> Then I did ask the hoste why he said the half and not the whole.
> And the Hoste answered in the yonge man's hearing 'Because he owes
> the half to me' ...
>
> ... Ther be many things in this country that be gross and
> superstitious: As that the people are of the opinion that Beyno and
> his cattle will prosper well.

It might well have been a survival of a greater idolatry than
Ansliss dreamed off. The sacrifice of a horned animal was part of
pagan ritual.

A contemporary of Beuno who would have been opposed to
any animal sacrifice or exploitation was Princess, later, St
Melangell. She is the patron saint of hares, and though her shrine
is just over the Gwynedd border in Cwm Pennant, Powys, she has
been adopted by a Gwynedd society dedicated to the welfare of

animals. The society, Cymdeithas Melangell, was founded by Mrs Morfydd Ceen, of Holyhead, in 1984 and has already attracted members from as far afield as Portsmouth and Birmingham. The Society's ultimate aim is to get legislation through Parliament that would declare first Gwynedd, and then the whole of Wales, a bloodsports-free zone. Mrs Ceen believes it is possible as a similar thing was done once before – by Melangell.

In the great tradition of female Celtic saints, Melangell ran away from an impending marriage. In a coracle she crossed the Irish Sea, fleeing from her irate father, an Irish King, and her disappointed bridegroom, to land on the shores of Gwynedd. She then made her way across the county into Powys, where she settled in the beautiful Pennant valley, near Llangynog. She soon became known in the area for her love of animals, particularly hares, which are to this day known as 'Melangell's lambs'.

One day in 604, Brochwel, Prince of Powys, was out hunting with his men near the valley when the hounds caught the scent of a hare. They chased it down narrow paths and through leafy woodland until it was exhausted. The hunt was nearly over when suddenly the dogs stopped dead in their tracks. When the huntsmen came up, they saw a young woman standing in a clearing with the hare, breathless but unafraid, at her feet, surrounded by the now still and silent hounds. Prince Brochwel ordered the woman, Melangell, away and commanded that the hunt should continue, but no one would move or attempt to touch the hare in her care. At last, impressed by Melangell's courage and her strange authority over his men and the dogs, he declared that from that day forward the valley where she lived would be a sanctuary to any person or animal in need.

After her death Melangell's cell became a place of pilgrimage. The rock where she made her bed can still be seen, carved with 'MONACELLA' – the Latin translation of her name – on its face. Not far away is the shrine containing her remains.

Melangell has already been referred to in a House of Commons speech made in 1949 by Mr Robert Richards in support of a bill to defend wildlife. He said: 'It is my prayer also that Melangell will take not only the hare but also the otter, the deer and the badger under her protection from henceforth.' Mrs Ceen, in her Gwynedd base where the saint landed, strongly believes that more will be heard of her in the future. Her society is complementary to the RSPCA, the main difference being that no one who takes part in, or supports, bloodsports of any kind may be a member.

The smallest church in Wales holds only six worshippers. It was built over a holy well by the monks of Aberconwy on the foreshore at Rhos-on-Sea and dedicated to St Trillo. Unlike most of the hermitages, this cell was reconsecrated on St Trillo's day, 16 June 1935. Although the cell measures only fifteen feet by nine, services are held there every Friday morning.

During the Owain Glyndwr rebellion in the early part of the fiteenth century, Wales, through Owain's agency, was drawn into the greatest controversy of the day, the Schism between the popes of Rome and Avignon. Gregory XII ruled in Rome but the Avignon Pope Benedict XIII was the candidate of Charles VI of France. And Glyndwr at his court in Harlech needed a French alliance. The bishops, Byfort and Trevor, who had deserted Henry IV to join him, were both appointees of Rome. If Gregory was successful in the contest for the papal throne, England, who supported him, would insist on their replacement. The third member of Owain's Cabinet, his chancellor Gruffyd Young, the Bishop of Bangor, was in favour of the Avignon pope for political reasons. Through him Young believed he could advance his Grand Design, a revolutionary programme to which bureaucratic Rome would never agree: he wanted a complete reorganization of the Church in Wales. St David's, in his scheme, would become a metropolitan church; only Welsh-speaking prelates and clergy would be appointed, and Welsh churches would be removed from the control of English monasteries, restoring the freedom they had enjoyed before the Norman occupation. Owain decided to support the King of France's Avignon candidate and wrote to him accordingly:

'... serene prince, you have in many ways from your innate goodness informed me and my subjects very clearly and graciously concerning the recognition of the True Vicar of Christ. I, in truth, rejoice with a full heart on account of that information of your excellency and because, inasmuch from this information I understand that the Lord Benedict, the supreme pontifex, intends to work for the promotion of a union in the Church of God with all his possible strength. Confident, indeed, of his right and intending to agree with you as far as is possible with me I recognize him as the true Vicar of Christ.'

It was a popular decision, for among the rights restored from the days of the old Celtic Church was the one that allowed priests to marry.

In Gwynedd the Welsh language is not so much a means of communication as a religious experience. It is both martyrdom and reincarnation. Paradoxically the martyrdom of the language came at the hands of a Welsh king and the reincarnation at the hands of a Liverpool-born librarian. In his Act of Union of England and Wales in 1536 King Henry VIII's Tudor Parliament declared:

Because in the same country [Wales] divers Rights, Usages and Customs be far discrepant from the Laws and Customs of this Realm and also because that the People of the same dominion have and do daily use a speech nothing like nor consonant to the Natural Mother Tongue used within this realm ...

... No person or persons that use the Welsh speech or language shall have or enjoy any Manner Office or Fees within this Realm of England, Wales or other the King's Dominion upon pain of forfeiting the same office or fees unless he or they use and exercise this English speech of language.

Twenty-eight years later, in the more tolerant reign of Elizabeth I, another Act was passed which permanently enshrined the language in the soul of the Welsh people. It ordered the translation of the Bible into Welsh. Within three years the first Welsh New Testament was on sale, and 1588 saw the publication of the majestic Welsh Bible produced by the Gwynedd cleric Bishop William Morgan and a group of North Wales scholars.

Bishop Morgan's birthplace, Tŷ Mawr Wybrnant, is between Penmachno and Dolwyddelan. It is now owned by the National Trust. They are hoping to have the cottage restored in time for the 400th anniversary of the publication of the Bible which is the source of modern Welsh. In the words of one commentator, his Bible linked the power of the language with the fervour of religion. The Bible was not solely a testament. It was a grammar. And Wales is obsessed with education. By the eighteenth century circulating schools with travelling teachers had taught a quarter of the population to read. Their pupils, adults as well as children, learned 'in six or eight weeks time not only to read tolerably but repeat by heart all the Church Catechism in their native language'. In the technological 1980s it takes far longer than eight weeks to teach illiterates to read, despite sophisticated teaching aids.

The schools had only one teaching aid, *y beibl bach*, 'the little Bible', based on Bishop Morgan's great work and costing only 5 shillings. Learning was not easy. One joiner's apprentice twice walked three hundred miles to attend a class. Generally classes were held in the parish church, the Bible and the catechism were used as readers, and the pupils were expected to attend church service. Yet there was opposition from the Church. Bishops and many clergy were against any education of the working classes. When the joiner opened a successful school on Anglesey, the vicar ordered it closed, and when the joiner asked him why, he replied: 'You preach in the hillside and lure the people there.'

The deep need for a Welsh Bible is illustrated by the story of Mary Jones, who saved for years and then in 1800 walked sixty miles from her home, Tŷ'n-ddal beyond Cader Idris, to Bala in order to buy her own copy. She had heard that in Bala the Reverend Thomas Charles was producing a vernacular edition, but she arrived in Bala to find that all the stock had gone. Charles was so moved by her determination that he gave her his own Bible. The incident prompted him to found the British and Foreign Bible Society.

It was that kind of enthusiasm which swept the Nonconformist tide through Gwynedd. In Merioneth George Fox preached the Quaker message and later sent two missionaries to assist the work of Morgan Llwyd of Maentwrog. Of the two thousand Welsh Quakers who settled in Pennsylvania, over half came from Merioneth.

In the early years of the nineteenth century the first turnpike roads, allied to the fusing of people into communities through the Industrial Revolution, brought travelling preachers into Gwynedd and produced the Methodist Revival. Lewis Rees founded a Methodist Society among the workers in the knitting industry in Bala and fervent groups were established among the Blaenau Ffestiniog quarrymen.

In the eighteenth century great religious leaders such as John Wesley and Hywel Harris, the Calvinist, had attracted large congregations. In Bala Harris fired the imagination of the local Anglican minister Thomas Charles, who became known as 'the man who gave God to Gwynedd'. The Reverend Mr Charles in turn encouraged his congregation to turn Methodist and himself became one of the founders of the Calvinistic Methodist Church. The theological college he also founded in Bala to train ministers still flourishes in the town. By the end of the century Calvinist chapels in Gwynedd far outnumbered those of any other Nonconformist group.

Wesley spoke no Welsh; Harris was fluent and fiery, so not surprisingly it was he who had the larger following in Gwynedd. In 1744 the first chapel opened on Anglesey at Mona, and within six years there were Nonconformist chapels over most of the island. By 1882 Gwynedd had seven hundred chapels, many of them in Anglesey. At first the groups met in farmhouses to hear Wesley and Harris but on Anglesey a third star joined the galaxy.

He was William Williams of Pantycelyn, Wales' greatest hymn-writer.

On the Lleyn, in mining communities in Snowdonia, at the slate quarries of Llanberis and the Ogwen Valley, Nonconformism was the great liberator of the intellect of a race that had been bullied and browbeaten for centuries. It unleashed an immense reservoir of talent: a prime minister, preachers by the peck, poets by the bushel, have flourished in the rich soil of Nonconformism.

It produced excesses too. One observer wrote of the Methodist Jumpers, an unorthodox sect in Caernarfon:

> Once and only once I have beheld the fantastical proceedings of these religionists, whose first care seems to be the erection of a pulpit, tribune and a due provision of preachers, able-bodied and having good lungs. As fatigue or any other calls succeed, the haranguer leaves his place, which is immediately occupied by a successor, and thus the stimulus of fanaticism is kept in full action until its effects are spread throughout the congregation. Ejaculation and sighs are first heard, then succeed an accruing murmur of groans, until at length the mass assembled swells into a storm of prayers and wild expression and jumping. The passion endured, the excitement and the fatigue ultimately produce an effect debasing to our nature and most disquieting to the bystander. Some are sick, some faint, some fall; and as they are led off, the women more particularly, the imagination seizes what may be supposed to be the appearance of a knot of witches exhausted by the orgies of their Sabbath's celebration.

But all was not lost: 'In narrowing these scandalous scenes ridicule has for once been beneficially employed, and the possessors of this abominable mummery are, I am informed, rapidly declining in numbers.'

But the sect was not quite as bad as it was painted: 'With respect to the charge brought against these people for profligate licentiousness of conduct during the night of their assemblies, I shall upon general grounds require the very strictest proofs before I would give credence to its existence, and above all to the manner of its existence.'

• CHAPTER 6 •

The quarrymen of Gwynedd have the most moving memorial of any industrial community in the world, the University College of North Wales, Bangor, founded in 1885.

The original college building, which opened in 1911 and stands like a cathedral on the ridge overlooking the town, was largely endowed by voluntary deductions from the quarrymen's pay over a period of many years. The pay was not good, and the sacrifice in many a home must have been immense, but in Wales scholarship is as much a passion as it is an intellectual activity.

The first premises provided in 1885 for the college's fifty-eight students and ten lecturers were in a former coaching inn, the Penrhos Arms. Then in 1902 the college acquired from the city council part of the bishop's park. Within nine years the college on the hill had been built, and since then it has been extended until today it caters for a student population of three thousand. What was the main college building now houses the administration, the department of Fine Arts and the splendid 350,000-volume library, also begun with the donations of quarrymen. There has been a considerable extension of the faculties. Today, in addition to the traditional disciplines, there are departments of Agriculture, Applied Mathematics and Computation, Biochemistry and Soil Science, Chemistry, Forestry and Wood Science, Physics and Pure Mathematics, Animal Biology and Plant Biology. There is a school of Electronic Engineering Science, a Botanical Garden and, across the straits in Menai Bridge, departments of Marine Biology and Physical Oceanography. The university has several halls of residence and it owns two boats, the ninety-foot RV *Prince Madog* and the forty-foot RV *Lewis Morris*.

When it opened in 1888, the Agriculture Department of the university was the first of its kind in Britain. Today it maintains its considerable reputation by having a university farm which covers the spectrum of farming experience with 371 acres (150 hectares) of mixed farming at sea-level, 445 acres (180 hectares) of enclosed hill grazing, and mountain grazing rights to a height of 1,094 yards (1,000 metres) in Snowdonia. It is a far cry from the early years in the Penrhos Arms, when the syllabus was restricted to Classics, Philosophy, Literature, History and Modern Languages and the basic sciences.

The university also runs a limited company, Industrial Development Bangor (UCNW) Ltd, which finds commercial applications for the pure research done in other faculties. IDB manufactures a wide range of electrostatic instruments and does work on cancer research. At the time of writing, the managing director, Professor Bob Paul, was co-ordinating research, with colleagues at Oxford, into the 300 m.p.h. magnetized train. The project looks at ways of using magnetized rail cars which will literally float on air. The principle involves huge magnets in capsules of heated liquid helium, producing 'super conductivity' and carrying, $2\frac{1}{2}$ inches off the track at speeds of up to 300 m.p.h., a forty-ton carriage with one hundred passengers.

Sophisticated research of this kind would have had those long-dead quarrymen reeling but they would have been heartened by another UCNW activity. Since 1962 the college has been formally bilingual. When the first classes were held, the language used in lectures was English. Now there are courses in Welsh in Biblical Studies, Drama, Philosophy, Education, History, Music, Social Theory and, of course, Welsh language, literature and history.

There is a touching link with one of those founder quarrymen among the books at Beaumaris and Bangor libraries. Albert Davies was in turn Calvinist, Catholic and Anglican. His several conversions came as a result of his passion for books on which he spent every penny he could scrape together. He worked at Penrhos Quarry in the nineteenth century. S. Baring Gould wrote of him:

> He lived in chronic hunger: and often was too poor to afford himself fire in the winter; every penny he could spare was spent in the purchase of books. He would read none but such as dealt with theology.
>
> At length he became so ill he had to be taken to the workhouse ... In the workhouse he received better food and comforts such as he had not been accustomed to as a poor and failing quarryman. Any little gratuity offered him he accepted to spend on his beloved books and in time his library was by no means inconsiderable. After his death by his express wish they have been divided between Bangor and Beaumaris libraries.

He was a man of rugged exterior with a head singularly like that attributed to Socrates.

One of the most bizarre of Gwynedd's scholars was Richard Jones, the son of an illiterate carpenter, who by the time he died at the age of forty had taught himself thirty-five languages. He was not the most elegant of scholars, it should be said. Someone wrote of him: 'He died as he had lived, a frowsy dirty peasant, or worse than a peasant; a loafer rather and a stroller, filthy in person, part medicant, part medicine man: one quarter idiot, three quarters genius.'

Dic Aberdaron's parents would not send him to the village school. He sneaked into the classroom after lessons were over and taught himself first Welsh and then English from the books he found lying about. He began wandering when he was twenty. Repeated beating by his parents had not succeeded in drumming any carpentry skill into him. On the road he met foreign tramps and tinkers and stayed with them long enough to pick up the rudiments of their languages. As news of the curious genius spread, people flocked to give him casual work and patronage. Dic accepted the work and the patronage and ignored the advice that went with it. He had no interest in making use of his unique gifts. He was obsessed by the construction of language; its uses went over his head. An Oxford don who tested him on the *Iliad* found his knowledge of the Greek language encyclopaedic but he was not interested at all in one of the greatest stories ever told. In fact, he got angry when the don questioned him about the characters in the tale.

Dic must have been a rare sight as he stumbled through North Wales, blowing a ram's horn and droning the song of Moses in Hebrew. His face peered out from a thicket of matted black hair. His hat was made of a hare's skin, and from the ears dangled scraps of paper and cloth inscribed with sentences in the classical languages. He wore a cavalryman's cast-off tunic in blue and silver and carried his library round with him in a capacious bag.

Though their beginnings were every bit as humble, the four Morris brothers of Anglesey achieved enormous academic distinction. The most successful of them was Lewis Morris, who was born in 1701 and rose from being a cooper's apprentice in Holyhead to owning a country estate in Cardigan and holding the position of HM Inspector of the Dominion of Wales. It was said of him that he could build a ship and sail it, frame a harp and make it speak, write an ode and set it to music.

His brother William was the least ambitious of the four. He stayed in Anglesey when his brothers Richard, John and Lewis left for London. Richard wrote in 1743 that he was learning Greek. His brother William wrote back that he had forgotten it. He was by trade a surveyor, and his charts of the Gwynedd coast are still in use. He and his brothers between them were beyond question the finest Welsh scholars of their day and would have a strong claim to be recognized as the fathers of Welsh antiquarian study.

The notebooks of Lewis Morris contain a list of 'Enquiries to be made by some Ingenious Inhabitant in every parish'. After listing questions into land and population, the questionnaire moved into more exotic areas:

An Account of ye most ancient people
What monstrous birth happened
Graves of Great Men
What ancient mss on vellum or paper
What inscriptions on grave stones
What fiery meteors, Corpse candles
What strange appearances in ye heavenly bodies
What ancient superstition
What fairy circles
What hidden treasures
What birds frequent the place
Insects, serpents
Country lanes
What rivers and their country names
What plants or herbs
What medieval springs
What stones and fossils
What ochres or earths for painting
What coal and other materials for fires
Gentlemen's seats
What Roman urns
What tumulis

The list gives a notion of the wide area over which Lewis Morris's mind ranged. So far as Anglesey is concerned, the notebooks show that, greatly aided by William, the brother who stayed at home, he tried to carry out the project on the island.

No description of the scholars of Gwynedd could possibly be complete without a further mention of 'Keeper' Williams of Conwy who became Archbishop of York. From early youth he needed only three hours sleep a night. So great were his achievements that a book was published recently arguing that it was Williams, not Bacon, who wrote the works of Shakespeare. The brothers George and Bernard Winchombe argue persuasively, and what emerges from their thesis is yet another prodigy of learning who, in 1592 at the age of ten, spoke several languages, was a gifted musician and singer and was, in addition, captain of Ruthin School.

In a biography published in 1700, Ambrose Phillips wrote of Williams' arrival at school: 'He came up better stocked with Latin and Greek than with good English.' At university he mastered several sciences as well as Greats. Once, in a spirit of scientific inquiry, he jumped from the town walls of Conwy onto the sea shore, hoping that his coat would bell out like a parachute. It did not and he fell with some force on his belly on a jagged stone. Phillips used the incident to deny a story current at the time that the doctor was born a eunuch. Borrowing a phrase from Williams' protégé, Bishop Hacket, he wrote: 'This caused an infirmity better understood than described.'

Archbishop Williams' monument is in the parish church at Llandegai. Nearby is the steel helmet he wore both to defend Conwy and to attack it. His epitaph reads: 'Eminently versed in all branches of knowledge, a treasure of learning in nine languages, the marrow of pure and unadulterated theology, an oracle of political judgment, the head and jewel of religious, canonical, civil and municipal law; in eloquence a very cymbal; a man of most retentive and superhuman memory and a storehouse for knowledge of all history ...' All the qualities, in short, you would expect to find in Shakespeare.

Gwynedd encourages unique human beings, even in this present tawdry age.

Aled Jones was a Bangor Cathedral chorister who lives in Llandegfan, Anglesey, whose hobby it was to compete in singing contests at Gwynedd eisteddfodau. His voice was unique but until Sain Recordiau (Records) of Llandwrog, near Caernarfon, made a long player, at the suggestion of a neighbour who wrote to tell them of the young singer, he was unknown outside the county. BBC Wales were sufficiently impressed to send Aled, in private life the archetypal mischievous schoolboy, to the Holy Land for a Christmas programme with the BBC Welsh Chorus.

Aled had been singing treble since the age of six. In 1982, at the Pwllheli National Youth Eisteddfod, he won the Solo and Cerdd Dant under twelve. With the programme *Born in Bethlehem*, in which he sang with a purity that raised neck hairs all over Britain, stardom was instant, as was the recognition of the masters of his profession. George Guest, the director of music at St John's College, Cambridge, said of his voice: 'It is one of the best treble voices I have heard.' In the months that followed, he was in demand all over the country. He sang with Stuart Burrows, Joan Sutherland and Sir Geraint Evans; he appeared before the Queen at a Royal Gala in Edinburgh; golden disc followed golden disc; he recorded 'Memory' from the musical *Cats* with Andrew Lloyd Webber. It took him less than an hour where other international singing stars had needed a week in the studio. Lloyd Webber said of him: 'About a hundred singers have recorded *Cats*. I think Aled's was the best.'

Compliments abounded. Critics agreed that the voice of the Anglesey schoolboy, who is as happy on the football field as on the concert platform, was the most perfect ever recorded. He is the perfect performer. On stage he shows no trace of nervousness. His interpretation of music astonishes the experts. In 1985, at the age of fourteen, he made record after record. But his parents, Nest and Derek, were determined that his feet should remain firmly on the ground. His programmes and recordings were arranged so that he did not miss his lessons at the David Hughes Comprehensive School in Menai Bridge. When the BBC wanted him to go to Cardiff to receive a gold disc, they had to send a helicopter to collect him after school.

Though 1985 was an *annus mirabilis* for the engaging boy, it was also a time of considerable strain. He went on the stage not knowing whether his voice would break before the end of the concert. When I interviewed him on my radio programme, he was philosophical. 'I don't worry about the voice breaking,' he said. 'What's the point? There is nothing I can do about it.'

Stuart Burrows advised him to rest for at least two years before attempting to train as a tenor – or whatever he turned out to be – and warned him of the danger of putting too much strain on the voice in the months before it cracked. Yet not a trace of this intolerable worry appeared in the boy's behaviour. The reason, I believe, is that God gave Aled Jones three gifts. No one who has heard him would doubt for a second that his voice is a gift from Heaven in the way that Mozart's talent was Heaven-sent. In his father and mother, fiercely protective, warmly loving, he has two gifts that Mozart lacked. I have never known a family so united and locked up with each other. Visiting them at their home overlooking the straits is a great spiritual restoration, if you can resist the toasted sandwiches which Aled presses on you, made with the electric toaster which is the only status symbol this golden-disc winner insisted on buying. His current ambition was to meet Daley Thompson, the Olympic athlete. He achieved it at the Royal Gala, where he was astonished to discover that Daley Thompson wanted *his* autograph.

The eisteddfodau in which Aled sings are not just serious music festivals. The englyn was never better described than by my friend and Crowned Bard, T. Glynne Davies, the poet when we were sharing the commentary box at the National Eisteddfod. He explained:

> At its simplest the poetic form of Cynghanedd which includes the englyn is a matter of having the same consonants in the same order at the end of the line as you have at the beginning. My teacher used to tell me that it was like an old woman's mouth with only two teeth, one at each end.
>
> The Englyn is a four line, thirty syllable, stanza with complex internal rhymes. It has ten syllables in the first line, six in the second and a pair of sevens. And it must consist of cynghanedd which is an alliterative pattern.
>
> A real master of the art thinks in cynghanedd. It is possible to write them in English whatever you are told. Gerald Manley Hopkins was very successful'.

T. Glynne a brilliant poet and a natural broadcaster decided the best way to demonstrate the art was to write one in English. Whilst we were conducting, with TV presenter Hywel Gwynfryn, a three-way two-hour conversation and commentary live on air he wrote the following example:

> So to gloat, I say T. *Glynne* [or perhaps
> Poor Hywel Gwynfryn]
> They say, in a way, he'll win
> Rich Uncle from Brynsiencyn.

Hywel offered examples from his favourite poet Dic Jones of Anglesey, a master of cynghanedd who wrote of the Modern Miss:

> Her suit a hairy sweater; in a pod no pea was tighter
> No frills and no lace for her
> Unruly rock and roller.

and of the night:

> No hymn of birds no tremor, save the sea's sad tenor
> The stars ascend in splendour and the dark creeps round the door.

The Eisteddfod prompts exchanges like that, even in the Radio Wales commentary box. The happy face of culture is the Eisteddfodwr, any one of the vast rumbustious crowd who spend a week following the great timber and steel pavilion, the heart of the Eisteddfod which is transplanted every year in a different part of the Principality. Although it is a national celebration of Welshness it doesn't confine itself to the Celtic heartland. In 1985 it was held at Rhuddlan near Rhyl, by an irony on the very field where in his statute Edward I laid claim to Wales, and a predominantly English-speaking area. It is a curious and lovable festival. The only one in Europe, perhaps in the world, where an audience comprising for the most part ordinary working people listens attentively at a poetry festival to hours of adjudications and never gets to hear even the winning poems. It is a serious music festival where rock and roll is encouraged. An Art exhibition where you can buy T shirts with slogans. A cultural celebration of Welshness where the most popular food on sale in the booths are pizzas, doughnuts and Breton pancakes. There are ritual demonstrations against whoever the Welsh Office sends down to represent it. But these are teenage tantrums and once the demonstration is over the Welsh Office representative is left to wander happily through the many attractions of the day. Almost certainly he will have a relative competing since Wales is not so much a country as a family.

The Eisteddfod is in fact two festivals. The poetry and music competition and the Gorsedd of the Bards of the Islands of Britain. The Gorsedd is perhaps the most scoffed at public ceremonial in Britain. There have been endless jokes about the bards in bedsheets cavorting round a ring of stones. Yet it might be argued that all ceremonial is silly. Think of the Procession of the Knights of the Garter at Windsor Castle. A gaggle of old men with hats like tea cosies, going outdoors in their dressing gowns with their supporters club badges sewn on the pockets. Or what of the Trooping of the Colour. A crowd of aggressive young men in red tunics and risible fur hats doing the military equivalent of 'Come Dancing'. All pageantry is absurd; an entertainment designed not so much for the audience as it is for the participants. The Gorsedd does have the merit of greater antiquity. Most of the great State Occasions date no further back than the reign of Victoria. The Gorsedd was found in 1792. It is amongst pageants the ultimate absurdity. It is not even Welsh. The first Gorsedd was celebrated on Primrose Hill in London and its ceremonies were invented almost single handed by a forger named Edward Williams, a stone-mason-cum-bookshop-owner who was born at Penmon in the Vale of Glamorgan and took the bardic title of Iolo Morganwg. The son of a stone mason he never had a day's schooling in his life and taught himself to read by watching his father cutting epitaphs on grave-stones. Yet he became a literary forger of such brilliance that people are still unsure which of his manuscripts are forgeries and which general medieval documents.

In the eighteenth century with the poem *Ossian*, a so-called ancient Celtic epic that was in reality the work of another forger, a Celtic craze swept Britain and Iolo saw his chance. He claimed with a man from Aberdare to be one of the two last surviving druids, the descendants of the college of Celtic priests. He revived that college, the Gorsedd, in an article in the *Gentleman's* magazine in 1789, holding the first ceremony three years later.

He put forward what he claimed was the ancient ritual, all the dazzling invention of his own brain. He claimed the Gorsedd has three sections: druids who wore white robes, bards and musicians who wore blue and ovates who wear green.

The stone circle at which the bards meet represents the twelve tribes of Israel and the centre stone the Ark of the Covenant. Iolo claimed that the first stones had been taken from the bed of the River Jordan and that the first Eisteddfod was held on its banks by the Israelites. The unsheathed Eisteddfod sword which is carried at all Eisteddfod ceremonies, is the symbol of Iolo's pacifism. Ironically the motto of this fraudulent ceremonial is Truth Against the World.

And yet it is a moving ceremony. It does pluck at the heart even of the anglicized observers. A useful ceremony too. In our day bards and ovates are elected for their services to the arts and culture in Wales. It is the Welsh equivalent of the Honours List. One Archdruid, Geraint Bowen told the audience at his election: 'The purpose of the pageant of the Gorsedd is to remind ourselves, remind the Welsh and the world, of the ancient nature of the Welsh language and of the devotion of the nation to the arts of this island.'

Wicked old Iolo's fraud has come to have serious meaning.

The scholars and artists which Gwynedd did not grow it imported from England.

Lord Clarendon, Dr Johnson, Thomas Gray, were among the visitors. According to his biographer and friend, Lord Orerry, Dean Jonathan Swift not only visited Gwynedd, he walked across it. The Earl wrote: 'He generally chose to dine with waggoners, ostlers and persons of that rank; and he used to lye at night in houses where he found written over the door "Lodgings for a Penny". He delighted in scenes of low life. The vulgar dialect was not only a fount of humour for him, but I verily believed was acceptable to his nature ...' Not always acceptable. On 25 September 1727 the Dean penned this sad ode in his Holyhead Journal:

Lo here I sit at Holy Head
With muddy ale and mouldy bread
All Christian vittles
Stink of fish
I'm where my enemies would wish.
Convict of lies is every sign
The inn has not one drop of wine.
I'm fastened both by wind and tide,
I see the ship at anchor ride.
The captain swears the sea's too rough
He had not passengers enough
And thus the Dean is forc'd to stay ...

Others found Gwynedd more to their taste. That very droll and vastly underrated scholar Thomas de Quincey came to Wales believing he was escaping arrest over a missing postal draft. In fact, there was no evidence of a crime. He was, as usual, all but penniless when, in 1802, at the age of sixteen, he walked from his home in Manchester to Caernarfon. His account of the journey is a minor comic classic. Most nights he slept in a tent he had made himself which was no bigger than an umbrella. In Bangor, where he rented a tiny room, he toyed with the idea of challenging the bishop to a duel in Greek and had an unfortunate experience with a herd of cows. The account of the hilarious hike can be found in his *Confession of an English Opium Eater*.

Paul Sandby was the first painter to give pictorial definition to Wales with his 'Twelve Views in Aquatinta', one set showing South Wales, the other North. But it was J.M.W. Turner who evoked the romantic qualities of Gwynedd. He came to Wales in 1790, influenced by Thomas Gray's nationalist 'ode', 'The Bard', which was first published in 1757. In 1798 he began a painting tour of North Wales from Dolgellau and the Mawddach estuary to Harlech, Criccieth and Caernarfon. He painted the principal peaks and passes in Snowdonia, and the castles of Harlech, Criccieth and Caernarfon. He crossed the Straits to draw Beaumaris, then crossed back to travel the Conwy road. At Dolbadarn Castle he was inspired to poetry, and again at Caernarfon, where he wrote:

And now on Arvon's haughty towers,
The bard the song of poetry pours
For oft on Mona's distant hills he sighs ...

The poetry was less than inspired but the paintings had an enormous success.

The trickle of tourists became a flood which threatened the very culture they came to admire. Coleridge and Wordsworth came and were suitably impressed by Snowdon's rugged beauty. Painters' easles sprouted from every crag. As early as 1802 de Quincey had noticed that little inns were springing up on the roadsides where travellers were welcomed. And that was thirty years before George Borrow 'discovered' *Wild Wales*, a curious title for a book which celebrated a civilized and creative nation that stretched back to its Roman creators, a so-called subject race that took the Normans two hundred years to conquer.

Lord Macaulay, the great historian, enjoyed himself in Wales to such a degree that, in the face of considerable opposition from Wordsworth, he wrote one of the worst ever poems on Wales. In fairness, it was intended to amuse his schoolgirl sister.

Up and down through all the day
On the hills of Wales I stray
And at night it is my habit
For to sup on a Welsh Rabbit.

Dr Johnson's visit to Wales with his patrons Mr and Mrs Thrale and their appalling daughter Queenie was not a success. The doctor and Mrs Thrale had already fallen out three times before they reached Gwynedd, where Mrs Thrale had inherited property on the Lleyn at Llangwnnadl. He saw little in the country which impressed him. Llyn Padarn and Llyn Peris: 'The lakes have no great breadth, so that the bark is always near one bank or the other.' The inheritance at Bodville: 'This species of pleasure is always melancholy. The walk was cut down and the pond was dry. Nothing was better.' Conwy: 'In all these old buildings the subterranean works are concealed by the rubbish.'

In the next century Percy Bysshe Shelley was much more enthusiastic. But then Shelley was *always* an enthusiast. He came to Tan-yr Allt, a mansion at Tremadog, as the tenant of its owner, the entrepreneur Alexander Madocks, who was responsible for the great embankment and port of Porthmadog. Shelley was among Madocks' friends who rallied to his aid when the first embankment was washed out to sea by giving him money and organizing public meetings to collect more. At a meeting in Bangor, reported in the *North Wales Gazette* in September 1814, Shelley announced: 'I publicly pledge myself to spend the last shilling of my fortune and devote the last breath of my life to this great, this glorious, cause.' Five months later the Shelleys hurried unceremoniously out of Wales after what his wife Harriet described as 'a night of horrible events'. In a letter to a friend she told how Shelley surprised an intruder:

> I had been in bed three hours when I heard a pistol go off. I immediately ran downstairs, where I perceived that Bysshe's flannel gown had been shot through and the window curtain.
>
> Bysshe had sent Daniel to see what hour it was when he heard the noise at the window. He went there and a man pushed his arm through the glass and fired at him. Thank God the ball went through his sleeve.

Few local people believed the story. Poor Harriet, not for the first time grossly deceived by the feckless Shelley, thought she knew why: 'There is a man of the name of Leson who the next morning went and told the shopkeepers of Tremadog that it was a tale of Mr Shelley's to impose upon them; that he might leave the country without paying their bills.'

Curiously, a glance at the files of the local newspaper shows that at the time of the supposed attack there was great alarm in the country following the escape from Chester Gaol of a local man who had committed a particularly brutal murder. If the attack was not, as has been pretty widely accepted, a figment of Shelley's imagination or, as he later claimed, a visitation by government agents pursuing him for his revolutionary ideas, perhaps it was the escaped prisoner looking for food and shelter and finding instead a tiny fragment of literary immortality as the man who attacked Shelley.

It would be impossible to mention all the outstanding or otherwise impressive poets, painters, artists and singers that Gwynedd has fostered, either as her own or as exiles from another land. Contemporary artists whose works are known to a wide gallery-going public include Kyffin Williams, who lives in Anglesey on the edge of the Menai Straits, Gwilym Pritchard, a chronicler on canvas of Snowdonia in all its moods, and Charles Tunnicliffe, the celebrated bird- and wildlife-painter who came from Cheshire to live in a house overlooking the Malltraeth marshes. After his death in 1981 his collection of measured drawings was bought by Anglesey Borough Council so that the work he did on the island might eventually, when a gallery is found, be exhibited as a whole.

In recent years Ed Povey has made his mark as one of the most provocative artists of the many working in Gwynedd. Born in 1951 and an exile from London, Ed first came to notice in the 1970s, when he painted an exotic medieval mural, complete with jester and dancing bear, on the outside wall of a friend's house in Upper Bangor. To their credit, local councils in Arfon, Anglesey and Aberconwy recognized an unusual talent, and he was commissioned to paint public buildings, such as the library wall at the entrance to Caernarfon, an amazing seventeen hundred square feet, depicting the history of the town. Other commissions from various sources in Porthmadog, Holyhead, Conwy, Bangor and Aberystwyth followed, and now Ed's paintings are tourist attractions. Since 1980 BBC Wales TV has been following his progress, and a documentary will, no doubt, result soon.

Ill health, partly brought on by painting murals sixty feet up a ladder in the North Wales climate, forced Ed to emigrate to the tropical West Indian island of Grenada, where he arrived just in time for the revolution, but every year he returns to Bangor to give an exhibition of his work. His heart, he says, is still in Gwynedd, which gave him his first chance as an artist, but increasingly his paintings, now mostly on canvas, are in demand on the international market. In 1984 a New York collector, who bought some of his works to hang between his Rembrandts and his Goyas, described him as one of the greatest twentieth-century painters. He then commissioned a $10,000 altarpiece from him. At this rate it seems that Ed's painted walls in Gwynedd will soon be worth more than the buildings they grace.

His paintings are always crowded – with people, symbolism, activity. They are complex and colourful and, unusually for an artist, when someone commissions a painting, Ed gives him, or her, all the sketches and reference material that led up to that picture. And with every painting comes a written story or explanation. When Ed started painting in Bangor, he always wore a jester's suit. It symbolized, he said, the wise man and the fool. Now he prefers the black and white of the mime.

The Archdeacon of Bangor, the Most Reverend T. Bayley Hughes, is a cartoon artist of national standing who from time to time makes the cathedral aisles ring with laughter with exhibitions of his highly entertaining work. A long-standing member of the Cartoonists Club of Great Britain, he finds himself called on to act as chaplain at their annual conventions.

The most enduring cartoon character of them all must be

In 1986 Gwynedd artist Ed Povey's paintings were the centre-piece of the New York Expo Spring Exhibition. Exactly ten years after he painted this shop-front mural 'Storage Jars' in Holyhead Road, Upper Bangor

Both Telford with his suspension bridge and Stephenson with his railway bridge tried to harmonize their work with Edward's great castle at Conwy

Sensitive restoration of Caernarfon's slate wharf has left this terracotta and yellow-brick office façade

An archive view of a Caernarfon street. A new Ludwigian County Council complex now complements the mock-Gothic law courts

Rupert the Bear. Alfred Edmeades Bestall, who for thirty years drew and wrote the strip cartoon for the *Daily Express*, set all Rupert's mountain adventures in Snowdonia. Mr Bestall, who lived, until his death in 1986, in a tiny cottage surrounded by rhododendrons in the woods near Beddgelert, took over the Rupert series from its creator, Marie Turtel, in 1935. He retired in 1965 but carried on with the annual until 1973, then contributed three pages a year until his eyesight began to fail in 1983. In 1985, at the age of ninety-two he was awarded the MBE in the Queen's Birthday Honours for the joy he had brought to millions of children and adults as the artist and story-teller of Rupert. Interviewed on that occasion by a local paper, he admitted that he had often pictured Rupert in pre-carious situations 'as he enjoyed mountain climbs – and these were always in Snowdonia'.

THE BUILDERS OF DREAMS

Mighty great winds, that for the most part therein doe rage, and the spired hills clustered together so neare and so high that shepherds upon their tops falling at odds in the morning, and challenging the field for fight before they can come together to try out their quarrel the day will be spent.

John Speed, *Atlas of Wales* (sixteenth century)

• CHAPTER 7 •

Gwynedd entered recorded history with the coming of the Roman General Suetonius Paulinus in AD 59. His soldiers were the first occupying army, setting a precedent that was to be frequently repeated during the succeeding thousand years. None surpassed, and few equalled, the murderous cruelty of the XX and XIV Legions.

The legions, marching behind their standards, must have been a terrifying sight to the Britons as they tramped across Gwynedd. Metal-covered men, heavy leather sandals hobnailed and striking sparks, wooden shields slung, short stabbing swords bouncing at their hips, they must have seemed unbeatable. The first soldiers that Gwynedd's tribesmen would have seen were the cavalry, probing and scouting the mountainsides for ambush. Then perhaps the general on the white horse of a staff officer. Behind Suetonius, the legions. And then the siege trains, trundling noisily on wooden wheels. *Ballistae*, flame-throwers that could send a blazing dart into a target two thousand feet away; onagers which hurled boulders and shrapnel bags of smaller stones, and, last of all, long, flat-bottomed barges for the crossing of the Menai Straits.

It is likely that the Romans made their camp on the banks of the straits at Llanfairisgaer ('St Mary's Church below the Camp'). The barges were carried down to the water's edge, and the cavalry prepared their horses for swimming them across. Then a strange thing happened, a thing unheard of amongst these veterans who had fought their way across Europe. The legions panicked. They stared across the straits and they were horrified. Tacitus, whose father-in-law Agricola was to lead a second campaign against Anglesey, records the scene:

> On the opposite shore stood the Britons closely drawn up and prepared for action. Women were seen rushing through the ranks in wild disorder, their dress funereal, their hair loose to the wind,

flaming torches in their hands and their whole appearance resembling the frantic rage of the Furies. The Druids were ranged in order, with hands uplifted, invoking the gods and pouring forth horrible imprecations.

The strangeness of the sight struck the Romans with awe and terror. They stood in stupid amazement, as if their limbs were paralysed, riveted to one spot, a mark for the enemy.

Their terror was understandable. They had been told how the British bathed their altars with the blood of their prisoners and in the entrails of men sought to find the will of the gods.

Tacitus wrote of Suetonius Paulinus: 'He proceeds always against the vanquished, even after they had surrendered, with excessive vigour. Justice under his administration had frequently the air of personal injury. Indeed his public proceedings and his private passions became so mixed that he was recalled to Rome.' All his savagery was released that day in AD 59 to force his legions to fight. 'Exhortations of the general soon diffused new life through the ranks and by mutual reproaches incited each other to deeds of valour. They felt the disgrace of yielding to a troop of women and a band of fanatical priests. They advanced their standards and attacked with impetuous fury. The Britons perished in the flames they had themselves kindled. The island fell and a garrison was established. The sacred groves of oaks were cut down, the Druids were burned in their own fires and hundreds of men, women and children were killed.' The carnage lives on in folk memory to this day.

The Romans probably landed at the Ferrymen's Inlet, now a land drainage outflow on the shore below the ruined church of Llanidan. Little has changed and there are few more pleasant excursions than to have a home-cooked luncheon at the Groeslon Inn at Brynsiencyn crossroads, followed by a stroll down the leafy lane across the road from the inn down to the shore. The silence is broken only by the murmuring bees and bird song. Everything is peaceful now but a glance at the map will show that it was not always so. The first large field on the right after leaving the inn is still called the Field of the Long Battle; below it is the Field of Bitter Lamentation; a few hundred yards to the left down another lane is Bryn-y-Beddau ('the Hill of the Graves'). According to the eighteenth-century antiquarian the Reverend Henry Rowlands, who was the vicar of Llanidan, writing in his book *Mona Antiqua*: 'Just on the shore there is a place called the Rhiedd, "the Chief Men's post", at which place the other day were taken from under a stone near the sea shore a bundle of British weapons.' Even today stone arrowheads are sometimes found among the pebbles and fossils on the beach.

There are other links with the Roman past in the district, notably the cottage of the Black Witch (*Gwrach Ddu*). Locally this is believed to be not the home of a curse-throwing crone but a memory of the Roman camp. With their impregnable armour, sophisticated weaponry and the more civilized skills, both medicinal and practical, of Roman civilization, the dark-skinned Spanish legions must indeed have seemed like witches to the indigenous tribesmen. Fortunately Suetonius Paulinus' garrisons were not to stay long. After two years the general had to march eastwards to fight Queen Boudicca and the Iceni. For, as Tacitus said, 'The whole island of Britain had risen.'

For two years the Britons lived in peace until Agricola led another legion into Gwynedd. The soldiers were from the XX Legion with reinforcements from the XIV, auxiliaries mostly with a few seasoned veterans, the First Cohort of Vardulli, the 'Loyal' from Northern Spain, spurred on by the brazen trumpet of one Januarius, bugler in Victor's century, whose pottery dish was discovered during excavations at the wooden fort they built at Segontium overlooking the estuary of the Seiont at Caernarfon.

The first invaders had marched across virgin country. Agricola's men marched along a well-made military road which entered Gwynedd at Caerhun, the legion post Canovium. That road, still in use by ramblers to this day, extends from the village of Roewen along the flanks of the Snowdon massif to Abergwyngregyn. It is made, in part, of sandstone the Roman engineers brought on carts from their legion headquarters at Chester and in part from local rock. The Roman road followed roughly a Bronze Age trackway over the mountains, and for three hundred years it was the most important road in Wales, linking Deva fortress in Chester with Segontium and the Flintshire lead mines. From Abergwyngregyn it took the line of the present coastal road to Caernarfon. A secondary road linked the Roman fort at Bryngyfeilian, which in its turn was linked at Tomen y Mur with a road to Caernarfon which the A4805 now covers. It formed an arterial box linking the two coastal forts with Maridunum (Carmarthen) and Isca (Caerleon). There was a fourth Roman road from Chester through Bala to Brithdir, where it joined the western coast road. It was the first in a long line of dazzling displays of engineering in Gwynedd.

The next building programme also had a military purpose. That was the ring of stone castles built by Edward I during his conquest of North Wales. It is difficult not to see these fortresses as status symbols. Far too sophisticated for the role they were required to fill, a much simpler structure would have over-awed the natives and served as a garrison. But Edward loved his toys, and he was never happier than when he was playing soldiers. In the twenty years which followed his campaign against Llewelyn, ten new castles, some with towns attached, and four lordship castles were built and three native castles and several border strongholds restored.

The castles were built in three stages which corresponded to the military campaigns mounted between 1277 and 1295. Conwy, which was built between 1283 and 1301, cost £13,761.9s. 10d.; Caernarfon, which was built at the same time, £12,308.3s. 9¾d.; Beaumaris, 1295 to 1300, £11,389.0s. 9d.; Harlech, 1285 to 1301, £8,190.2s. 4¼d.; Criccieth, which was also rebuilt over the same period, cost £318.17s. 4¾d.

The castles were built to the plans of Master James of St George, whom Edward had poached from his cousin Philip of Savoy with the promise of a salary of £54 a year, which, incidentally, was £14 more than Edward paid the Chief Justice of England. The designs were brilliant. Conwy, for example, could be defended by fifteen men-at-arms and sixty archers. St George called in the master craftsmen who had helped him build castles in Savoy for his first master: Philip the carpenter, Stephen the painter, Master Monasser de Vaucoulers the mason. To assist them, the kingdom was scoured for men and materials. Builders came from all over England, dykers from the Fens; the materials, freestone from Pembrokeshire, lime from Tenby, limestone from Anglesey, lead from the mines of Snowdonia and the Isle of Man, sea coal from Clwyd, iron and steel from Newcastle-under-Lyme. These raw materials, the money to pay for them and the wages of the men had to be brought through the 'enemy lines', loaded on pack mules. It was a great undertaking, and the result was a chain of cathedrals of war so formidable that three centuries later Oliver Cromwell smashed them into ruins lest they be used by Royalists to defy his rule.

The castles played a dual role in the subjugation of Wales. They were both fortifications and political symbols. Caernarfon particularly was designed to give the English Crown the respectability of precedent. It was not the first time the tactic had been used. The Norman kings had commissioned Geoffrey of Monmouth to invent an entire ancestry to give them proof of descent from an ancient British royal line. Edward chose a similar tactic. The Roman usurper Maximus, a Spaniard who was declared emperor by his troops in Britain in 383, lived in

Caernarfon and married Elen, the daughter of a British chief. Maximus appears in the *Mabinogion* as Macsen Wledig. There is a legend that the Emperor dreamt of a castle overlooking an estuary in which sat a lovely lady.

> And he came straight to Arfon: and the emperor recognised the land the moment he saw it. And the moment he saw the castle of Aber Seint, 'See yonder,' said he, 'the castle wherin I saw the lady I love best' and he came straight to the castle ...
>
> The maiden he had seen in his sleep he saw sitting in a chair of red gold. 'Emperor of Rome,' said she, 'all hail.' And the emperor threw his arms round her neck and that night he slept with her.

After this hasty courtship the couple were married, '... and she chose that the most exalted stronghold should be made for her in Arfon, and soil from Rome was brought there so that it might be healthier for the emperor to sit or move about.'

The legend had everything Edward needed to confirm the royal antecedents. He claimed to have found in the excavations for the castle of Caernarfon the bones of a Roman Emperor. Unfortunately he got his emperors mixed up, following, no doubt, an error in the twelfth-century *Hanes Gruffydd ap Cynan*. In this the original castle of Arfon is described as being built in the old city of the Emperor Constantine, son of Constans the Great. It was these unlikely remains that Edward announced he had found and re-buried with considerable pomp. Unfortunately there is no record that Constantine was ever in Gwynedd. Edward went further. Today visitors notice that the castle of Caernarfon is different from his other castles. Its towers are not round like the others; they are polygonal. The walls are patterned with bands of different-coloured stone. There is a precedent for them. They are copies of the tile-laced Theodosian walls of Constantinople, the great city Constantine built as the capital of the Roman Empire in the East. Constantinople had a Golden Gate. So did Caernarfon. What is now the Water Gate is in Welsh *'Porth yr Awr'*, 'gate of gold'. And the stone eagle which gives the castle tower its name does not commemorate the room in which the future King Edward II was born: it was the imperial eagle of Rome.

Nothing was to be omitted to bolster Caernarfon's claim to be the Constantinople of Wales. The actual Caer Aber Saint, the Roman fort Segontium, can still be traced in fascinating ruins on the outskirts of the town. It is listed as a fort and the terminus of a road in the Antonine Itinerary. Segontium was first revealed by accident during building work in the mid-nineteenth century. It is still not fully excavated but many of the finds of the series of digs that have been held there can be seen in its excellent little museum.

The route of the Roman road was traced by Sir Mortimer Wheeler during his time in Caernarfon. He found that, after leaving the north-eastern gate of Segontium, the road ran almost directly for $2\frac{3}{4}$ miles along the ridgeway dividing the Cadnant Valley from the Seiont, following the line of the modern road to the hill fort of Dinas Dinorwig, where a milestone of Trajan Decius was found. From Llandeiniolen the road went to a farmhouse, Ty Coch, on the west bank of the River Cegin, where a second milestone, this time of the period of Caracallus, was found.

Sir Mortimer thought it likely that from here to Aber (now called Abergwyngregyn) the road followed a straight line before climbing into the hills along the lower slope of the hill above Gorddinog, where there is another hill fort, Maes y Gaer. Further on, two more milestones belonging to the reigns of Hadrian (117-38) and Septimus Severus (207-9) were found at Rhiw Goch on the Gorddinog estate, near Aber, by the then landowner, Colonel H. Platt, Bangor's first mayor. He gave both milestones to the British Museum. The Hadrian milestone is one of the prime exhibits of the Romano-British gallery of the British Museum, but the Severian milestone, which has been returned to Bangor, had not been exhibited at the Museum since before World War II. It is exhibited alongside a plastercast of the upper part of Hadrian's milestone. The Bangor Museum also houses a third Roman milestone, found at Madryn Farm, Abergwyngregyn, in 1959. The fourth stone is on exhibition at the National Museum in Cardiff.

As has been seen, part of the Roman road followed the tracks between villages made by the native Britons. In Gwynedd the Romans seldom built outside the safety of their own strongholds. The only vernacular architecture we have from the period came from the natives. The foundations of their circular huts, grouped in a neighbourly way on hillsides and river banks, can be found all over the county. The most impressive is Tre'r Ceiri (the town of the giants) on one of the peaks of Yr Eifl, or 'the Rivals' as they have become known by corruption − *'yr eifl'* in fact means 'the prongs of a fork' − at the gateway to the Lleyn Peninsula above Llanaelhaearn. The Giants' Town was circled by a great wall which is in part fifteen feet high and ten feet wide. Behind this immense defensive wall are the remains of a hundred circular houses covering an area of five acres.

Much of the ruin and the demolition of stone walls which prevents careful investigation of the site is due not to time but to greed. In the first half of the nineteenth century an old woman of Llithfaen nearby dreamed that a copper cauldron full of gold was buried under Tre'r Ceiri. In the miniature gold rush that followed, much valuable archaeological evidence was destroyed.

Similar villages are found on high ground elsewhere. The huts are mostly circular, though there are elliptical and oblong varieties. What remains are the foundations. These comprise double rows of stone, with earth and pebble infilling, once surmounted by thatched roofs.

In the hut circle on the hillside above Cable Bay on Anglesey traces can be seen of hearths, stone tables and beds, even paved floors. There is about them a sort of rugged cosiness. And whilst the intelligence admits that such sites were chosen for defensive purposes and because the valleys were covered at that time in marsh and forest, the heart hopes that the spectacular view played some part in the builders' reckoning. On either hand the cliffs of Anglesey tower, and across Caernarfon Bay can be seen the peaks of Giants' Town and the glistening coast of Lleyn.

The people who built these huts were the descendants of Gwynedd's first engineers, New Stone Age tribes of the time up to 300 BC. They built the elaborate burial tombs, the cromlechs, houses of the dead whose walls were massive upright slabs of stone, roofed with a single capstone weighing many tons, covered with mounds of earth.

One of the finest of North Wales cromlechs is on the Cable Bay headland near the hill village. Barclodiad y Gawres has a twenty-three-foot aisle which leads into a domed central chamber. There are three side chambers which once had sliding stone 'doors'. The dome of the central chamber is built up from overlapping stones; the upright stones of the walls are dovetailed into the roof 'beam', and five of the upright stones are decorated with chiselled designs.

In the eighteenth century Thomas Pennant in his *Tour of Wales* wrote of a cromlech in Vortigern Valley, hard by Tre'r Ceiri. His description of the spot is chilling; 'Embosomed in a lofty mountain, on two sides bounded by stony steeps on which no vegetables appear but the blasted heath and stunted gorse: the third side exhibits a most tremendous front of block precipice with the loftiest peak of the mountain Eifl soaring above: and the only opening to this secluded spot is towards the sea, a northern aspect where that chilling wind exerts its fury.'

Traditionally it was to this valley the Saxon King Vortigern fled from the anger of his subjects and where he died when his castle was consumed by lightning. In the seventeenth century what was thought to be the mount of Vortigern's castle was excavated under the direction of the local parson, the Reverend Hugh Roberts. To the diggers' delight they found 'a stone coffin' containing the bones of a tall man. The description suggests to modern scholarship that he had lived several hundred years before Vortigern. In fact, what they had found, and largely destroyed in doing so, was another of the mysterious cromlechs.

Another Anglesey 'Passage Grave' is Bryn Celli Ddu, Brynsiencyn, one of the last megalithic tombs on the island. This is built inside a henge which was of much earlier construction. Here the henge, upright stones built in a circle, connects to the grave in the centre by a ceremonial path. Though smaller than that at Cable Bay, the frame is every bit as impressive. Inside the chamber is a tall, circular pillar decorated with abstract symbols.

A third henge can be found on Penmaenmawr. Meini Hirion consists of two circles of stones, imperfectly preserved. In the seventeenth century it was much more impressive. Sir John Wynne noted that the stones were surrounded by a wall. He went on: 'And neare to this circle there are three pretty big stones. Upon their endes, standinge tryangle wiese like a tribbet, where upon as they say was sett a greate caudron to boyle meat in and surely the three stones doe looke as yf they had been longe in a great fyre.' Amongst the stones which remain is one roughly in human shape which is called the Deity Stone; one with a basin hollowed in the top is the Stone of Sacrifice. Between the first large circle and the second smaller one there used – again according to Sir John – to be three stones of different colours. One was red, one white and the other blue. The local tradition is that they were three women who winnowed their corn there on the sabbath. As a punishment, the legend went, they were turned into stone the colour of the clothes they were wearing.

After the Romans left, there was no major civil engineering project for over a thousand years, and five hundred years after Edward I built his seaside castles the sea was still the safest way to travel to most parts of Gwynedd. Roads scarcely existed. Where they did, mostly on the coast, they were hazardous.

Until late in the seventeenth century the stretch round the crags of Penmaenmawr was scarcely more than a track covered in loose stone which climbed up the face of the precipice. Parts of it were crumbling away, and none of it was protected from the sea sixty feet below. At low tide the preferred route for coaches was over the sands at the foot of the two Penmaens. If the tide was missed, travellers rode over the crags, leaving their coaches to be manhandled over later. The system – it was said to have been introduced by the Earl of Clarendon – was to set the horses one behind the other in single traces, pulling the coach behind them. Behind the coach three or four men prevented it from slipping backwards.

Either by boat or by road the journey was dangerous. In the seventeenth century a parishioner of Llanfairfechan, Sion Humphreys, arranged to meet his sweetheart Anne Thomas at Conwy Fair. He decided to walk over Penmaenmawr; she thought she would be safer in the ferry. He fell off the mountain and she fell out of the boat. Both survived, as did the vicar of Llanelian, the Reverend Mr Jones, when he fell off the crag at the steepest point whilst riding his horse and carrying a midwife behind him. The horse and the midwife were killed, Jones escaped without a scratch.

When Penmaen had been crossed, there were dangers still to be encountered. In the days before the Menai was bridged, the ferry journey across the strait or, at low tide, the walk across the Lavan Sands, was perilous. In 1755 a Scots pedlar was drowned when the ferrymen refused to go out for him. They went out the next day and robbed his corpse.

The Quaker preacher George Fox met little better treatment on the ferry after preaching the Word at Beaumaris. He recalled:

'I bid John get his horse into the Ferry Boat but there having got in a company of wild gentlemen as we called them which we found to be very rude men, they with others kept him out of the boat. I rode to the boat's side and spoke to them, shewing them what unmanly and unchristian conduct it was. As I spoke I leapt my horse into the boat amongst them, thinking John's horse would have followed, but the boat being deep it could not do so, wherefore I leapt out again on horseback into the water and stayed with John on that side till the boat returned. Having crossed we had forty two miles to travel that evening and when we had paid for our passage we had but one groat left between us in money.

In 1774 Dr Samuel Johnson and the Thrales made the journey over Penmaenmawr by the new road. It held no terrors for the Doctor, who noted in his journal: 'We set out in some anxiety but we came to Penmaenmawr by daylight; and found a way, lately made, very easy and very safe. It was cut smooth and enclosed between parallel walls; the outer of which securing the passenger from the precipice, which is deep and dreadful. This wall is here and there broken, by mischievous wantonness. The inner wall preserves the road from the loose stones, which the shattered steep above it would pour down. That side of the mountain seems to have a surface of loose stones which at every accident may crumble.' That danger at least is still present. In the winter of 1984 the coast road was blocked for several days after a minor avalanche had swept down the mountain.

In 1776 the first Turnpike Act was passed and a road of sorts built from Tal-y-Cafn ferry through Conwy, Bangor and Caernarfon to Pwllheli and from Caernarfon through Beddgelert to Aberglaslyn. After the second Turnpike Act in 1786, the road was extended from Tal-y-Cafn to Llanwrst and from Beddgelert to Pwllheli and Porth Dinllaen.

With the roads came the coaches. One Royal Mail went through Conwy to Holyhead, another from Betws-y-Coed through Capel Curig with a heavy passenger carriage following the same route. A waggon from Chester came to Conwy once a week, and another from Shrewsbury via Capel Curig. For the rich-in-a-hurry post chaises could be hired at Conwy, Bangor, Capel Curig, Porthmadog and Pwllheli.

The Capel Curig/Bangor coaches ran nightly from the Bull and Mouth Inn in London. The coach was drawn on the 279-mile journey by Cleveland bays travelling at nine miles an hour. It took thirty-eight hours, and each coach carried a maximum of three pasengers outside, to be increased later to seven. The mail service was the idea of a Bath theatre manager, John Palmer, who was Surveyor and Controller of the Post Office from 1786 until his dismissal in 1793 and replacement by an aristocratic blockhead, General Lord Carteret. Palmer at least got a generous redundancy payment, £50,000, a handsome fortune in the eighteenth century.

Neither Palmer nor his coaches were popular with the turnpikes. Not only did the coaches pay no tolls: if the Mail was delayed at the gates, dilatory keepers had to pay a heavy fine. Tolls were levied on vehicles, horsemen and even animals. It was a profitable source of revenue. The amount of money collected annually at the Llanfairpwll tollhouse increased from £86 in 1827 to £343 in 1848. However, as more and more people used the new Britannia railway bridge, opened in 1850, there was a decline in the amount of traffic on the road, and in 1895 all the tollhouses on Anglesey, among the last in the country, were closed.

Coachmen protected themselves from the cold on their box seat behind the team by drinking large quantities of hot punch. Birch Reynardson, the authority on coaching in its golden days, recalled a coachman called Winterbotham of the Chester-Holyhead Mail

The railway bridge across the Conwy Estuary, built like the Britannia
Bridge by Robert Stephenson. Both bridges were built at the same time
and opened within six months of each other in 1826

getting 'amazing fresh': 'He approached rolling about like a
seventy-four in a calm: or as if he were walking with a couple of
soda-water bottles tied to his feet.' Reynardson was so alarmed
that he bundled Winterbotham inside the coach and took up the
ribbons himself. The coachman slept through the journey along
the Gwynedd coast road, including the dreaded Penmaenmawr,
and awoke just as the Mail clattered into St Asaph. Reynardson
heard him muttering to himself: 'I think I'd better get outside
now. I aren't used to doing my travelling like a gentleman and
inside the Mail to be sure. Never travelled inside the Mail or any
coach before, and I dare say I never shall again. Don't think I like
the inside of a coach much.'

Another famous driver of the Chester and Holyhead was Old
John Scott, who used to 'boil up a trot' to get up Penmaenmawr.
His advice to new drivers was, 'Hit 'em sly. Hit 'em sly. If the
'osses 'ear the whip before they feel it they'll never be got up.'

Not everyone was disquieted by the terrible aspect. A coach
party which contained the celebrated eighteenth-century actress
Sarah Siddons got out of their vehicle at the foot of
Penmaenmawr. Mrs Siddons' companion, Betty Wilkinson, wrote
in her diary that the party went to a bridge commanding the

fullest view of the landscape: 'A lady within hearing of us was in such ecstasies that she exclaimed: "This awful scenery makes me feel as if I were only a worm or a grain of dust on the face of the earth." Mrs Siddons turned round and said: "I feel very differently".'

There is no question as to the name of the greatest road-builder in the history of the county. It is Thomas Telford, whose Holyhead roads from Shrewsbury and Chester were so superbly conceived that, although the 107 miles from Shrewsbury to Holyhead ran through Snowdonia, the gradients were so gentle that no horse needed to slow to a walk. At its highest over the mountain summit and down the Nant Ffrancon pass, the gradient never exceeds 1 in 22. And at a time when recently laid motorways are crumbling, it is salutary to notice the few repair gangs on the Telford road, built over a century and a half ago. As with his roads, so too with his bridges. I cross the Menai Bridge daily without a qualm. The faults in the new Severn Bridge and the unfavourable reports on it are sufficient to send me on a forty-mile detour to avoid it on journeys from Cardiff to Bristol.

Telford built in the Roman style. First he levelled and drained; next a solid Roman-style pavement of large stones was laid, broad end down and closely set, their surfaces levelled. On top was placed a layer of stones the size of walnuts. Telford always stressed the importance of properly grading the stone which he stored in bins at the roadside.

Mention is often made of Telford's most famous bridges, the Menai and its prototype in Conwy, conceived as a drawbridge over a 'moat', the River Conwy, yet there are two more Telford bridges that have their claims. There is the exuberant Waterloo Bridge at Betws-y-Coed, its spandrels filled with the national symbols, the leek, the rose, the thistle and the shamrock. It bears the proud inscription: 'This arch was constructed in the same year that the Battle of Waterloo was fought.' The Stanley Embankment, which bridges the Inland Sea on the outskirts of Holyhead, is another little miracle of engineering.

An earlier road had been planned to cross the strait which separates Holy Island from the rest of Anglesey at its narrowest point, Four Mile Bridge. Telford would have none of this. His road runs along an embankment 1,300 yards long, 16 feet high, 114 feet wide at the base and 34 feet at the top. Its walls are covered in rubber to prevent erosion. Yet it took the contractors, Gill & Hodges, only a year to build it.

The road to Holyhead begins at the Marble Arch in London and ends at the Marble Arch in Holyhead, a forlorn sight in its Doric

Abstract sculpture? Actually a central-heating system Roman style. The hypocaust in the Commandant's House at Segontium, the Roman fort of Caernarfon

Reflected in the waters of its swan-haunted moat, Beaumaris Castle, one of the most satisfying of Edward I's castles in North Wales, now designated among the world's top ten Heritage Wonders

Harlech maintained its fighting role longer than any other of Edward's castles. In the Civil War it was the last castle defended by the Royalists

Inigo Jones, a local boy who made good, designed this graceful bridge over the River Conwy at Llanwrst once a fresh-water pearl fishery

The tollboard at Llanfair PG still in position on the side of the tollhouse. The prices seem less reasonable when you remember that in 1820 when the board was in use it would take a labourer four days to earn enough to take a horse through the gate

Tolls to be taken at
LLANFAIR GATE

s. d

For every Horse, Mule, or other Cattle, drawing any Coach or other Carriage, with springs the sum of 4

For every Horse, Mule or other Beast or Cattle, drawing any Waggon Cart or other such Carriage not employed solely in carrying or going empty to fetch Lime for manure the sum of 3

For every Horse, Mule, or other Beast or Cattle, drawing any Waggon, Cart, or other such Carriage, employed solely in carrying or going empty to fetch Lime for manure the sum of 1½

For every Horse, Mule, or Ass, laden or unladen, and not drawing, the sum of 1

For every Drove of Oxen, Cows, or other neat Cattle per score, the sum of 10

For every Drove of Calves, Sheep, Lambs, or Pigs per score, the sum of 5

For every Horse, Mule or other Beast drawing any Waggon, or Cart, the Wheels being less than 3 inches in breadth, or having Wheels with Tires fastened with Nails projecting and not countersunk to pay double Toll.

A Ticket taken here clears Carnedd Du Bar.

marble magnificence, standing in the rubble and wire netting of the town's dockland on Salt Island. The arch celebrates an accidental visit by King George IV, who put into Holyhead on the royal yacht in August 1821 whilst in passage to Ireland to meet up with the Royal Yacht Squadron. When his ship sailed into the harbour, he was met with such demonstrations of loyalty, such crowds and wild cheering that the King, who was more used to being booed by his disloyal subjects, decided to land. He then went by coach to Plas Newydd, the home in Llanfairpwll of his cavalry commander at Waterloo, the Marquess of Anglesey. The Marquess could be relied on to let the King pretend that he, too, had fought in the battle.

The King had intended to stay only one night but the weather worsened, and it was five days before the yacht *Royal George* could put to sea. So grateful were the Anglesey gentry for the royal condescension that they built the Holyhead Marble Arch from stone brought by boat from Red Wharf Bay. They lacked, however, the driving power of Telford's builders. The arch took three years to build.

It would be nice to think that from the lawns of Plas Newydd the King looked down along the coast to where, perhaps two miles away, for the first time in history the Menai Straits were about to be bridged, despite, it should be said, bitter opposition from his host. Telford had first produced proposals for the Menai Bridge in 1810. They were turned down by the Admiralty because the bridge allowed insufficient headroom for the Navy's men-of-war. Eight years later the government were at last persuaded that the straits would have to be crossed, and Telford was asked to re-submit plans. This time there was to be no problem for ships. Telford proposed a suspension bridge with a span of 579 feet with 100 feet headroom, carried across by two suspension towers 153 feet above the straits at high water, pierced by arches for the two twelve-foot carriageways.

The opposition to the scheme was orchestrated by three landowners, the Marquess, a quarry-owner called Assheton-Smith and a third man, Owen Williams of Craigy-y-Don, who used their influence to get work halted. Within a year the government ordered it restarted, heavily lobbied, no doubt, by Irish MPs who had first demanded a good road from London, so uncomfortable was the coach journey from London to the Irish ferry.

By 1823 the piers were at roadway height, and Telford, who was then sixty-nine, wrote that 'work was also proceeding satisfactorily' on the Conwy bridge which he was building at the same time. It was the largest undertaking of its kind and without precedent. Almost everything Telford did had never been attempted before, yet nothing ruffled him, even though the problems were awesome. The links for the suspension chains were forged on the Shrewsbury canal at Upton Magna, carried by barge to Chester, shipped to Menai and assembled on site. The first chain was tested by slinging it across the River Cadnant which flows into the straits.

Watched by hundreds of flag-waving spectators, at 2.30 p.m. on 26 April 1825, an hour before high water, the first of the sixteen chains, each suspended portion of which weighed $23\frac{1}{2}$ tons, was laid on a raft 450 feet long and six feet wide. It was lifted into place on the tower by cables mounted on a capstan worked by a team of 150 men to the tune of a fife band. The operation took two hours twenty minutes.

As soon as the chains were in place in Menai, the crews and tackle were moved to Conwy to raise the chains there. The tide was too swift to float the chains across on a raft, but once again Telford's ingenuity saved the day. He had ropes slung from the tower on the Conwy bank to the one at Llandudno Junction. On the ropes he built a timber platform, and the chains were assembled from the links *in situ*.

In January 1826 the Menai Bridge was opened, the Conwy Bridge in July of the same year. There was no official party. Telford hated parties. Local people were less inhibited. When the first chain at Menai was set, three workers, Hugh Davies, a stonemason, John Williams, a carpenter, and William Williams, had drunk the quart of ale which all the workers were given by Telford to celebrate. Then one after the other they ran along the nine-inch-wide chain from Anglesey to the mainland. A local cobbler next crawled along the chain to the centre, where he sat and cobbled a pair of shoes. After the final chain had been winched into place, a military band played first from a special platform built high on the Anglesey tower and then marched down planking laid precariously on the chains to the centre of the bridge where they played the National Anthem one hundred feet above the swirling straits.

The first coach to cross the completed Menai Bridge was fittingly the Holyhead Mail, with David Davies holding the ribbons and with William Read as guard. At the outskirts of Bangor it had been flagged down by William Provis, Telford's resident engineer. He took the coach to the Ferry Inn in Bangor where an impromptu party was being held. After some spirited carousing Provis led a party to the coach, and at 1.30 a.m., lit by oil lanterns, the Menai Bridge was officially opened by a coachload of revellers, the first of many it has carried over a century and a half since.

Telford's great roads and the spectacular bridge did for the mail coach what the turbo prop did for the sports car. May Day was traditionally the day on which the coachmen raced each other to set up records. On one such occasion the Holyhead Mail was timed at $10\frac{1}{2}$ miles per hour from London, including stops. 'The Wonder' did the 153-mile journey from London to Shrewsbury in $15\frac{3}{4}$ hours. The Mail from London to Holyhead, via Chester, was never as fast. Its record time, without passengers, as on all May Day events, was $9\frac{1}{2}$ miles per hour. To increase the speed by only a mile and a half an hour, the horses would have had to gallop the greater part of the way, as they did in the shafts of the Shrewsbury Greyhound on the Holyhead Road, which travelled 153 miles two furlongs from London to Shrewsbury at the rate of twelve miles per hour. The supreme coaching record was set by the Independent Tally Ho running between London and Birmingham on May Day 1830. The Tally Ho covered the 109 miles in seven hours thirty minutes.

There were accidents, of course. The Holyhead Mail once tried to pass the Chester Mail by galloping furiously past on the wrong side of the road. The driver of the Chester Mail retaliated by pulling his leaders across those of his rival, and both coaches crashed.

A luckless passenger on another occasion was one M.W. Davies of Holywell, who took the coach to visit Anglesey because he had been frightened by the sinking of the *Rothsay Castle* earlier in the year and thought it would be safer by coach. He was wrong. As the coach left the White Lion Inn at St Asaph with the coachman 'springing his cattle', Mr Davies fell off. Reporting the incident, the *North Wales Chronicle* went on: 'Strangely enough neither passengers, guard nor coachman took the slightest notice of the unfortunate young man who was discovered quite by chance by a lady out walking. He died in agony two days later.' Small wonder that the patrons of the Holyhead Mail were moved to write letters like this to their morning papers:

Whoever takes up a newspaper in these eventful times it is even betting whether an accident by a coach or a suicide first meets his eye. As the month of November is fast approaching, when from foggy weather and dark nights both these calamities are bound to increase, I suggest the propriety of any gentleman resolved on self-destruction trying to avoid the disgrace attached to it by first taking a few journeys by some of these Dreadnoughts High Flyer or Tally Ho coaches: as in all probability he may meet with as instant a death as if he had let off one of Joe Mantan's pistols in his mouth or severed his head from his body with one of Mr Palmer's best razors.

Today much of Telford's road has been replaced by a new Expressway from Chester to Holyhead. In a graceful tribute to Thomas Telford the company which is building the new road, Alfred McAlpine Construction, took out a half-page advertisement in the *Daily Post* when after three years they reached the borders of Gwynedd. Over a picture of Telford was the headline: 'Right Up Your Street, Thomas.' A second line in heavy type read: 'Tomorrow it opens. Wish you were there, Thomas!'

He would no doubt have found much to interest him. The new route is called the Daffodil Highway. Acres of the national flower have been planted along the road's verges by the Welsh Office at the urging of the Prince of Wales' committee. Cynics claimed that each bloom represented a pound note spent on the road. It had cost Telford's backers in the government £250,000 to build the road from Chester to Holyhead. The Expressway, which runs over a similar distance, will cost £400 million. Of this nearly £90 million will go on the cost of a tunnel under the river at Conwy. When the road was first planned, in the 1960s, the intention was to cross the Conwy by a bridge over the Deganwy Narrows. It would have cost only £1½ million. Engineers and surveyors alike were surprised when Peter Thomas, the Secretary of State for Wales, decided on the far more expensive tunnel. It has been suggested that the decision was affected by the vigorous lobbying of golfers whose course lay in the path of the approaches to the bridge. It will be the first tube tunnel to be constructed, and it may be completed by the end of the decade. At present the motorway ends on the far bank of the Conwy and begins again at Llanfairfechan. The dreadful bottlenecks of traffic are the worst Conwy has experienced since the last road-improvement scheme nearly half a century ago.

There have already been considerable delays in starting the tunnel. When test borings were made in the estuary bed, it was found that running under the salt-water estuary, and separated from it by a table of rock, is another river, this one fresh water.

River crossings on the Conwy have never been without trouble. In 1822, when Telford built the first bridge over the Conwy, the novelist Mrs Hemans wrote to a friend: 'I can easily imagine your indignation at the sight of stage coaches amongst such scenery. You will therefore, I trust, sympathise with my feelings on finding upon my last visit to Conwy the ci-devant picturesque little island in the midst of the river metamorphosised into something like a raised pier for the support of the proposed bridge.'

In time the townspeople became fond of the bridge. When in 1848 Robert Stephenson in his turn built his tubular railway bridge, there was another uproar. Stephenson's ugly tube, people insisted, would ruin the view of Telford's graceful suspension bridge. In the 1950s, when the present writer was reporting on Welsh affairs for the *Daily Mirror*, a third bridge, this time for vehicles, provoked yet another storm of protest. This time fishermen complained that the bridge piers would alter the estuary currents and silt up the river.

Robert Stephenson's father, George, the inventor of the steam engine, had been commissioned by the Chester and General Company in 1838 to survey routes for a railway to link with the Dublin Ferry. There were two possible sites for the railway terminus. One was Holyhead and the other Porth Dinllaen, near Nefyn, on the Lleyn Peninsula. Stephenson chose Holyhead because it offered better gradients and was less costly. At a public meeting in Chester in January 1839, convened so that he could explain his choice, he was enthusiastically supported by the mayor of Chester – not on grounds of either practicability or cost: if Porth Dinllaen had been chosen, Shrewsbury and not Chester would be the gateway to Ireland.

In 1840 a rail link between Crewe and Chester was opened, and two years later Robert Stephenson was appointed Chief Engineer to carry out his father's plans. He made two major changes. At Penmaenmawr Stephenson senior had recommended tunnelling but this proved far too expensive, and Stephenson junior chose to go round the mountain on a terrace mounted on stilts. The second and much more serious problem was bridging the Menai Straits. George Stephenson's solution was to uncouple the locomotive at the mainland side of Telford's bridge and draw the carriage across with horses. Robert, like Telford before him, decided to bridge the straits, though he confessed: 'I stood on the verge of a responsibility from which I confess I had nearly shrunk.'

Stephenson had in many ways a much more difficult problem than Telford. The suspension bridge had already occupied the narrowest point in the straits, and the railway bridge would have to stay rigid in all weathers. The 'give' in a suspension bridge would be fatal in a rail crossing.

In 1841 Stephenson had made a bridge for the Hertford and Ware branch of the North-Eastern Railway Company which had

The Britannia Railway Bridge over the Menai Straits during its construction in 1849. Hot rivets were thrown forty feet to the men working on the top of the tubes. And when (below) these giant tubes were lifted into place, there was only $\frac{3}{4}$ inch to spare when they were fitted into their slots in the pillars, so accurately had they been built

been built of wrought-iron 'cells' riveted together with angle irons. It came to him that a similar tubular construction would give him the strength he needed on his Britannia Bridge. This was confirmed in a curious way. At her launching the steamship *Prince of Wales* became stuck, with 110 feet of her heavy iron hull suspended in mid-air. It was thought that the hull would buckle under her own tremendous weight of iron. It did not: a simple demonstration of the basic scientific truth that a tube is stronger than a rod of equal length and circumference.

Stephenson was inspired by the incident to experiment with different shapes and materials. He settled on a rectangle with strengthening cells above and below. The first tube was 472 feet long and weighed fifteen hundred tons. In the two tubes nine hundred tons of rivets were used. The sheets of iron from which the tubes were made had to be flattened by hand to $3\frac{1}{2}$ inches. Rivet boys, most of them not even in their teens, had to be trained to throw red hot rivets forty feet in the air from the fires on the ground to the rivet crews on top of the tubes. It was also the first time in recorded history that a weight of fifteen hundred tons had been lifted one hundred feet. Like Telford, Stephenson decided to float the four tubes one by one to their position below the bridge and then lift them into place. Isambard Brunel was among the VIPs who watched the first attempt. The idea had been to swing the tube from the Anglesey shore out to the central pier. The first time it was attempted, the tow broke under the strain. On the second attempt a cable snapped and crowds fled to avoid being crushed by the great tube as it swept down the Anglesey shore. On the third attempt a capstan jammed and the weight of the tube dragged the winch from its foundations. The foreman, Charles Rolfe, called on the crowd to lay hold of the loose rope, and eventually they were able to secure it in its place at the base of the tower.

The actual lifting took several days. Stephenson insisted the tubes be lifted a few inches at a time to prevent damage. When they had been hauled to their place one hundred feet high, it was found that they were built so accurately that they fitted into their slots in the tower with only three-quarters of an inch to spare.

The last rivet in the bridge was put in by Stephenson himself on 5 March 1850. Then he rode through his airborne tunnel in the first locomotive to cross. To test its strength, before the tunnel was open to the public, a goods train loaded with two hundred tons of coal was halted in the centre of the bridge.

Just how important that rail link became to Anglesey was demonstrated 120 years later, on 23 May 1970, when the bridge was put to the torch by teenage vandals looking for bats. The effect on the island's economy was disastrous, and it is doubtful that Holyhead will ever recover from the blow which immediately put three hundred men on the dole. Rebuilding the tunnel cost £3,250,000, and it took three years. The new bridge has a road deck running on top of the rail tunnel and is now part of the Chester to Holyhead Expressway.

Holyhead came within an ace of losing its ferry. A single vote in Parliament defeated a project to move the packet station for the Irish service to Porth Dinllaen on the Lleyn. Holyhead is only six miles nearer to Ireland than Porth Dinllaen but it is thirty miles further from London. It was arbitrarily chosen in Elizabethan times as the last overland stage on the 'Pony Express' route from London.

The quarry-owner Assheton-Smith of Vaynol wanted the ferry moved to Porth Dinllaen to remove the need for Telford's proposed bridge over the Menai. But the most powerful advocate of change was W.A. Madocks, the landowner and member of Parliament who had built Porthmadog. He realized that if the mail coaches came to Porth Dinllaen, they would bring greater prosperity to the Lleyn Peninsula. The decision to back Telford's scheme was a blow to Madocks and his friends but they did not give up. In 1835 Henry Archer, the manager of the Ffestiniog Railway, announced plans for a railway from London to Porth Dinllaen, where a Dublin packet service would be launched. Within a year more plans were announced, this time for a railway from Chester to Orme's Bay, the easiest and cheapest route. The route would run over level land, the Cheshire plain and the coastal strip, to the Orme, but there were two major disadvantages: the sea crossing was thirty miles longer than from Holyhead, and in 1836 Llandudno was nothing more than a collection of cottages. It was not until three years later that the company which was eventually to be successful, the 'Great Holyhead Railway', was launched. It was a battle of giants. While Stephenson worked on his line, Isambard Brunel was called in to survey a line from Didcot through Worcester and Newtown to Porth Dinllaen. Henry Archer returned with yet another scheme for a line from Bangor to Porth Dinllaen. But the government decided to back Stephenson, and Holyhead was saved.

The first railway in Gwynedd had been drawn by horses and was not designed for passenger traffic. It was laid down in 1801 by Lord Penrhyn, and its purpose was to carry the slate from the quarries in the Ogwen Valleys to Penrhyn Port. Despite recession and the heavy taxation levied to pay for the war with France, the

This man-made 'mountain' of waste slate at Blaenau Ffestiniog is a maze of tracks, tramways and steps, though the narrow gauge tramways system is derelict and the main line at its side is used primarily to transport nuclear waste from Trawsfynydd power station

This slate quarry locomotive has ended its life as an exhibit at the quarry museum at Blaenau Ffestiniog

Nostalgia? The engine 'Edward Thomas' is old enough as she stands at the platform in Great Western colours, but the station on the Tal-y-Llyn railway at Abergynolwyn was only finished in 1969

Craig Lledr railway bridge was built in Scots Baronial Gothic as a sop to conservationists led by Tennyson who thought that a railway would ruin the valley. Now conservationists fight to save railways

slate industry in Snowdonia was selling vast quantities of writing slates which were made in the factories Lord Penrhyn had built next to his port, using money from the family sugar plantations in Jamaica. It was a wise investment. Soon every Victorian schoolchild was using Snowdonia writing slate.

Thomas Assheton-Smith, the owner of the slate beds of Dinorwig, opened his own railway in 1828 running from Nantlle to Pen-y-Groes and from there to Caernarfon. Within a few years, in 1832, the most famous of Gwynedd's Great Little Trains, the Ffestiniog Railway, came into existence by Act of Parliament.

In the early stages trams free-wheeled from the mines to the coast carrying along with the slate the horses which would pull the train back to the mines, but by 1850 the Maelwyn range had been tunnelled, and later steam engines were introduced. Other railways opened. In Merioneth the Tal-y-Llyn and Dulas Valleys had their own railway system. The Corris railway through Dolgellau was closed only in 1948, when the valley was virtually buried under slate waste.

Most of the quarry lines eventually joined with the loveliest railway route in Wales, Great Western's Cambrian Line, which linked West Wales with Shrewsbury and is now happily being partly restored by British Rail. Restored too is the Tal-y-Llyn lakeside railway. It had opened in 1866 to carry slate from Abergynolwyn to Tywyn on the coast, when it joined the Cambrian railway. The slate quarries which it served closed after World War II but in 1952 the $6\frac{3}{4}$ mile stretch of line was taken over by volunteers. The Tal-y-Llyn has unique engineering features. At Abergynolwyn, where the station is higher up the mountain than the village, an ingenious cable incline lowered goods down to a track which ran along the backs of the houses. From Abergynolwyn the line climbs the slope of the Fathew Valley and crosses a viaduct to Dolgoch station and to Tywyn, where there is a fascinating narrow-gauge railway museum.

For me it is the Ffestiniog Railway which is the greatest of the Little Trains. I was one of the guests when, in 1963, the Ffestiniog Preservation Railway Society celebrated a century of steam locomotion by recreating a Victorian journey. Not least of the day's delights were drinks in the station buffet at Victorian prices. Twenty years earlier the line had closed, apparently for ever. Railway enthusiasts, mostly from Manchester and the Midlands, thought otherwise. It had been the labour of years rebuilding the line, in some cases literally hacking through jungle. Now it is possible to travel from Porthmadog to Llandudno by linking into the British Rail system. It is an exciting journey, and varied. The train runs along Madocks' embankment and makes an almost continuous climb along the flanks of Snowdonia to the terminus in Blaenau Ffestiniog where passengers change to BR for a trip down the Conwy Valley.

The most spectacular Little Train Ride is on the Snowdon Mountain Railway, the only 'rack' railway in Great Britain, now under new management. The rack system involves toothed racks in the centre of the track which engage cogs under the carriages. There is a speed limit of five miles per hour and therefore time enough to enjoy the panoramic scenery over the mountains from Anglesey in the north to Cardigan Bay in the south.

The two-mile-long slate railway which runs by the lakeside at Llanberis may not be as spectacular as the Snowdon railway but it has great charm and superb views of mountains reflected in the water. There are picnic areas in the woods by the lake at Dinorwig terminus.

The Cambrian Line from Pwllheli to Shrewsbury runs along the Cardigan coast by a recently rebuilt viaduct over the River Dyfi, across the Mawddach estuary to Barmouth, Harlech and Porthmadog.

At Shrewsbury the Central Wales line – the only surviving rail link between North Wales and the south – runs to Llanelli.

The majority of the passengers on all these lines are, as might be expected, holidaymakers. This is nothing new. A handbill, printed in Caernarfon in 1892, which advertises the Snowdon and Beddgelert District North Wales Railways, proclaims:

> Starting from Dinas Station, 3 miles from Carnarvon on the London and North Western Railway the line ascends for 2 miles on a gradient of 1 in 48 to Tryfan Junction whence a branch goes up to Bryngwyn rising for $2\frac{1}{2}$ miles at an average gradient of 1 in 40.
>
> From Bryngwyn a magnificent view is obtained extending over Carnarvon, the Menai Straits and Anglesey and the fine mountains known as the Rivals: and the access to Moel Tryfan is easy. This mountain is of great interest from the pre-historic sea-beach deposited on its summit now 1,400 feet above sea level ...

In addition to its railway system, Gwynedd had a number of tramways, but the only one which remains is that on the Great Orme at Llandudno which was built after the success of the cliff railway of Scarborough, the first funicular railway in Great Britain.

The first horse tram in North Wales was at Wrexham, the second nearer home in Gwynedd at Pwllheli. Pwllheli declined in the latter 1890s, when her harbour began to silt up. She was saved by holidaymakers, brought by the Cambrian Railway to the station which was built in 1867 'as a temporary building'. It has just been given an award as the best restored station in Britain and is now a listed building.

The first horse-drawn trams in Pwllheli were owned by a quarry-owner named Solomon Andrews who built the west end of the town in the year the station was opened. He converted a tramway he had built to carry stone to the houses into a passenger service. In 1896 the enterprising Andrews bought a mansion at Llanbedrog, $3\frac{1}{2}$ miles along the coast, which he converted into an art gallery with four hundred paintings including some by the great masters. He landscaped the garden, built a monkey house and extended his tramline to the house. He enjoyed a great success until 1927, when the tramway, which ran for most of its length along sand dunes on the high-water mark, was washed out to sea in a gale.

Alas, the only trace which remains of the other horse-drawn tram at Pwllheli, which was run by Pwllheli Corporation, is the Tourist Board Information kiosk in Station Square. It is converted from one of the old tramcars, rescued in 1969 by Pwllheli Borough Council from a farmyard on the Lleyn where it was being used as a chicken house.

The tramway which ran from Llandudno to Colwyn Bay from 1899 struggled on until 1956, when the high cost of electricity forced its closure.

• CHAPTER 8 •

Beauty in Wales is received more readily through the ear than through the eye. It is primarily a country of poets and makers of music. The visual arts fall some way behind. Wales has never produced a painter of the first rank, its architecture is frequently derivative: the classic façades of Cardiff, Gwynedd's pseudo-Norman castles and above all the Georgiana of eighteenth-century England.

The new council offices in Caernarfon are a delight. Their magic casements seem to open onto faery seas forlorn. They are medieval to the point that one expects a princess at every window. But the tradition of the building is European, not Welsh.

In the tribal days the natives of Gwynedd had no use for towns. When, after two hundred years, the Normans at last succeeded in the partial conquest of this troublesome land, they had to begin at the beginning and build the first Welsh towns.

Edward I came next, building castles and towns in a piece for English tenants. The Welsh were unceremoniously dumped wherever they would be out of the way. When Beaumaris Castle was built, the population of that pleasant and sheltered spot was herded onto the exposed coast at Newborough, where it was not long before their village was buried in sand dunes.

When Shelley's Madocks built his new towns, Porthmadog and Tremadog, his purpose was more benevolent. In 1625 Sir John Wynne of Gwydir had seen the advantages of enclosing and draining the marshes Traeth Bach and Traeth Mawr with an embankment which would link Caernarvonshire with Merioneth. He tried to interest his cousin, Sir Hugh Myddleton, a London alderman who had brought water to the capital by the New River project. Sir John wrote to Sir Hugh: 'I may say to you what the Jews said to Christ. "We have heard of thy great workes done abroad, doe now somewhat in thine own country".' But Sir Hugh declined the offer. He wrote back: 'The scheme you propose would require a whole man with a long purse.'

In 1770 there was another attempt at an embankment at Traeth Mawr as part of a turnpike road from Bala to Porth Dinllaen, but it was not until the arrival of Madocks, who bought the Tan-yr-Allt estate in Penmorfa in 1791, that a serious attempt at enclosure, one of the last and the biggest in Wales, was attempted.

Madocks is an appealing figure. He already owned one Welsh estate in Clwyd, he was a member of Parliament and a well-known barrister. His personality was engaging. He was a romantic visionary, a sentimentalist, just the sort of man to whom the notion of draining and enclosing nearly ten thousand acres of land in two great schemes would appeal. All he was short of was ready cash. The first embankment took most of his fortune. He was able to finance the second by prudently marrying an heiress, the great-niece of the Revivalist Hywel Harris.

The first draining scheme was a comparatively modest one, extending an earth embankment covered in turf from Porthmadog to Tremadog. Porthmadog itself was almost an accidental product but Tremadog was planned. It was the year of the Union of the British and Irish Parliaments, when it was clear that traffic between the two countries was bound to increase. The notion of a post road from Bala to Porth Dinllaen had been revived in 1802 at a meeting of landowners at the Bull, Crown and Anchor Inn, Pwllheli. Madocks had been present and had taken a £400 share. His interest was kindled and the result was Tremadog, which, incidentally, was to come to fame years later as the birthplace of Lawrence of Arabia.

With its pleasing houses, the coaching inn – and a tavern too for the peasants – Madocks' town is designed for people to live in. He wanted a prosperous community so he built a woollen mill, powered by water, a fulling mill and acorn mill. He wanted tourists to come to his coaching inn, so he built a theatre and a race course. There is a chapel and an Anglican church.

Over the years Porthmadog has eclipsed Tremadog. For all that, it is not Porthmadog with its bustle and its railway station but the quieter community of Tremadog which is the lasting monument to this remarkable man.

Madocks would have got on splendidly with Clough Williams Ellis, a fellow of infinite jest, of most excellent fancy. The son of an ancient Welsh family, he was asked by his fellow-Guardees what he would like as a wedding gift. 'A folly,' he said, 'on a mountain crag.' The folly was built, only to be eclipsed in later years by the most magnificent folly in Britain, Portmeirion.

Nothing is what it seems in this Italianate fantasy where, before the war, the future Edward VIII brought his mistresses, where

Noel Coward wrote *Blithe Spirit*, where almost every British author, painter, musician of note, has come for rest and inspiration. Portmeirion was a fitting background for the incomprehensible cult TV series *The Prisoner*. In a country which has appeared as locations for films as diverse as *Carry on Up the Khyber* and *The Inn of the Sixth Happiness*, Portmeirion must hold the record for screen appearances.

Parenthetically, I once interviewed Roman Polanski, who made an extraordinary film of *Macbeth* here, during which his publicist assured us that the script was the joint work of Polanski and Shakespeare. It was the latest of a long line of films that have been made in Snowdonia, a range that has gone on so long that a Gwynedd man who had been out of work for as long as anyone could remember described himself in a court appearance as a 'retired film actor'.

The first film to be made here was *The Drum* with Sabu, the elephant boy. Charlton Heston was here to star in *The Chairman*. Pondering all this, I asked Polanski the attraction of this stretch of countryside to film-makers. 'Iss no pylons,' he replied, 'and mebbe they like staying at Portmeirion.'

It was in the early years of the century that Clough Williams Ellis discovered a derelict mansion above a sheltered beach and set about creating the magnificent, frolicsome, fantastic village which he described as 'his love affair with life'. He bought the house and the surrounding land with the single splendid purpose of putting forth his ideas of fitness and gaiety and beauty. Nothing that gave him pleasure was neglected. A plaque on a statue of Hercules on one of the walls celebrates 'The Summer of 1959. In honour of its splendour.'

Williams Ellis was a successful architect with a London practice, though he had only three months formal training. He was an unlikely figure in twentieth-century Wales, a swashbuckler in breeches and yellow hose, a Renaissance prince in the wrong age. When he died, he wanted his ashes sent up in a skyrocket over Portmeirion.

He called Portmeirion his 'Home for Fallen Buildings'. The slates set in the pavement are cut-offs from lavatory seats; the great copper dome on the town hall cupola is an upturned pig-food boiler; a belvedere covers an electricity sub-station; a balustrade from a Liverpool seamen's home fronts the mansion. The barrel roof in the town hall dates from Tudor times. Williams Ellis bought it when a stately home in Clwyd was being demolished.

He also called Portmeirion 'an illusion, a microcosm of the world outside'. A boiler-house chimney is hidden behind a dome;

Llandudno with the Great Orme in the background was one of the first
purpose-built holiday resorts. It is still one of the most elegant

cherubs and urns in their niches are single-dimension cut-outs;
windows are painted on the walls. He controlled the number of day
visitors by varying the cost of admission. When there were more
visitors than he thought good for the village, he kept raising the
price until the crowds went away. Then he brought it down again.

Though the village was his first love, his services were always in
demand in the world outside. In Russia he was offered a three-year
contract, a private train and a staff of his own choosing to tour the
country on stately reconnaissance, picking sites for new towns. In
Ireland he built a model village, a school and a Christian Science
church, in China official residences for the Communists. In
Gwynedd he built a Methodist chapel. When his neighbour and
friend Lloyd George died, it was Clough Williams Ellis who was
called in to design the gates of the memorial museum, pick the spot
for the grave on the banks of the River Dwyfor and erect there the
monument to the only prime minister Gwynedd has produced.

No one has challenged Llandudno's claim to be the Queen of the
Welsh resorts. When Arnold Bennett brought his hero Denry
Machin to the town in *The Card*, he called it 'the Queen of the
Western Watering Places'. Though his fiancée Ruth Earp thought
Llandudno 'more stylish than Blackpool', characteristically Denry
saw it as a place to make money: 'In Llandudno fifty thousand

souls desired always to perform the same act at the same time: they wanted to be distracted and they would do anything for the sake of abstraction, and would pay for the privilege. And they would all pay at once'. This great thought was more majestic to him than the sea, or the Great Orme and the Little Orme.

Llandudno was the success of the age and an obsession with the writers of the period. Hawley Smart in his thriller *The Great Tontine* has a character, Paul Pegray, who creates a holiday resort by buying unwanted land at £30 an acre 'in the vicinity of the Orme's Head, nothing better than a little fishing village; but at last the great colonising agent of our times the railway touched it ... Lodging house keepers and shopkeepers flocked from the surrounding towns to start in business in the new watering place. The first hotel was already dwarfed by a gigantic rival ...'

The truth about Llandudno has an improbability that fiction could not hope to get away with. In 1843 a Liverpool surveyor called Owen Williams, with a fancy for sea breezes, accompanied a friend, a shareholder, to the Annual General Meeting of the Tŷ Gwyn Copper Mine on the Greater Orme.

In those days the population of Llandudno, less than a thousand miners and smallholders, lived in miserable cottages, caves and hovels round the base of the Orme. They had even lost their 955 acres of common land. They had been tricked out of it, their only asset, by their MP, Edward Mostyn. He had introduced the Eglwysrhos, Llandudno and Llangystennin Enclosure Acts into Parliament. The Acts gave the greater part of the acreage to the principal freeholders. They had been represented by the Bishop of Bangor, the Right Reverend Christopher Bethell. For his reward the bishop got eighteen acres of prime building land but 832 acres went to the MP who had introduced the Bill, Edward Mostyn.

On the day that the common land was mapped for the enclosure award, it was also being surveyed for an auction of leasehold building land. Looking down from the Great Orme at the MP's acres, it had struck surveyor Williams that they would make a splendid site for a holiday resort. Over lunch at the King's Head he mentioned the notion and then presumably forgot it. But the idea had fallen on receptive ears. The company secretary of the Tŷ Gwyn mine, John Williams, was also agent to the Mostyn Estates, and he passed it on to Edward Mostyn. Some months later Williams and Mostyn met for the first time on the beach at Llandudno and in a boatman's hut planned Llandudno as it stands today.

In the King's Head at the terminus of the Great Orme railway, still an admirable eating-house, there hangs a painting of the

Porthmadog harbour in the evening light. Fishing fleets now are all on charter to part-time anglers. The grounds have been fished out of everything except dogfish – and monsters

Capel Peniel, Tremadog, is acknowledged to be one of the finest chapels in Wales but it was built as a theatre. It stands opposite the birthplace of T. E. Lawrence

Mawddach Estuary and on the far bank Cader Idris from the
look-out spot at Coes-faen, Barmouth. Holidays were invented
in order to enjoy views like this

Portmeirion, the most extavagant folly ever built. Its architect, Clough William Ellis, built this collection of delightful whimsical visual jokes for the sheer pleasure of it. Countless thousands – including kings and superstars – have shared it since

Nothing is what it seems here where even the petrol pumps give you knowing looks and (*right*) the decorative ironwork turns out to be wood

Llandudno that Owen Williams and the elder Mostyn planned. It differs little from the Llandudno we see. But in 1854 Williams was no longer responsible for the plans of the new resort. That year a local Act of Parliament had given powers to Llandudno's first Board of Improvement Commission. Its chairman was Thomas Mostyn, the son of the MP who had by that time succeeded his father both as member of Parliament and as local wheeler-dealer. Williams' job went to a London firm, Wehnert & Ashdown. It was that firm which designed, following Williams' original plan, the promenade where, in 1854, St George's Hotel was built. The speculator was, for once, a local farmer's son, Isaiah Davies, who inherited the King's Head by marriage to the innkeeper's daughter. According to powerful local tradition, he got the valuable building plot on the promenade by cancelling the drinking debts of Mostyn's agent, John Williams.

The pier which separates the promenade from the Marine Drive is 2,295 feet long and is one of the few remaining in Wales. The present four-mile-long Marine Drive follows the line of a toll way, Custs Path, a route so dangerous that in 1868 the Prime Minister, William Gladstone, had to be blindfolded before he could pass over it. A company was formed to develop the Drive as a toll road in 1872 but it took three years to raise the capital. After twelve years of private ownership it was bought by the urban council.

In recent years Llandudno has seemed in danger of losing its pre-eminence. The new Expressway, which brings it within easy shopping distance of Merseyside and the Wirral, will alter that. Already two major investment schemes for shopping centres are planned behind the graceful façades of Mostyn Street, one backing onto the library and the other the town hall.

The town hall scheme, likely to get off the ground towards the end of 1986 and be completed during 1988, is a highly imaginative one, in keeping with the Victorian elegance of the rest of the town. Developed by Haden Refurbishment, Development and Construction of Warrington, a multi-million pound company with an international reputation, the scheme envisages a spacious shopping centre, with marbled halls and columns, Victorian malls and a main entrance in Mostyn Street – Llandudno's main shopping thoroughfare – decorated with a canopy that complements the wrought-iron work found on other buildings in the street.

Few town centre schemes can have posed so many architectural challenges. Not only does the development front onto a street of listed buildings but it incorporates three other major listed

Change in Llandudno must be subtle. When the town hall and adjoining Ebenezer Chapel were incorporated in an £8½ million shopping mall they still had to present an unchanged façade

buildings, the town hall, an Edwardian chapel and an early cinema. Part of the interior of the town hall, dating from the beginning of this century, will be demolished under the scheme to provide shops at ground-level, but Haden has drawn up plans to refurbish completely the imposing façade of the building. The Ebenezer Chapel, said by Professor Anthony Jones, principal of Glasgow School of Art and the acknowledged expert on Welsh chapels, to be one of the finest examples of Edwardian chapel architecture in Wales, will also be restored by Haden and then handed back to the town council to use as they wish. Local architect George Hedges, who has drawn up the plans for Haden, sees this as a major work of restoration since the chapel has been allowed to fall into a bad state of repair in recent years and is at present closed to the public. The frontage of the Palladian cinema on the opposite side of the development must also be preserved. Part of the vast interior that in its heyday accommodated an audience of hundreds will be turned into a market hall.

The whole project, costing in the region of £8½ million, has been warmly welcomed by traders in the town, who believe it will restore and reinforce Llandudno's claim to be the shopping mecca of the North Wales coast. And conservationists, initially worried

about the impact of a super-modern shopping centre on a Victorian town, now say it shows 'considerable promise'.

Competition is keen for units in the centre, and many national operators, not already represented in the town, are seeking space there. This, along with the 450 jobs the construction and later servicing of the scheme will bring to an area of high unemployment, is certain to set Arnold Bennett's 'Queen of the Western Watering Places' firmly on her throne.

Commented Haden's development manager Mr Douglas Leech in a local newspaper: 'Llandudno is a unique town, conceived and planned as a single entity in the last century, round one of the loveliest bays in Britain. We want to develop in our scheme the ideas of the brilliant men who planned this little jewel in the crown of the Welsh coast.'

In total the centre will cover eighty thousand square feet with parking space for three hundred vehicles. The library scheme, to be developed by the Land Authority for Wales and Mostyn Estates, is on a smaller scale, 47,000 square feet.

The happy image of 'Bond Street by the Sea' which was coined by Douglas Leech is not inappropriate. Since its early days the fashionable have flocked to this loveliest of resort towns. It has been claimed that the shops in Mostyn Street have held more royal warrants than those in any other street outside London.

Two queens stayed in the town. Queen Rambai Barni of Siam lived in the Imperial Hotel until 1940, when the building was commandeered by the department of Inland Revenue. Queen Elizabeth of Romania, a romantic figure who wrote novels under a pseudonym, spent five weeks at the Marine Hotel in 1890. Her description of Wales as 'a beautiful haven of peace' lives on in the town's motto: '*Hardd, hafan, hedd.*'

Every famous politician from Lloyd George to Churchill has visited the town to address political rallies. Guests at the St George's Hotel have included Napoleon III and the Empress Eugénie, Bismarck, Disraeli, Gladstone and Churchill. They moved freely about the town in a way that is not possible today. When Margaret Thatcher attended a Conservative Party conference here in 1985, death threats so alarmed the police that the SAS were called in. They had to guard against terrorist attacks from the sea.

In more civilized times Dean Liddell and his family, including his daughter Alice, the 'onlie begetter' of *Alice in Wonderland*, had a holiday home in what is now Gogarth Abbey Hotel. Despite Alice's strenuous denials, there is a persistent tradition that the seaside scenes of *Wonderland* are rooted in the sands of Deganwy.

Codman's Punch and Judy shows which have been a summer feature on the promenade for over a century have another literary claim. Thomas Codlin, the puppet man in Charles Dickens' *The Old Curiosity Shop*, was modelled on an earlier Codman.

The town goes to considerable lengths in protecting its own image. The first Professor Codman had to fight for years to get the Improvement Commissioners to waive their ban on 'Punch and Judy, his dog and all the noisy paraphernalia belonging thereto'. Since then bans imposed by the Commissioners have included nude bathing, bathing within two hundred yards of the opposite sex, the Liverpool Liberal Conference, preaching on the beach, a popular song 'Ain't it grand to be blooming well dead', a circus, jazz music, sky-writing and boxing. In 1984 a hotel-owner had to move a robot, which was in a trailer parked outside his hotel advertising a 'Space City', because it spoiled the visual amenity of the town.

There has been a long musical tradition in Llandudno. Jules Rivière, a former French Army musician who began his musical life conducting a seven-man band in an open bandstand at the end of the pier, was able, after considerable argument, to persuade the Pier Company to allow him to give concerts in the Pier

Pavilion itself. So successful were his concerts that they soon achieved a national reputation. An impressive figure, he conducted facing the audience, seated in a gilded armchair with a bejewelled ivory baton. Amongst those who came to study his style was the young Henry Wood. One of his successors was an even more famous musical dandy, Sir Malcolm Sargent, who conducted the pier orchestra for two summer seasons. When Sir Thomas Beecham heard the orchestra, he was so impressed that he poached one of the players, a young musician called Paul Beard, who went on to become leader of the forerunner of the London Philharmonic.

• CHAPTER 9 •

The rocks of Gwynedd are among the oldest in the world but the county has always stood in the vanguard of technology.

In 1943, when a Conwy-born architect and civil engineer, Hugh Iorys Jones, was commissioned by Winston Churchill to design a portable harbour for use by an invasion force, he remembered the isolated Morfa outside his home town. And for seven months, though nine hundred men worked in shifts in pre-fabricated workshops and it was tested in the Conwy estuary, Mulberry Harbour was one of the best kept secrets of World War II. The project remained a secret until the early 1950s, when a director of the firm which was responsible for the steelwork came to spend his retirement in Deganwy.

During the war Bangor was the centre of the diamond-polishing industry. Craftsmen from Belgium and Holland moved there and worked on millions of pounds worth of stones in rooms over Burton's tailor shop in the High Street. Most of the wartime radio comedy shows came from the same town, for early in the war the BBC evacuated its Light Entertainment department to Bangor. Amongst the shows which were presented and transmitted from the Penrhyn Hall, now, alas, demolished, was probably the most famous comedy series in the history of broadcasting, ITMA. By happy coincidence my broadcasting colleague, the versatile Roger Worsley who has taken the admirable photographs which enhance this book, is the son of the producer of ITMA, Francis Worsley. It was Roger who gave the show one of its most famous characters, 'Funf', the German spy. He showed his father the latest craze at his Bangor school, speaking into a glass to produce a sinister voice. 'This is Funf speaking' joined 'Don't forget the diver', 'Ta-ta for now' and other immortal catchphrases from that much-loved programme in the folklore of radio. There is a persistent local tradition too that the diver in ITMA was based on a one-legged diver who performed on Bangor pier.

Bangor still maintains a strong broadcasting presence, with a

Radio Cymru and Radio Wales complex of studios. Another colleague, a local journalist and son and grandson of Gwynedd newspaper editors, Angus McDermid, went on to become one of the Corporation's most distinguished foreign correspondents. P.J. Kavanagh, the poet, spent some years at school in Bangor, where his father, Ted, wrote the ITMA scripts.

More warlike activities went on at Valley on Anglesey. Gwynedd has always attracted aviators. In World War I there were two airship stations, one in Bangor and another on Anglesey. Their station commanders celebrated the Armistice in 1918 in startling fashion by flying dirigibles under the arches of the Menai Bridge.

In those days Llangefni airfield was a large meadow, carrying the grand title Airship Station, Anglesey, a detached unit of the Royal Naval Air Station Malahide, stationed in Dublin. From 1915 anti-submarine patrols, non-rigid airships of the Submarine Scout Zero type, flew out of Llangefni over the Irish Sea. The first commanding officer, Major G.H. Scott CBE, AFC, who piloted an airship under the Menai Bridge, went on to command the airship B34 on its historic Atlantic crossing. As Deputy Director Airship Development he flew to Canada in another historic crossing in the R100 in 1930. He was killed in a crash in the R101.

When in World War II it was decided to re-activate the airfield on Anglesey, the first problem for the commanding officer of RAF Rhosneigr was finding the place. Security in the village was so tight that no one would tell Wing Commander J.C.W. Oliver DSO, DFC, where his station was. When he at last convinced the Rhosneigr policeman that he was not a German spy, he was surprised to be asked: 'Can you ride a horse?' He said that he could and, clutching the station documents under his arm, was soon galloping across the beaches and over thirty-foot-high sandhills in the wake of the equestrian policeman. He arrived to find work on building the airfield at a standstill. Sandstorms had clogged the engines of both the bulldozers which were being used to dig out a landing-strip. It was a presage of things to come.

The first squadron at RAF Valley was made up of Czechs flying Hurricanes; then came Belgians with Spitfires; even the Beaufighter night-flying British squadron which followed had an international flavour. Air crew included Canadians, Poles, Czechs, Dutchmen and Belgians. Two squadrons of Australians followed.

The early Spitfire sorties were virtually suicide missions. Pilot training went no further than lessons in taking off and landing. Yet, though barely more than boys, they flew long, dangerous hours, protecting convoys through the Irish Sea and the Western Approaches. There were no air-sea rescue launches or helicopters to pick them up if they were shot down, and aircraft performance was unreliable. The drifting, clogging sands at Valley fouled the engine filters and intakes. The Rolls-Royce Merlin engines had to be completely overhauled every fifty hours. On other fighter stations the engines needed servicing only every 150 hours. Hurricanes and Spitfires repeatedly failed to return from patrol. The mortality rate among the Valley pilots was higher than that in squadrons engaged in the Battle of Britain.

Sometimes planes crashed within yards of the strip, on one occasion with horrifying results. At 11.30 a.m. on 28 August 1941, a Botha twin-engined bomber with a Polish crew of three crashed in the surf off Rhosneigr beach shortly after taking off to defend a convoy against U-boat attack. The crashed aircraft was only yards from the shore but a full south-westerly gale lashed the waves. It took the Porth Dinllaen lifeboat an hour and a half to make the short passage across the strait from Caernarfon to Rhosneigr.

The first boat to put off from the beach capsized. A coastguard was drowned and the other occupant, an airman, was swept ashore barely alive. PC George C. Arthur, the village policeman, called for volunteers and launched a whaler. As it came under the lea of the plane, the whaler was hit by a beam sea, and it too capsized. Only three of the crew of seven survived. From the beach fourteen servicemen swam out to rescue them. Four were drowned. In all, fourteen people lost their lives in the rescue. Despite valiant attempts by two schoolboy athletes, Stuart Wood of Chester and his friend Derrick Boynham, who were on holiday at Rhosneigr, the Polish crew of the plane were among the casualties. The boys, who were awarded George Medals, launched a dinghy but it took them three-quarters of an hour to row through the breakers the two hundred yards to the aircraft.

Nothing could be induced to grow to cover the sand-and-rock airstrip until the bed soil from three adjoining lakes was dredged up and spread over the sanded strip. As soon as the grass grew, the casualty rate dropped dramatically.

In 1943 a detachment of the USAF arrived at Valley, and within a year it had become a major terminus for trans-Atlantic flights.

A mountain rescue team, one of the first in the RAF, was founded there in the same year and in its first operational year answered four hundred call-outs in Snowdonia. It remains as one of six such teams throughout the UK. Although it was formed to

Dolgyn, Meir: the entrance to Darby's ironwork complex

Detail of the splendid iron casting done by Darby of Coalbrookdale to a design by Thomas Telford for the Waterloo Bridge at Betws-y-Coed. Still looking just as marvellous as it did in 1816 it nevertheless carries traffic well beyond the weights it was designed to support. A miniature engineering masterpiece

An unlikely view of the world's largest hydro-electric scheme. In fact Dinorwig's's generators are in massive caverns hollowed out from the rock below the slate quarry remains shown here.

rescue the crews of aircraft which had crashed in mountainous country, it is kept at a state of readiness by the constant call on its services, never refused, to rescue civilian climbers. In this work it is often assisted by 22 Air-Sea Rescue Squadron. Since its arrival in 1955, this squadron has been called out on over three thousand rescue missions over Gwynedd, saving hundreds of lives.

There are two flying-schools operating out of Valley. The Central Flying School Helicopter Detachment trains all the RAF's pilots, winchmen and crewmen for search and rescue duties. The other training wing, No. 4 Flying Training School, is the only advanced Jet Flying School in the RAF. Student pilots who have been picked to fly high-performance jets come to Anglesey. There they complete a twenty-two-week course with eighty-five hours flying Hawker Siddeley Hawks with a range of 1,735 miles and a top speed of 535 knots.

It is nerve-tingling to watch these young pilots flying their planes at breath-taking speed below the peaks, almost along the valley floors, of Snowdonia. It is difficult to believe that the unit has flown 85,000 hours with no loss of life.

Less well publicized than its warlike activities are the charitable services RAF Valley performs for the county, which have won it the freedoms of Anglesey and Bangor, and in 1981 the station was awarded the Wilkinson Sword of Peace for its community work. Every two years the profits from the station's bi-annual Open Day, which are usually in the region of £30,000, go to Gwynedd charities. Station wives have a thrift shop for Anglesey charities, the sub-aqua club works with Gwynedd coastguards, the mountain rescue teams instruct climbing-clubs. The search and rescue helicopter unit runs courses for St John's Ambulance Brigade, the station sea angling club has adopted the Gwynedd Guide Dogs for the Blind, and the airmen take parties of disabled people on tours of the station. Small wonder that when a minority of Anglesey borough councillors objected to the airmen exercising their freemen's right to march through Llangefni with fixed bayonets there were howls of protest against the councillors and support for the station from all corners of Gwynedd.

During the war there was a second large RAF presence in Gwynedd, the establishment of which has repercussions which continue to this day. In 1936, to the delight of local people, the government announced that it was to build an RAF bombing training school at Hell's Mouth, near Pwllheli, on the Lleyn Peninsula. To the local people in an area of terrible depression and endemic unemployment the news meant jobs and regular wages. To a minority, few of them living either on the Lleyn or in poverty, it represented yet another intrusion into Welsh culture by the English.

On 7 September 1936 Saunders Lewis, the Liverpool-born founder of the Welsh Nationalist party, D.J. Williams, a Fishguard schoolmaster, and the Reverend Lewis Valentine, a North Wales Baptist minister, set fire to wooden buildings at the school and gave themselves up to the local police. The three were brought to trial at Caernarfon Assizes, where the jury failed to agree and the case was sent to the Old Bailey for re-trial. There Saunders Lewis, who was the spokesman for the three, refused to recognize the right of the court to try him because it had been transferred from his own country. All three were sent to prison for nine months. After their sentence Williams returned to his school, Valentine to his church, but the University of Wales sacked Saunders Lewis from his post as librarian. Even those who thought the three men had acted with considerable silliness were united in believing that the university's treatment of Saunders Lewis was a piece of humbug.

The hollow mountain stands somewhere between folklore and the far frontiers of advanced technology. The concept of a mountain being hollowed out by blind mechanical moles so that magic fire can be produced by a giant waterfall is quite in keeping with Gwynedd's mythology. But in this case it is hard fact: the Dinorwig Pumped Storage Power Project. Even the names of the firms who carried it out, MacAlpine, Brand and Zschokike, sound vaguely Peer Gyntian. Dinorwig is the largest pumped storage scheme in Europe and the first in the world that can boost the supply of electricity to the national grid from zero load to full power in ten seconds.

The power station is hidden in a huge cavern, twice as long as a soccer pitch and sixteen storeys high, in the heart of the mountain. It has been used as the location for a science fiction film. Above it on the peak is Marchlyn Mawr, a reservoir capable of holding 1,540 million gallons (7,000m³) of water: 85,000 (386,410 litres) gallons of water can be channelled along a horizontal concrete-lined low-pressure tunnel 1.05 miles (1,695 metres) long to surge ponds at the head of a vertical shaft. This shaft, 484 yards (443 metres) deep and 10.4 yards (9.5 metres) in diameter, links the low-pressure tunnel in the mountain peak with a high-pressure manifold system which, in turn, feeds the reversible turbines. Once through the turbines the water flows into Llyn Peris and Llyn Padarn.

From the power station the electricity passes through enormous underground cables embedded in water-cooled concrete to a sub-station six miles away at Pentir.

The whole complex covers twenty-five square miles. There is a machine hall and a transformer hall joined by a gallery. Smaller galleries connect machine halls with the pump-turbine and motor generator complexes. The station cost £310 million but it will pay for itself within six years. It took 2,500 men, the vast majority of them local, many descended from quarrymen, seven years to build. Output equals the combined production of the two nuclear power stations of Trawsfynydd and Wylfa. It could supply the whole of Wales with electricity and, barring earthquakes, will last one thousand years. Besides the two enormous caverns four miles of tunnels were bored and 10 million tons (10.16 million tonnes) of rock and shale were excavated. The builders' shopping list included a million tons (1.016 million tonnes) of concrete aggregate and 200,000 tons (203,000 tonnes) of cement and pulverized ash.

When they commissioned the work, the Central Electricity Generating Board specified that at least seventy per cent of the hourly paid labour force must have lived in the Dinorwig area for at least five years. It proved a wise policy. Like the Expressway from Chester to Holyhead, all so far completed ahead of schedule, the Dinorwig project was finished well within the target time and with the minimum of industrial upset. Industrialists could do worse than come to Gwynedd.

Only marginally less impressive is the 144.4 mile (232-kilometre) long oil pipeline which runs under land and water from Shell Petroleum's refinery at Stanlow, in Cheshire, to a marine terminal at Amlwch on the coast of Anglesey.

The closing of the Suez Canal, with the consequence of a long sea journey round the Cape, led to the commissioning of larger tankers to keep oil prices down. These supertankers could not make the passage up to the Tranmere terminal on the River Mersey where the $8\frac{3}{4}$ yard (eight-metre) tide rise and fall makes loading a matter of precise timing. Even a short delay in berthing at high water means that comparatively small tankers of seventy thousand dead weight tonnage run the risk of being grounded on the low tide.

Amlwch was considered as a terminal only after Liverpool City Council turned down the request by Shell Petroleum to site their single loading mooring at the Mersey mouth. In 1972 Anglesey Council seized the opportunity in the hope that it would bring employment and attract a healthy income to the island. In the event, comparatively few local people were used in the construction of the terminal and even fewer in its running. Initially Shell agreed to pay the council £600,000 a year in oil revenues. These were to be used for 'amenity purposes' on behalf of the ratepayers in Anglesey. However, in 1985, when the council was on the verge of pledging the revenues to build and equip an £8½ million art gallery, Shell dropped a bombshell. They said they wanted substantial reductions in the oil royalties. It was even suggested the levy might be dropped altogether. This followed an announcement that the company was laying off one thousand men at the Stanlow refinery. Demand for oil had dropped by thirty-five per cent since the beginning of the decade and, as a Shell negotiator pointed out, although when the terminal was built it was estimated that it would be carrying 25.4 million tonnes (25 million tons) of crude oil a year, in fact it had never piped more than 10.16 million tonnes (10 million tons) and the figure in 1984 was 7.1 million tonnes (7 million tons). Shell asked that the £1,900 pilotage charges per ship be dropped and suggested the royalty reduction. It seemed the set-up was no longer economically viable for the company.

When discussing plans for the £8½ million gallery, Anglesey's chief executive, Mr Leon Gibson, has assured councillors that, when the current eight-year agreement with Shell ran out in 1988, 'it is anticipated we will receive at least the equivalent of the 1987-8 allocation with inflation.' Fortunately, opposition to the gallery was so vociferous that wise counsels prevailed and plans for that particular scheme were dropped.

Negotiations on the royalties are proceeding between Anglesey and Shell but whatever their outcome it would be churlish to undervalue the impressive engineering that went into the Amlwch terminal. The mooring off Amlwch took the biggest supertankers in service. The buoy is 27.9 yards (twenty-seven metres) in diameter and weighs 492 tons (five hundred tonnes). From the tankers the oil goes down 39 inch (one thousand millimetre) diameter submarine pipelines to Amlwch port. From Amlwch it is carried 3.1 miles (five kilometres) underground to the storage tankers at the main pumping station at Rhosgoch. This station has ten storage tanks with total capacity of 915,600 cubic yards (700,000 cubic metres). The site provided for eleven more holding tankers which will not now ever be needed. Electric pumps send the oil down 35.1 inch (900 millimetre) pipes under every imaginable obstacle on its 78.9 mile (127-kilometre) journey. Amongst the natural hazards are the Menai Straits, Snowdonia and three rivers, the Conwy, the Clwyd and the Dee.

The surveyors had to get the co-operation and approval of five counties, the Landowners Association, the National Farmers' Union and the Farmers' Union of Wales. Negotiations and surveys had to be carried out on four hundred properties. There had to be payment of rates for easement, loss of crops and land-usage while the pipe was being laid. At the time that Shell were surveying their pipeline, Anglesey Aluminium opened its smelter plant at Holyhead which at its peak employed 1,250 local workers and produced a hundred thousand tons of aluminium a year.

Gwynedd in the twentieth century sees itself as the home of the sunshine industries. The county's industrial record is good. There are few disputes and workers are quick to pick up new skills.

At Bangor there is the seventy-acre Llandegai industrial estate which links into the Expressway and through it to the English motorway system: similarly the Cibyn industrial estate on the outskirts of Caernarfon lies alongside the North Wales coast road, and the Gaerwen industrial estate on Anglesey opens onto the London-Holyhead trunk road which provides access to freight and passenger ships and woefully under-used container-traffic facilities. From Holyhead British Rail operates a daily service to major industrial centres throughout Britain. Air facilities for executive travel are available at RAF Valley, and there are landing facilities at Caernarfon, Llanbedr, near Harlech, and Mona on Anglesey. Penamser industrial estate at Porthmadog links to the rest of the UK by road and rail. Smaller industrial locations are available at Bala, Blaenau Ffestiniog, Amlwch, Dolgellau, Penryndeudraeth, Llanwrst, Pwllheli, Tywyn and Llandudno Junction. All these locations have government financed multi-purpose factory units ready for immediate occupation. In addition the local authority provides small workshops.

Operating costs are significantly lower in Gwynedd, and commercial rents are a third of those in southern England. There are technical colleges at Llandrillo, Llandudno, Llangefni, Bangor and Dolgellau, and the council offers mortgages and council houses to key workers. The Electrical Engineering Science department at the University College of North Wales in Bangor is one of the foremost in Europe. The Industrial Development Board has already been mentioned earlier in this narrative.

The nuclear power generators at Trawsfynydd and Wylfa are nearing the end of their operative lives. The CEGB's proposal to replace them with a skyscraper complex makes conservationists fear for the landscape around them. It was announced in 1985 that they would be among fifteen power stations in a nuclear grid designed to free industry from its dependence on coal.

During 1984-5 the Wylfa power station had its most successful year since operations started in 1971, functioning for 8,200 hours out of a possible 8,600. But it was not able to get rid of its nuclear radiated fuel waste, and it was stored on site. When four of the five purpose-built storage tanks holding fuel waste had been filled and the other was one-third full, the station superintendent, Mr Ray Razzell, said: 'We can probably hold out until the beginning of the new year but if we cannot solve our problems by then the station will have to be run down.'

Normally nuclear waste from the station is sent in specially constructed flasks to the Sellafield reprocessing plant, but none have been able to leave the site since September 1984. This is because a crane which normally handles the flasks is having to be redesigned for safety reasons.

Gwynedd is no stranger to technological innovations. Somewhere in the cellars of Windsor Castle are two barrels which once contained genuine Welsh Whisky distilled at Frongoch, near Bala.

The Welsh whisky industry was started in the nineteenth century by the eccentric squire of Rhiwlas, R.J. Lloyd Price, and Robert Willis, with a capital of £100,000. Squire Price was a man who thought big. He once bought the largest bulldog in the world, but unfortunately its journey from its home in the Balkans to Wales took it through Paris, which, at the time (1870-71) was under siege by the Prussians, and it was stolen and eaten. Squire Price had better luck with horses. When his fortunes were at their lowest ebb he backed with his remaining cash a horse called Bendigo which won the Derby. The Squire commemorated the win by presenting a lychgate to his church which carried the legend: 'And now to heaven my soul will go. Thanks to the good horse Bendigo.' When the Bishop of St Asaph came to bless the new gate, he was furious. Obligingly Squire Price had the offending verse removed. When the Bishop left, he had it replaced.

The idea of a Welsh distillery was sound. The peaty land and the crystal water of the Tryweryn valley are unrivalled even in the Highlands of Scotland. Unfortunately for the squire and his partner, Bala was staunchly Nonconformist and deeply religious. Delivery had to be made to local suppliers at night for fear of what their neighbours would do.

Whisky was not the only enterprise undertaken by the Squire. Advertisements for whisky carried such footnotes as: 'Rhiwlas Aluminous Earth. Useful to the Boiler Composition Makers, so sought after by the colour trade as a basis for paints, by paper makers as a fitting superior to Kaolins; by cement, polish and polishing powder and disinfectant makers. Unequalled for de-odourising purposes and for use in Earth Closets.' Or: 'Not far from this distillery is situated the Rhiwlas Game Farm, instituted in 1880 by a sportsman for sportsmen. Cheapest and best pheasant eggs: Partridges eggs. Live Grouse. Pheasants for shooting and breeding ...' The Squire went in for advertising copywriting: 'Eyes Front. 'tenshun. At the word of command the warrior vintner Captain Mears will stand and deliver. This Cambrian Cordial regimental motto: Taste and Try, before you buy.'

He was not slow to advertise his own family. The Welsh lady on the bottle label was a portrait of his wife. On one advert she rides – modestly side-saddle – a winged barrel of Welsh whisky, with this noble piece of copywriting:

Tidings of Priceless Price I bring
Mounted on my Thais
Welsh Whisky's praises loud I sing
From this lofty dais.
Drink it! 'Tis brewed on, here's the tip,
Th'estate of Price of Rhiwlas
'Twill Scotch the Irish so a nip
Take each old man and new.

Squire Price is my favourite Welshman. On my shelves I have one of the books from his library, a volume of Baring Gould's *British Saints* which carries the Squire's bookplate. But the plate has been stuck in the back of the book. Upside down. It must have been very good whisky. Certainly Queen Victoria favoured it. When she was staying near Bala, she was presented by the Squire with a cask of the Cambrian Cordial, which retailed at 3 shillings a bottle. Wrote a contemporary: 'Judging by the letters of enquiry received by the company from the keeper of the cellars as to when it will be permissable to tap the barrel, the Queen is uncommonly anxious to taste her own whisky.' The Queen was no amateur in the matter. Her standard tipple was whisky mixed with claret.

A second barrel of the Cambrian Cordial went into the royal cellars. It was presented in 1894 to the Prince of Wales, later Edward VII, in his capacity as Worshipful Grand Master of the English Masons, by the 'Brothers of the Bala Lodge of Free Masons'. I know of only one other bottle. It was one owned by my old friend and prince of story-tellers Bob Semple, the landlord of the White Lion and Royal Hotel in Bala in the 1950s. I could never persuade him to open it for research or any other purpose. Where it is now I know not, alas.

Sadly the Distillers Company were too strong for the spirit of Wales. By 1914 the brewery was empty, and during the war it was a POW camp. The final irony came in the twenties when it was a concentration camp for Irish prisoners, guarded by Scotch soldiers. I think Squire Price would have appreciated the joke. He might even be glad to know that there is still a Welsh whisky, though unhappily it is distilled not in Gwynedd but in Brecon.

The growing audience of the TV programme *One Man and His Dog* and other programmes about sheepdog trials owes a considerable debt to Squire Price, for it was he who invented them. The first recorded sheepdog trial was held on his land in Bala on 9 October 1873. A plaque which commemorates the trial on the Garth Goch and Rhiwaedog Fields was erected on the site at the commemorative trials in 1979.

On the first trial, although the shepherds were predominantly Welsh, the prize was won by a Scotsman with his dog Tweed. The competition would be a walkover for today's shepherds. It was in two parts. The pen was five hundred yards from the fold and six feet wide. In the second part of the competition dog and man drove in view for eight hundred yards. Three hundred spectators watched with mixed feelings as the Scotsman won. (It is nice to record that a Welsh shepherd won the commemoration trial.) But Thompson, the Scotsman, bragged so noisily and crowed over his Welsh fellow shepherds so much that they issued a challenge. They declared they would meet Scots, or indeed shepherds from any country, to see who had the best dogs.

With a small committee Squire Price set about organizing the competition. And on 30 June 1876, under the auspices of the Kennel Club, the first international sheepdog trial was held at Alexandra Palace, London. The top prize was £15 for the best working dog; there was a prize of £5 for the best-looking dog and £2 for the quickest time.

Now, of course, through the medium of television, the sport is watched by millions. And what a delight it was for me in 1985 to commentate on the Welsh National Open Championships for BBC Wales with my colleague and the country's leading authority on trials, Eric Halsall. For the trials are still held at Rhiwlas Home Farm at Bala on the land of Squire R.J. Lloyd Price, still farmed by a descendant of the Squire, the amiable Robin Price.

At the age of eighty-six, Cadwallader Roberts is one of the few remaining people alive who can remember Squire Price. Still active, he was Course Marshall at the 1985 championship. It is his boast that he has been the tenant of six succeeding generations of the Price family, '... and every one of 'em a gentleman in every way'.

'The trials of a sheepdog.' Though not to scale this diagram gives an idea of what a typical course looks like. The dog races away at the shepherd's command, taking care to circle the sheep and not to disturb them, separating certain marked ones from the rest and bringing these on for final penning near the shepherd. The least number of movements made by the shepherd, the speed and style at which the movements are accomplished … all these count in the awarding of points that make one of them top dog

It is entirely typical of Squire Price, or, to give him his full but little used name and title, Mr R.J. Lloyd Price of Rhiwlas, that he should have been the founder of such an amiable sport as the sheepdog trial.

For thousands of years the shepherd kept the secrets of his craft to himself. When he generously agreed to share them, there was born what I believe is the only intelligent spectator sport, more dignified than football, more skilful than darts and much less noisy than snooker. No wonder so many people prefer it. No sheepdog in history has ever hugged and kissed his master when the flock are penned; they don't, thank God, say 'Magic' as a substitute for conversation. And their supporters are contemplative.

Surprisingly border collies have not been around very long. Fifty years ago a shepherd would not have recognized one; they were acknowledged by the Kennel Club only in 1976. The first recorded mention of the name was in an insult three hundred years ago. An Aberdeen bishop was said to be like a collie because he kept coming to dinner uninvited. But no one knows what the word means. Sheepdogs came from any breed or no breed at all. All they needed was intelligence and a pronounced hunting instinct. When the old drovers found a good sheepdog, they crossed it with a mastiff to herd the sheep to market and with a terrier for a guard dog.

'Dog and Stick' farming is one of humanity's more benign occupations. For one thing it leaves the countryside as it finds it. Sheep don't churn up the ground, rip out the hedgerows or poison the land. A flock of sheep cropping a field encourages wild flowers. And no landscape of distant hills worth its salt was ever painted without a prospect of sheep.

The partnership between man and dog persuades you – in the face of formidable evidence to the contrary – that mankind is not all that bad. I have to say that it is the only agricultural partnership between man and the dumb creatures that I can think of which doesn't end with the creatures being eaten. Even cows and horses end up as a hound meat.

And the implements the shepherd uses are so aesthetically pleasing. There is nothing pretty about a tractor, and it is difficult to rave over the beauty and symmetry of a combine harvester. The shepherd's crook is not only a thing of great beauty, it is wonderfully practical. The little hook on the end to hang a lantern on; the way the crook narrows on itself so that a sheep can get into it but only with determination get out again. The length. I always assumed that shepherds' crooks were long so that the sheep could be reached with ease. My friend Hughie 'Bugail' Williams, a man who combines his shepherding with being a police constable in Bangor, North Wales, put me right on that one. The crook is a third, longer leg for the shepherd. Very useful to push yourself forward on a mountain slope.

I like shepherds. They are thoughtful men. Spending your life away from other men with only a flock of Sunday dinners to keep you company induces reflection. And they are hardy too.

The shepherd, his crook and his flock have been symbols of caring and tranquillity since the days of antiquity. When the Greeks wanted to describe Arcady, the heavenly place, they used the symbol of the shepherd boy tending his flock. The Good Shepherd is a powerful image in Christianity.

Shepherds know that when sheep look stupid they are acting. What is happening out there is living chess. The sheep are testing the dog, probing for its weaknesses, trying to outsmart it. Wyn Edwards of Ruthin, a Blue Riband Trials winner, tells me that a sheep can spot a weak dog in a minute. And of all the cunning tribe of sheep there is none so cunning as a Welsh ewe. It is not long since a band of those fleecy females learned to cross cattle grids by tiptoeing on the bars.

In the matter of sheep I am one with Bo-Peep. If we lost them, I'd cry my eyes out. Watch them as they move out of range of the dog. Balletic. No chorus line ever achieved such unison of movement. And the look they give you. The only other place you will see a look like that is the bridge table. It's the look of an animal that has just discovered that the world has gone barking mad. Literally. It's a look that says 'Stop the World I want to get off'. The look of someone who has just put his foot in something unpleasant called life.

I'm fascinated by the lovely simplicity of the sheepdog trial. Think of the field as a clock face with the sheep at its centre. The shepherd stands at six o'clock, and the dog works round the rim, clockwise, anti-clockwise, at command. The sole aim of the sheep is to humiliate the dog in front of all those people; the sole aim of the shepherds to prevent it. The dog's path is pear-shaped up towards the sheep and then round them. Careful not to spook. And an experienced handler can so read the ground that he knows what is going to happen before either dog or sheep do. He spots mistakes before they happen. Everyone knows where they are and where they are going. Oh, that there were such symmetry in other sports. Such langourous logic.

One thing, I confess, distorts this peaceful image. I get very worried about the dogs. And so do the sheep. Because the dog is not controlling the flock so much as hunting it. Dogs stalk sheep as lions stalk game. When you watch sheepdogs, working, what you are seeing is the race memory of the wolf. When it crouches, it is not planning its next move. It is preparing to spring. The cleverness of those first shepherds thousands of years ago did not lie in teaching the dogs to cut out the sheep they wanted to move; the dogs already knew how to do that. They had used the tactic in the wild. The shepherds' cleverness was to talk them out of diving for the throat of the prey. And dragging it off into the bush.

A sheepdog trial is potentially as lethal as a bullfight. Only the generosity of the dog, its willing co-operation with man and the skill of generations of shepherds prevent this pastoral scene from becoming a bloodbath. No *corridas*, of course. Just corridors of post and rail fencing and binding twine. No suits of light. No capes. Just cloth caps and sheep-stalkers. No fancy footwork from *matadors*, but a complicated footstep just the same, and one that only farm folk seem able to master. A sort of purposeful amble, as though the body is content to leave the navigating to the feet.

Touches of the dandy, though only the initiated can spot them.

Mostly the carvings on the crook handles. Whistles, crouching dogs, thistles and daffodils, but hardly ever a sheep. You can tell the dogs that are going to the Internationals too. They are bi-lingual. Home dogs work only in Welsh.

THE JEWELS IN THE CROWN

Yet gladly showe, to straunger great good will:
A courteous kind of love in every place
A man may finde, in simple people's face.

The Worthinesse of Wales by Thomas Churchiard
(sixteenth century)

• CHAPTER 10 •

Caernarfon Castle, revered by medievalists, loathed by Nationalists, guards the gateway to an older Wales.

The Lleyn Peninsula has changed little over the centuries. Fiercely Nonconformist, using the language as a means of communication rather than status, it is determinedly, admirably Welsh. Its beauty catches the heart; it is preoccupied with its own affairs and the old Welsh tradition of hospitality to the stranger. And it is guarded by Caernarfon, mysterious and in an odd way sinister in its dark elegance.

It was disclosed recently that the master spy Juan Garcia chose Caernarfon as the headquarters for the mythical spy ring which he used to fleece his Nazi spymasters. Although he never moved from his home in Spain, Garcia, it was revealed at the D-Day celebrations in 1984, persuaded the Nazis that he was actually living in Caernarfon. Since the town was then headquarters of the Welsh Nationalist Party, whose pre-war leaders had praised Franco, Mussolini and Hitler and opposed the British war effort, Garcia was readily believed. (And not only in Nazi Germany. For many years Whitehall refused to release any details of Garcia's work, a piece of buffoonery which led many people in Britain to believe the Nationalists ran a spy network. This was monstrously unjust. In fact a Nationalist, Arthur Owen, who did spy for the Abwehr, the German Intelligence agency, was 'turned' by the British. Another 'Nationalist' spy who turned up in Spain was in truth a South Wales police inspector.)

British Secret Intelligence intercepted the despatch Garcia sent in July 1941 in which he announced his arrival in Caernarfon and explained he would be sending future despatches by courier to Portugal for onward transmission. This signal would explain why all future despatches about his British activities originated in Spain. This satisfied the Germans but it greatly worried the British Intelligence Community. Ironically the reason Garcia set up as a freelance spy was that he had been turned down when he offered his services as an agent to the British. When next he offered them his services, he was taken up and brought to Britain. He worked with an organization in the SIS called the Twenty Committee – XX or Double Cross.

Garcia's agents' successes were all planted by the Twenty Committee. The deception was thorough. When the Abwehr once complained that he had not warned them of preparation in Liverpool for the allied invasion of North Africa, he explained that his Merseyside agent had died suddenly and sent as proof an obituary notice which the Committee had inserted in the *Liverpool Daily Post*. His greatest *coup* was persuading the Nazis that the D-Day landings in Normandy were only a decoy designed to draw the Germans from the real invasion which would take place in Calais. Believing him, the Nazi High Command pulled out troops from Normandy, and as a result casualties on D-Day were far lower than they would otherwise have been.

It is easy to see Caernarfon as a centre of the secrets trade. It is like no other town in Wales. A place where even the Welsh language is not Welsh enough and they speak a Welsh dialect unknown in the rest of the country, based on the cockney slang of the London militiamen who were stationed there in the nineteenth century.

As you walk under the castle walls, there is a distinct sense of 'goings on.' It may be the walls themselves, modelled as they were on the walls of Constantinople; it may be the streets of superior guest houses, their identical Regency façades and glittering door furniture giving them the air of embassies, or at least consulates, of Ruritanian powers. Behind the lace curtains, one feels, the Merry Widow still holds admirers spellbound, and it would be no surprise to read among the bed-and-breakfast signs another which read: 'Kings of Zenda Imprisoned' or 'Special Rates for Spies'.

Caernarfon looks at life obliquely; it sees things differently from the rest of Wales. During the Investiture of the present Prince of Wales in July 1964, a TV reporter asked a local man in the street for his views on 'The Prince of Wales.' 'Don't ask me,' the man replied. 'I've been barred from the place since the end of the war.'

The first twentieth-century investiture of a Prince of Wales, the man who was later to abdicate the throne before his coronation as Edward VIII, was organized in 1911 by David Lloyd George, whose statue stands on the roof of a public lavatory in the Castle Square. He was MP for the Caernarfon borough for fifty-five years. His home was at Llanystumdwy, near Criccieth. His museum there was little visited until the showing of a TV series based on his colourful life. Now it does a roaring trade.

Criccieth might be dominated by its castle, built by Llywelyn the Great, strengthened by Edward I and laid waste by Owain Glyndwr, but it is Lloyd George who is the *genius loci*. Though born in Manchester, he spent his childhood with his widowed mother in a small cottage, still standing, opposite the Feathers Inn. In his prosperity he built a much larger house, Brynawelon, where the family still live.

The oldest building in Pwllheli, chiefly famous now as a yachting marina, is the Penlan Fawr, an inn which dates back to the early 1600s. In the days when Pwllheli was a busy port, it was a dockside pub, but as the harbour silted up and the land-reclamation programme began, the sea receded almost out of sight. In its day the Penlan has been a theatre, a town hall, a chapel and a school. The stage still exists at the rear of the building on which the eighteenth-century actress Sarah Siddons appeared during a tour of Wales. The great preacher Hywel Harris held services in the streets outside, and Dr Johnson stayed at Penlan Fawr with his friends the Thrales on their tour of North Wales.

In Abersoch little but English is ever heard. It is the most anglicized of the Lleyn towns and the playground of the middle classes from Cheshire and the Wirral. In the summer the lanes are choked with sports cars, and the bay is filled with motor launches and wind-surfers. It is virtually indistinguishable from any small resort on the south coast of England. Aberdaron, on the other hand, is quintessentially Welsh, though it, too, is packed every summer with visitors from England. For all its popularity as a camping site, a charabanc rendezvous and a place of resort, it still evokes the pilgrims who every day congregated there before they made the hazardous crossing across the tide race to Bardsey Island, the resting place of over a thousand saints.

In 1985 a local Roman Catholic priest started organizing pilgrimages once again to Bardsey, with sailings from Pwllheli, but he found that many trips had to be cancelled because of the treacherous seas.

Understandably, before the pilgrims of old embarked from Aberdaron they prayed in the church of St Hywyn, the cathedral of Lleyn, as it was once known. The church stands just above the beach on the site of a Celtic oratory, the cell of St Hywyn, the confessor to the monks and one of the saints who founded the monastery on Bardsey Island. The oldest part of the church dates back to the twelfth century, when it would have contained, near the altar, a Chair of Peace. Under Welsh law, once a fugitive reached this seat he was safe from his pursuers. It was in those days and until at least the thirteenth century a monastic college of priests, but there have been slips from grace in its long history. In July 1623 after a visitation from his superiors at Bangor, it was noted in their report: '... the vicar came to read a prayer upon a Sunday and was not well: but seemed to be overseen by drinke ...' The care of souls has been in more responsible hands since, including those of the distinguished poet the Reverend R.S. Thomas who was vicar here until his retirement in 1978.

The road across the National Trust headland overlooking Bardsey Island leads to the coastguard station at the cliff head, where the views are superb, but the less adventurous will be content to picnic in the lower car-park, infrequently full, and enjoy the view of Bardsey across the wicked stretch of water, Bardsey Sound. Many mariners have lost their lives there over the centuries. The account of one passage by Hilaire Belloc in his *Cruise of the Nona*, the yacht given to him by Lord Stanley, makes excellent reading when you are sitting comfortably, glass of wine in hand, on that headland and thinking of Belloc out in a wild sea in a very old cutter, slow and only thirty feet long. Happily all was well.

How much worse it must have been for the first monks and the pilgrims that followed them in the early times. Little wonder that three pilgrimages to Bardsey across the two-mile stretch of water were the equivalent of one to Rome. As late as the eighteenth century the ferrymen ceased rowing as they neared the island and began to pray. Pennant, the eighteenth-century traveller, thought it was the holiness of the island which had affected them. More likely it was a prayer of thanksgiving for deliverance.

Although only five hundred Welsh saints have been identified, as many as twenty thousand are supposed to have been buried on Bardsey. It was certainly a popular place of pilgrimage. The great and very readable authority on North Wales, A.G. Bradley, gives this account of the pilgrims of Bardsey: 'For generations, probably for centuries, men from all parts of the West limped and crawled and dragged themselves along the rude roads ... Every church, upon both shores (of the Peninsula) became a shelter and a refuge for the pilgrims.'

Perhaps the reason Bardsey was so popular can be found in Giraldus Cambrensis' book: 'Beyond Lleyn there is a small island inhabited by very religious monks called Cuellbes or Culidei. This island either from the wholesomeness of the climate, owing to its vicinity to Ireland, or rather from some miracle obtained by the merit of the saints, has this wonderful peculiarity, that the oldest people die first, because diseases are uncommon and scarcely any die, except of extreme old age. Its name is Enlli in the Welsh and Bardsey in the Saxon language.'

The island is still popular with tourists. A Trust took over in 1981, and since then all twelve houses owned by it have been renovated and are now able to take paying guests throughout the summer. During Whit week in 1985 thirty-five visitors stayed on the island, although some stayed at the bird observatory. Commented warden Mr Dafydd Thomas at the time: 'Last summer over three hundred people stayed with us, and a further two hundred stayed in the observatory, and prospects are even better.'

Thomas came to the area as an evacuee during the war and has farmed at Criccieth since 1962. One of his most important jobs now as warden is to look after *Bugail Enlli II*, the Trust's recently acquired Cyclone 26 type boat, which is vital to the island. It carries not only the island's passengers on the eighteen-mile voyage from Pwllheli in one hour flat but also all the materials needed to improve the properties.

No less fearsome than Bardsey Sound is Hell's Mouth Bay. The drive to it from Aberdaron or Sarn across Rhiw Mountain is spectacular on a clear day. The long stretch of golden sand looks inviting but the seas are extremely dangerous for swimmers, and many ships have been wrecked there, which no doubt accounts for its sinister name. In Welsh it is called Porth Neigwl, Nigel's Beach, after Nigel of Lorraine who landed there after being given the towns of Pwllheli and Nefyn by the Black Prince. One of the loveliest views of the bay is from the gardens of Plas-yn-Rhiw, a delightful sixteenth-century house and estate which were given to the National Trust by three remarkable sisters, Eileen, Laura, and Honora Keating.

In the 1930s Clough Williams Ellis had found the house. He wrote: 'Such was the appealing charm of the whole bowery oasis in that austere and empty landscape that I had no difficulty in persuading a romantic friend of mine that this was indeed the home he had been seeking for so long.' Unfortunately the owner, an elderly eccentric, lived abroad and did not answer letters, so the plan had to be abandoned. The Keating sisters were more tenacious. They had seen and fallen in love with Plas-yn-Rhiw. When eventually the house was put up for sale, though it was derelict, they bought it and dedicated the rest of their lives, using local labour, to its restoration. As any portion of the old estate, which had been sold separately, came up at auction, they bought that too, with the sole aim of giving it to the nation to enjoy as a memorial to their parents.

Between 1939 and 1957 they managed to restore the manor house and buy back 325 acres of the estate. Since their deaths the Trust has bought from the University of Wales the 145-acre common at Mynydd Rhiw which affords breathtaking views of Anglesey, Snowdonia, Cardigan Bay, even the Wicklow hills of Ireland. The Trust has dedicated the land to the memory of the Keating sisters. In 1985 it completed their work with a £45,000 restoration programme on the house, which contains a holiday flat for rent throughout the year.

The Keatings were quite obviously besotted by the Lleyn, where they had spent their holidays since 1919. It is a state of mind easily achieved. I know of no more pleasant holiday than wandering on the Lleyn, taking in walks like Porth Neigwl's $3\frac{1}{2}$ miles of beach and a meal at the splendid Lion Inn at Tudweiliog, where you can barbecue steak supplied by the landlady in a flower-filled courtyard.

There is Llangian, which was the best-kept village in Wales by official consent in 1964 and has remained so by common consent ever since. The churchyard has a tombstone which bears an inscription in Latin: 'Melus the Doctor, son of Martin, lies here.' It is the only tombstone ever found commemorating a sixth-century Christian burial on which the occupation of the person is mentioned, and it is one of the earliest references to the profession of doctor.

At Porth Oer the sands whistle under your feet. At the curiously named Porth Iago the cliffs and sands are carefully tended by its owners, a local farming family. They make a very small charge for passing through their farmyard to an ample grass car-park.

Llangwnnadl I wrote about in the introduction to this book. The sixteenth-century parish church, simple, three-aisled, all flowers and beeswax, the Welsh incense, is the most perfect little church I know. Its sister church at Bryncroes, a mile or so inland near Sarn, is pure magic. Christmas Evans, the evangelist, was married there, and in 1906 one of the most dramatic of restoration programmes was completed there with the happiest of results. The walls appear to be made of slate, dark and glowing. Blades of light pierce through the Norman windows. The effect is indescribably dramatic, especially when you first walk into the church, lovingly cared for by Mrs Mary Thomas, who lives across the lane from the churchyard.

Among the joys of this tiny stretch of jewelled coastline are its remarkable eating-houses. Some are well known, such as the Dive Inn at Tudweiliog, famous for its monster lobsters, its wine cellar and above all a superb Maltese fish soup so crowded with every kind of seafood that it would be no surprise to find trawler fleets fishing from the rim of the plate. Others are less well known but are well worth seeking out. None is a disappointment.

A once derelict and virtually inaccessible village, Nant Gwrtheyrn, in the shadow of the Rivals near Llithfaen, has been reconstructed in a unique cultural experience as a Welsh language centre. The village, which was the home of quarrymen, is built on a grassy ledge at the seaward end of a wooded valley. Now students sleep in the restored cottages, and the chapel is a social centre. At present thirty-two students at a time can be accommodated for courses in Welsh language, history and legend. There is also a specialist course 'Welsh at Work' for local government employees. It is said by students to offer the most efficient way of learning Welsh. English is *not* spoken there.

Across the sea from Lleyn, visible on all but the darkest day, is the coastline of Anglesey, the enchanted isle of the Phoenicians, the furthermost outpost of the Roman Empire, the capital of the medieval kingdom of Gwynedd. It is a low land, sea-hugging. It has a greater proportion of lowland than any other district in Wales: nowhere is higher than 720 feet above sea-level, and only two hundred acres are over five hundred feet above sea-level. It is the plainsman's paradise.

Anglesey has given the United Kingdom the greatest dynasty of kings, the Tudors, but it is primarily an Isle of Skies, of baroque cloud architecture and Turner sunsets over its western coast. When St Dwyn was dying on Llanddwyn Island, God obligingly split a rock which was blocking her view of an Aberffraw sunset.

It is the driest borough in Wales, with between thirty-five and forty inches of rainfall a year, and one of the sunniest, with an average of 1,550 hours of sunshine. Spring comes early and the winters are not harsh. Its few industries are modern but there is about the island a sense of ancient place. There are eighteen neolithic tombs (4,000 to 2,000 BC), thirty-two Bronze Age barrows, nine Iron Age forts and one magnificent memorial to the golden age of the Celts, the great votive treasure of Llyn Cerrig Bach, near Valley. It was discovered in 1943 by workmen digging up peat from the bottom of the lake to build the grass runway for RAF Valley. The peat was left to dry before being loaded onto lorries and taken to Valley. It was only then, when it was ready for spreading, that the treasure was found. The first artefact to come to light was a Bronze Age chain used to manacle slaves. It was so strong that workmen on the site used it to pull free lorries that were trapped in the mud.

Fortunately four of the workmen, W.O. and R. Roberts, W. Jones and W. Rees, realized the importance of the artefacts they were finding and they alerted the scholars. In all 144 objects were found on the bed of the lake and in the peat that had been dredged from it. They came from all over Britain, costly and of superb workmanship, weapons and military accessories. Their position in the lake suggests that they were all thrown in from the same place, a rocky platform on the shore. They included chain harness and chariot traces, slave chains, shields, spears and eleven swords. The presence of the latter has suggested to some archaeologists a connection with the Arthurian legend of Excalibur, thrown into just such a lake as Llyn Cerrig Bach.

Anglesey is a place where legends are at home. Any parish on the island can produce a clutch of them. On Puffin Island, off Penmon, the community of early medieval monks lived by pickling and salting the puffins, a great delicacy, and sending them to Chester market, where they sold at 4 shillings a barrel. But Giraldus Cambrensis says that if ever there was dissension in the community the island would be overrun with a plague of mice. Curiously, some years ago Lord Langford, from Rhuddlan, marooned on the island after a boating accident and probably the first person to land there in years, found the island heaving with rats.

Across the tide race at Penmon a religious community was founded by St Seiriol, whose cell can still be seen near what was once the monastery fishpond. Nearby is the largest dovecot in Europe.

Two miles to the south-west of Penmon, where the River Lleiniog meets the Menai Straits, was fought, in 1084, the battle between the Viking King Magnus and Hugh 'the Fat', Earl of Chester. Descendants, who, not surprisingly, sought a more romantic name, called the Earl *'Lupus'*, but according to legend the name came not from the Latin for a wolf, as might seem obvious, but from the jubilant cry of Magnus when one of his archers put an arrow into the Earl's eye. *'Leit loup,'* he called. 'Let him dance', a punishment, the legend says, 'for his cruelties on the poor inhabitants'.

Beaumaris (locally it is pronounced 'bew') grew up round Edward I's castle on the site of a Viking port, Porth Wygyr.

There are three curious memorials on this coast of the island.

Nowhere on Anglesey is the island's spirit of ancient place more vivid than at Penmon Priory. The ruins of the thirteenth century Augustinian priory, reconstructed in this sketch, include St Seiriol's crystal well, the vibrant church, the monks' fishpond and a substantial stone dovecote

Behind Beaumaris, rising surprisingly in a meadow, is an obelisk erected to a local landowner, Sir Richard Williams Bulkeley, in 1875. On the straits, between the two bridges, looking slightly puzzled, is a statue of Lord Nelson. The memorial was sculpted by Admiral Lord Clarence Paget in 1873.

The third and most imposing memorial of all was erected under the Admiral's supervision to his famous ancestor the first Marquess of Anglesey, who lost his leg in action at Waterloo when he commanded the cavalry for the Duke of Wellington. Atop a 91-foot stone, Doric column (on the site, incidentally, of Craig-y-Dinas, a Celtic fortress) stands the bronze statue of 'Peg Leg' in the uniform of a Regency cavalryman, his leg miraculously restored. There is a more homely memorial. It is a poem reputedly written by the MP George Canning after the leg was buried with great ceremony on the battlefield.

Here lies and let no saucy knave
Presume to sneer or laugh
To learn that mouldering in this grave
There lies – a British calf.

For he who writes these lines is sure
That those who read the whole
Will find that laugh was premature
For here, too, lies the sole.

And here five little toes repose
Twin born with other five
Unheeded by their brother toes
Who all are now alive.

A leg and foot, to speak more plain,
Lie here of one commanding
Who though his wits he might retain
Lost half his understanding.

And when the guns with thunder fraught
Poured bullets thick as hail
Could only in this way be taught
To give the foe leg bail.

And now in England just as gay
As in the battle brave
Goes to the rout, the ball, the play,
With one leg in the grave.

The first Marquess would have enjoyed the joke. He told the surgeon as he was in the act of cutting off the limb: 'I have had a pretty long run. I have been a beau these forty-seven years and it would not be fair to cut the young men out any longer.'

A third memorial to the Marquess was perhaps the most useful. He designed the first articulated artificial leg, which is now an exhibit in the Waterloo Museum at his home nearby, Plas Newydd. The house, which is said to be the most comfortable stately home in Britain, and the magnificent strait-side gardens are now owned by the National Trust.

In the dining-room at Plas Newydd is a *trompe d'oeil* mural by Rex Whistler, a frequent visitor before his death in action in World War II. Many of his theatrical designs and sketches are on display in the house. The present Marquess lives in a flat at the top of the house, which he aptly describes as 'living on the howdah while someone else feeds the white elephant'.

Llanfairpwllgwyngyllgogerychwyrndrobwyllllantysiliogogo-goch has the curious distinction of being the village with the longest name in the world. For many years its only practical value was to vandals who stole the destination sign from the railway station so often that it was moved to the museum at Penrhyn Castle, where it can still be seen.

In fact, the name is a Victorian invention with a commercial purpose. A Menai Bridge tailor suggested it when the railway came to Anglesey. He thought it would attract visitors. (What the locals felt about the change from the original and lovely name of the village, Llanfairpwllgwyngyll, may be fairly judged by the fact that it is still called by them Llanfairpwll.) The tailor did well out of the idea. He sold in his shops an envelope which was said to contain a cure for lockjaw. The cure was a slip of paper on which the name of the village was printed. In the century or more that followed, it was about the only imaginative attempt to amuse the tourists who were lured to get off the trains there. Until quite recently the village was nothing more than a ribbon of houses on the A5. In the past decade, however, since the departure of British Rail from the station site, there have been some attempts to make the village attractive to the rather bemused visitors for whom it has certainly been better to journey hopefully than arrive disappointed. A proposal to demolish the station, which was the only tourist attraction, and rebuild it in America came to nothing, and in 1985 villagers lost patience with entrepreneurs and formed a co-operative to buy the station themselves.

The village does have one enduring claim to fame of more substance and importance than its name. It was in Llanfairpwll that the first Women's Institute was founded in 1915, in a tin hut which can still be seen next to Telford's tollhouse.

Two people share the distinction for the establishment of the Llanfairpwll WI. One was Colonel Stapleton Cotton, a relative of the Marquess of Anglesey, who came to live at Llwyn Onn on the Plas Newydd estate after being wounded and paralysed in the Zulu war. He was a 'do-gooder' in the best sense. He founded a bacon factory, a bulb farm and an egg-processing factory all within Llanfairpwll. The other was a Mrs Watt, a Canadian lady who had seen the work of the Canadian Women's Institute and wanted to start one up in Britain. She tried and failed in England but later spoke about the Canadian group at a meeting of the Agricultural Organization Society in London, of which Colonel Stapleton Cotton was a member. After hearing her speech, Colonel Cotton asked if she would address a meeting in Bangor at the University College of North Wales. She did so in June 1915, and the following day the Colonel called a meeting of the ladies of Llanfairpwll, and Britain's first WI was formed. This first meeting was held at Graig, by permission of W.E. Jones, on Wednesday 15

The Penrhos Nature Reserve at Holyhead has the finest collection of owls in Europe. Local birds, like this barn owl on a cromlech on the reserve, also find love and care. All kinds of rare birds, including peregrine falcons like the one opposite can be seen on the reserve

June. After that, things spiralled quickly, and seventy years later there are almost nine thousand Women's Institutes in Great Britain.

The pleasures of Anglesey are contemplative – long walks over dune country, the two nature reserves at Abermenai and Newborough Warren, rambles down the aisles of the green cathedrals of the Forestry Commission. It is a landscape painted in a simple wash of blue skies, golden sand and green meadowland. The cottages are long and low and, for the most part, unobtrusively grey – or, at their most celebratory, whitewashed. Colour is provided by wild flowers in the hedgerows, the meadows and the small copses that are all that remains of Anglesey's primeval woodland. In early spring they are alight with snowdrops; then come daffodils and bluebells.

Orchids drift on the nature reserves, viper's bugloss lives up raucously to its name; there are swathes of valerian, a profusion of cowslips, rare elsewhere; wild roses and fuchsia, drifts of elder, explosions of scarlet berries from the mountain ash. Visit Anglesey and you will carry a bouquet in your mind for the rest of your life. The flowers bring butterflies in a profusion exceeded only on the Lleyn. And birds. Firstly, in February, the ravens searching for nest-building sites; in March shelduck gather, and oyster-catchers; the ringed plover are visible, and balletic flocks of turnstones mime their names in the rock pools. There are redshank on the bird tables; advance parties of guillemots arrive. April is nest-building time. Wheatears in empty rabbit burrows, rock pipits in the rocks, wrens in the ivy of tumble-down cottages. In late spring the high flyers arrive, the terns with wings like scimitar blades, including the rare roseates, followed by the martins, the swallows and miraculous swifts.

Anglesey is the best place to study owls. In the wild and in captivity too. At the Nature Reserve at Penrhos, Holyhead, the director, Ken Williams, has assembled the finest collection of owls in Europe, a think-tank in the trees, all egos and outraged dignity. Most rare avian visitors to Anglesey end up at the Nature Reserve, either in the casualty wards of the wildlife hospital or merely brought there by some nature-lover who has found them exhausted or injured, like the Greenland falcon which survived the crossing of vast oceans only to be shot by a wildfowler when it reached the safety of Anglesey. A sacred ibis once flew into the reserve, which has also given a home to pink flamingoes, peregrine falcons, even displaced badgers.

Williams is a rare character. A former village policeman, son and grandson of village policemen, he was a regular soldier, a sergeant in the Prince of Wales company of the Welsh Guards. And he makes no secret of the fact that he blackmailed an executive of Anglesey Aluminium into handing over the former Stanley sporting estate as a nature reserve. It was a case of 'Take me to your leaders or I'll get you with a motoring offence.' The meeting fixed, Ken sat up all night in his village police station at Trearddur Bay drawing up plans for a reserve to be presented next day to a board meeting of Rio Tinto, the owners of the smelter. It is part of island legend that PC Williams lectured these very tough tycoons with his cycle clips still circling his uniform trousers. The board agreed to his plans, gave him the land he wanted and in doing so won a public relations victory that a massive and expensive publicity campaign could never have given them. The reserve which Ken created, aided by his wife Chris, the daughter of a well-to-do Nairobi family, has been showered with awards and is one of the biggest tourist attractions on the island.

A frequent visitor to the reserve before his death was Charles Tunnicliffe, thought by many to be the best bird-painter of his generation. Tunnicliffe lived in a wide-windowed house overlooking Malltraeth Bay and the Cefni marshes, where the Vikings sailed their longships up river and where, in the eighteenth and nineteenth centuries, though it is difficult to believe it now of these acres of birdsong and marsh iris, there was once a busy shipbuilding industry.

The Malltraeth Cob was intended to do on a smaller scale what Madocks did on a much larger one at Porthmadog. The first embankment was started in 1788. It was made of furze faggots bound with cordage, covered with sand and turves on the land

Once a keeper's cottage, this is now the headquarters and warden's
home at Penrhos

side and on the seaward side a stone pavement. It was to be fifteen
hundred yards long, fifty yards wide on the base, four yards wide
at the summit and five yards high. Work was abandoned in 1796
when it was nearly complete after an unusually high tide
breached it, and it was not recommenced until 1811. The total
cost, £50,000, seems now to island dog-walkers a small price to
pay for a walk which combines the maximum exercise for the
animal with the minimum of exertion for the owner, whilst at the
same time giving unrivalled views in turn of mountain, sea, forest
and meadowland.

Holyhead, the last frontier of Rome, was for a while the mecca
for Irish shoppers who crowd the town since goods are so much
cheaper on Anglesey than in Eire that their savings on shopping
more than meet the cost of their trip. There was another
inducement. By an inspired piece of public relations on the part of
the ferry service, Sealink off-season travellers received a litre of
spirits free. Unfortunately, mean-spirited Irish bureaucrats have
insisted that their fellow-countrymen pay a £5 tourist tax for the
privilege of leaving their own country, and the trade has
diminished as a result.

The glories of Holyhead are the caverns of North Stack,
including Parliament House, so named because of 'the

disagreeable gabbling noise', though in this case it is made by sea birds. On South Stack a delightful castellated folly, Elin's Tower, has been converted into a nature museum and bird observatory. At the foot of the cliffs is the lighthouse which functioned until 1985, when it was closed by Trinity House and replaced with an automatic light. A precipitous stairway down to the lighthouse, carved in the rock, provides admirable watching-points to observe fulmars, razorbills and the improbable puffins. It is a good place, too, for spotting the grey seal. The west coast of Gwynedd gives a summer home to most of the world's population of grey seals.

The sea-bird population has two major enemies, climbers who smash nesting sites, ignoring guidelines laid down by the British Mountaineering Council, and marine pollution. Twice in 1969 there were tragedies from which the population of auks has not yet recovered. In March of that year five thousand auks died when six hundred tons of oil spilled into the water after a collision at sea. Another ten thousand dead birds were washed ashore later in the same year, killed by an unknown cause believed to be pollution from the paint and plastics industry.

Beaumaris is considered by its inhabitants to be the rightful capital of Anglesey. It is certainly the island's most stylish town. It maintains the tradition of robed mayor and corporation, and its impressive civic regalia can be seen in the town hall. At the Bull's Head Charles Dickens stayed, and Dr Johnson. It was the headquarters of the Roundheads in the Civil War and still maintains high traditions of hospitality with splendid beer and food served under the eye of its formidable owner, Mrs Dorothy Barnett.

Beaumaris has always been popular with visitors. The graceful Victorian terrace on the sea front was designed by Joseph Hansom, who also designed the Hansom cab; the old county hall contains a perfectly preserved Jacobean court room, still in regular use. The local opinion of lawyers over the years can be judged by a small plaster relief over the fireplace in the magistrates' retiring-room: it shows one farmer tugging the horns of a cow and a second farmer pulling its tail; between them, milking the animal, is a solicitor.

A surprising tourist attraction is Beaumaris Gaol, which has the only working treadmill left in Britain, and a whipping-room. Prisoners were hanged by walking them out of a second-floor room through a door which opened onto the air and left them dangling from a gibbet over the street below. Spectators could pay 6d each for a space in the flowerbeds of the gardens opposite to get a good view of the execution. When it was opened, in 1829, the gaol was seen as a great humanitarian step forward. Life inside the prison and workhouse was better than it was outside. Regular meals and plenty of work. In the ceiling of the women's workroom are a series of slots. Strings were attached to the cots of the babies in the nursery above and run through the slots to the work benches below. When a baby cried, the string was pulled by its mother, the cot rocked and the baby went back to sleep. In its day this was the height of benevolence.

Beaumaris retains a Jane Austen quality even in the twentieth century, when its streets are thronged. In the early nineteenth century, when the Reverend Thomas Roscoe visited the town, it was already a fashionable bathing place:

> When I was contemplating the motley group that sauntered away the morning on what is called the Green I turned to the waiter at one of the hotels. 'Why, see,' he said, 'this is the place where the reg'lars, as we call 'em, and the Short Allowance Gentlemen turn out ... The party before you taking so many strides as if, like the Colonel, they were walking for a wager, are the reg'lars who pay by the week for all the meals the day will offer and they are preparing themselves for the bell that will ring them at two o'clock to the dinner table. The Short Allowance Gentlemen, on the contrary, are those who pay for every separate meal which they take. These you will find, at this hour, earnestly contemplating Puffin Island as if they had just discovered some new beauties in the place and had no leisure left for eating on purpose that they may let the morning breakfast hold out till supper time.'

The journey made by Gras-y-Garth, an elderly lady ferry-boat keeper of Beaumaris, was out of the ordinary. When she was over sixty, she still worked the Beaumaris ferry. She was a short, thickset woman and the finest oar on the coast. In 1797 in a wild storm her ferry boat broke its moorings and was carried across the bay to Liverpool. When she heard where it had made landfall, Gras-y-Garth set off and walked the sixty miles to claim it. What is more, she rowed the seventeen-foot boat with only a single man to spell her through rough seas back across the bay to Garth Point on Anglesey.

Many, no doubt, spent the hungry hours contemplating the castle, which, at that time, was a romantic ruin. This, the last of Edward's eight Welsh castles, now considerably restored, came nearest to perfection in its design.

Across the straits from Anglesey is Bangor, the guardian of

The Castle Hotel remains but shops and offices have taken the place of the Albion Hotel, shown in this delightful drawing of a nineteenth-century market in Bangor

Snowdonia and a city of considerable antiquity. There was a flourishing monastery in Bangor in the sixth century, and the tomb of Owain Gwynedd, Prince of Wales, can be seen in the cathedral of St Deiniol, who founded the bishopric. The first cathedral and city – it was then called 'Y Cae Onn', 'the Ash Enclosure' – was destroyed by the Normans in 1071. In 1212 the cathedral was destroyed for a second time by King John, who took the bishop hostage. After the building was once again gutted by Owain Glyndwr, it lay in ruins for sixty years before it was rebuilt by two men, Bishop Harry Dean and his dean Richard Kyffin who, as rector of Llanddwyn island, gave counsel and aid to the Tudors as they prepared for the battle with Richard III. The unfortunate building was not even safe when it was being rebuilt. During one restoration the cathedral bells were stolen. The thief was struck blind on his way to the shore to watch the bells being loaded for shipment abroad. Finally it was restored in 1866 by Sir Gilbert Scott.

The Friars School in Bangor, where many famous men have been educated, is built on land granted to the Black Friars in 1277. When their house was burned down in 1552, the first Friars School was endowed. Bangor is a town of pleasant secrets. The gardens of the BBC offices were laid down in the days when the studios were a private house by its owner, a sea captain, and contain rare shrubs from all over the world. The city museum houses a remarkable collection of medieval woodcarvings, including a very rare example of a figure of St Uncumber, the only lady saint with a beard. Her true name is St Wilgefortis, and she grew the beard for the usual saintly reason, to discourage a suitor, in this case the King of Sicily. In England she was called Uncumber by wives who believed she would help them get rid of unwanted husbands. It made Sir Thomas More very cross. He was puzzled that the women attempted to bribe the saint's effigy with gifts of oats: '... whereof I cannot perceive the reason, but if it be because she should provide a horse for an evil husband to ride to the devil upon ... insomuch that women have therefore changed her name and instead of St Wilgefortis call her Saint Uncumber because they reckon for a peck of oats she will not fail to uncumber them of their husbands'. How this patron saint of feminists came to Bangor I have not been able to discover. Sheer luck, for it is a splendid, vigorous piece of carving of the German school.

Since it was 'discovered' by painters and poets of the Back to Nature movement in the eighteenth century, everyone has seen Snowdon through different eyes. To Dr Johnson it merely offered a diversion for the Thrales' appalling ten-year-old daughter, Queenie. Her father gave her a penny for every goat she counted grazing on the slopes of Snowdon. She counted 149. Of Snowdon itself, Dr Johnson, for whom all pleasure was centred in London, merely wrote: 'On the side of Snowdon are the remains of a large fort, to which we climbed with great labour.'

Others have been more impressed. Wordsworth was inspired to write some of his worst poetry by the prospect of Snowdon.

In one of these excursions (may they never fade from the remembrance)
Through the Northern Tracts
Of Cambria ranging with a youthful friend
I left Bethgelert's huts at couching time
And westward took my way to see the sun
Rise to the top of Snowdon
To the door
Of a rude cottage at the mountain's base we came
And raised the shepherd who attends
The adventurous strangers' steps, a trusty guide:
Then cheered by short refreshment sallied forth ....

The orientalist Elizabeth Smith, who climbed Snowdon in 1798, put it better. In her day it was fashionable to begin the climb at night and reach the summit just as dawn was breaking. Alone of her party Miss Smith finished the climb: 'I look up and see the upper part illuminated by a beautiful rose coloured light, while the opposite part still casts a dark shade over its base and conceals the sun from my view ... I arrived at the highest peak at a quarter past four and saw a view of which it is impossible to form an idea from description. For many miles around it was composed of tops of mountains of all the various forms that can be imagined: some appeared swimming in an ocean of vapour: on others the clouds sat like a cap of snow appearing as soft as down.'

The prospect did not always please. The Reverend Mr Roscoe wrote of his climb to the peak of Snowdon in bad weather: 'I saw the heavy mist rolling in volumes along the sides and summits of the hills and at times sweeping round and below us, producing the appearance of being enveloped in clouds. The prospect at that moment was bleak and wild in the extreme: and the sudden gusts, rushing at intervals through the glens and hollows producing a strange unearthly sound, mingling with the distant blasting of the mines and the cry of the ravens over our heads.'

In his book *Beauties, Harmonies and Sublimities of Nature*, the nineteenth-century travel-writer Nathaniel Bucke was quite carried away by the distant prospect: 'The four kingdoms one sees at once: Wales, England, Scotland and Ireland ... we take in these regions from the triple crown of Cader Idris to the sterile crags of Carnedds David and Llewelyn. Snowdon, rising in the centre, appears as if he could touch the south with his right hand and the north with his left.'

The mountains still continue to exert their pull. Every fine day they are festooned with climbers in highly coloured anoraks dangling from the crags like cheap Rasta beads indifferently strung; the pubs in Bethesda ring to tales so tall you would need pitons to climb them. Not a month, scarcely a week, passes without some tragedy on the slopes. The clatter of the rotor blades of the rescue helicopter has become, with the sound of the lawnmower, part of the summer litany of Gwynedd. One of the busiest cafés in the country is the one on the summit of Snowdon where, perversely, there was until recently a notice banning rucksacks. The day of the vast solitudes, in Snowdon anyway, is over.

In Conwy the curse is the motor car. Held up by the problems of laying a tunnel on the shifting estuary sands, all the traffic on the four-lane highway of the Expressway now squeezes through the town's narrow medieval gateway. A journey from Anglesey to Llandudno that takes half an hour in early spring becomes a $2\frac{1}{2}$ hour nightmare in high summer. The temptation to linger in Conwy, a gem of a walled town, is easy to resist when the town is choked with motor cars. And yet I confess to a *tendresse* for Conwy. It's a two-street town, and if it is not quite true to say that it is the only town remaining in Britain completely encircled by its medieval walls, nor wholly true to say that those walls are built in the shape of a Welsh harp, it is near enough true for me to believe it. Purists scoff at the cinema in the main street with arrow-slits where other cinemas have windows. I warm to the unknown architect who thought of that pleasant conceit. The nineteenth-century Castle Hotel is self-consciously Jacobean but I see nothing wrong in that. It boasts an elegant, neo-Georgian bar, and there is a charming tale in the pictures painted on the foyer panelling by an impecunious member of the Royal Cambrian Academy of Art in return for board and lodgings. The last painting is unfinished because he came into an unexpected legacy, dropped his brushes to celebrate and never took them up again. Across the main street is Plas Mawr, a stately terraced house which is just the house I would like to live in with its walled gardens and picture galleries.

Whenever I go to Conwy, I remember the philosophy of one of the classic gardeners of Japan. His name was Rikyu, and in the sixteenth century he designed a garden overlooking the sea. When his friends saw it, they were dismayed to find that the view of the sea was obstructed by a row of evergreens. It was only when they walked over the stepping-stones across a stream which led to the tea-room and stooped to rinse their hands in a stone water basin that they discovered the secret of the garden. As they raised their heads from the basin, they saw the distant sea shimmering through the trees and became aware that the whole garden was designed to be seen from this one unexpected place. As with Rikyu's garden in Sakai, so with Conwy. In the watchtower at the top of Plas Mawr there are small windows. Each one frames a perfect view of the roofs of the town and the castle towers, and beyond them the fishing-boat-bobbing estuary; or perhaps a single seagull, motionless on an ancient chimney; a formidable fragment of the city wall.

Walk through the arch down to the quayside with the coiled ropes and lobster pots; at low tide the masts of the trawlers line the walls of the quay, gradually rising with the tide until you can walk onto their busy decks. Parenthetically you can buy fish, still sea-wet, from a trolley on the quay. It is perhaps typical of the sturdy individuality of the town that the owner still deals in pounds and shillings and refuses to follow the rest of the country round the maze of metrication. At the other end of the quay is the smallest house in Britain where you will be welcomed by Margaret Williams, the biographer of Conwy's ghosts, not a whit incongruous in her tall Welsh steeple hat and traditional dress. Or buy a pint in the Liverpool Arms, where travellers on the packet boats from Liverpool once broke their journey. Take it to one of the benches thoughtfully provided under the town wall and admire on a summer's evening the silvered sea studded with small boats and sometimes large, stylish sea-going yachts. Take a pleasure boat yourself at the end of the jetty. Sail under the bridges and up the estuary, then look back at the castle on the shore under the wooded hill where once Glyndwr's men lay and waited for the English garrison to march out to church. There were markets then in the town, and there still are under bright cloth awnings. And when you are tired of the town there is still the Conwy Valley to explore.

To the right as you make your way up the valley are the peaks of Snowdonia, to the left the gentler border lands of the old county of Denbighshire, now forever Clwyd. On this river road the Romans marched into their fortress at Conovium, the halfway station between Bodfair in the Vale of Clwyd and their journey's end at Caernarfon. Conovium is a village now, Caerhun, but you can see fragments of the fort and the belongings the Romans left behind at the admirable little Rapallo Museum in Llandudno.

The valley lands between here and Llanrwst are richly meadowed and wooded. Outside the high summer season the roads are quiet and comparatively little travelled except by local folk about their rural business. It is sheep country mostly, dressed with coppices of oak, until you reach Maenan Abbey, a fishing hotel now on the outskirts of Llanrwst, where Edward II received the homage of the Bishop of Bangor.

Llanrwst was once the wool market of Wales and famous for its harp-makers. The river bridge here was designed by a son of the town, Inigo Jones, who may also have designed the magnificent mortuary chapel of the Wynne family behind the parish church on the river bank. In later years Llanrwst was most famous for its proximity to the fashionable spa of Trefriw, a quiet enough place but once thronged with the quality taking its mineral waters.

Beyond Llanrwst on the Betws road is Gwydir Castle – sold in recent years on the strength of a talk I gave on *Woman's Hour* – where Queen Elizabeth Tudor and Charles I both stayed. Though much restored, enough of the castle still remains to repay a visit. It was once the home of wicked old Sir John Wynne, whose spirit, you will recall, is imprisoned under the Swallow Falls 'to be purged, punished and spouted upon and purified from the foul deeds done in his days of nature'. That always seems to me to be hard on the man who left us a delightfully vain account of his genealogy which contains yet another example of the bad verse which Wales so often inspires. Sir John wrote of the devastating march of an earl of Pembroke:

In Harddlech and Dinbech every house
Was basely set on fire.
But poor Nany Conwy suffered more
For there the flames burnt higher.
'Twas in the year of our Lord
Fourteen hundred and sixty eight
That these unhappy towns of Wales
Met with such wretched fate.

Betws-y-Coed, with its Swallow Falls and Faery Glen, has been a place of tourist resort since the nineteenth century. It was an angler's paradise. At the time of writing this peaceful – except in high summer – place is the centre of angry controversy. The Wales Water Board wish to build a salmon ladder on the falls; the conservationists claim it will ruin a prime beauty spot. Curmudgeons like myself believe that, like almost every other beauty spot, it has already been ruined by the motor car and only visit it in the winter.

In the days before the internal combustion engine the area was very popular with watercolourists, notably David Cox, who for ten years from 1844 spent his holidays in the town. The signboard he painted for the Royal Oak now hangs inside the hotel, together with more of his watercolours.

This is a shamelessly subjective book, proudly partial. A ninety-thousand-word, love-letter to the county I believe to be the most glorious on the planet. And nowhere is it lovelier than the valley of the Mawddach estuary between Barmouth and Dolgellau. Barmouth is rather lovable than lovely: a jumble of gloomy granite and screaming plastic; rumbustious as befits a town which has been a port since the Middle Ages. The architecture is a mixture of the brash and the grimly condescending, as though a coachload of Blackpool shops and fun-fairs had arrived for a day out in a genteel Edwardian resort.

Barmouth does not prepare you at all for the beauties of the drive to Dolgellau. Even motoring along the estuary in the lowering summer of 1985, when the only change in the weather seemed from vertical rain to horizontal and the estuary was the colour of polished lead, it was haunting. Islands in its stream and on the far bank, its crags coming almost to the water's edge, Cader Idris. Above the road the wooded lower slopes of Snowdonia where rain-washed rocks the colour of lionskin glowed in patches through the trees. On brighter days the car would have been abandoned to take the New Precipice Walk through Farcllynys Woodland. Instead we motored across the Mawddach by the toll bridge at Penmaenpool and into Dolgellau, largely rebuilt in the nineteenth century for well-to-do English tourists who came to climb Cader Idris.

In parts Dolgellau is provokingly un-Welsh. Its hotels are built on neo-Georgian principles; the *patois* owes as much to Merseyside as Mawddach. Even on a wet day the place was a-bustle with tourists but I never came across waitresses more civil, nor car-park attendants and tourist information officers either for that matter. It is a measure of the town's amiability that dogs are allowed in most of the hotels. It is a place of lanes and secret cul-de-sacs more Cotswold than Cymru. The Royal Ship Hotel sails the middle of the main street, parting the roadway, whilst behind it, decked with flowers, is the Golden Lion Royal, which in its working days as a coaching inn, before royalty stayed there, was called simply Plas Isa.

Before the tourists came, Dolgellau's principal occupation was weaving flannel cloth, and remains of fulling mills can be seen along the banks of the River Aran, but the nineteenth-century developers' names for the streets fall awkwardly on Welsh ears: Baker Street, Finsbury Square, Smithfield Street and Lombard Street, Eldon Square and Meyrick Square, unlikely London imports to a county town which enthusiastically returned the Nationalist MP Dafydd Elis Thomas.

There was a time when Dolgellau rivalled Conwy for its traffic jams. Happily bypassed, it is now a town to stroll in and take your time. It was once the junction of the three Roman military roads. More peacefully it boasts the oldest cricket team in Wales, founded in 1841 by Frederick Temple who became Archbishop of Canterbury.

Two miles outside the town is Nannau, at seven hundred feet up the mountainside the highest stately home in Britain. It was once the home of Hywel Sele, a kinsman, but deadly enemy, of Owain Glyndwr, who is said to have murdered him and stuffed his body into a hollow tree.

Also near Dolgellau is Llangareth, the boyhood home of Tristan Jones, a best-selling author now and one of the most remarkable maritime adventurers Wales has produced for centuries. Jones was born at sea, fittingly. His father was a Merchant Navy skipper, and his ship was lying off Tristan da Cunha. Jones went back to sea when he was thirteen as a deckhand on a sailing barge, and he has been sea-going ever since. When he was sixteen, at the outbreak of World War II, he signed on for twelve years with the Royal Navy and suffered the terrors of HMS *Ganges*, the Royal Navy's savage training-school for boys. He had three ships torpedoed under him before he was eighteen. After the war he transferred to the Royal Hydrographic Service. In 1952 an inshore survey vessel on which he was serving was blown up in Aden by terrorists, and he suffered a severe spinal injury which left him paralysed. He was discharged and told he would never walk again.

Since that time Jones has sailed 345,000 miles in boats under forty feet in length, 180,000 miles of that single-handed, crossing the Atlantic eighteen times under sail, nine times alone. On one voyage he dragged his boat across a hundred-mile desert. In 1984 he wrote what will unquestionably be among the classic books on naval warfare. *Hearts of Oak* tells graphically the story of the war from the lower deck which makes it almost unique since most of the stories of war at sea are written by officers.

Jones now lives in Key West, San Diego, but when I talked to him for a radio programme he still remained heart and soul a Gwynedd man. It is fair to say that his adventurous life has not done much for his health but it has fostered a magnificent spirit.

Gwynedd is a county caught in water. Its northern frontier is the Conwy, its western the sea and in the south the Dyfi. The road from Dolgellau to Machynlleth, which stands at the head of the Dyfi estuary, skirts Cader Idris and runs through more spectacular valley land down the Tal-y-Llyn pass through Abergynolwyn, where you can see scratched in the parapet to the bridge the fish that a village policeman poached. And so on to Machynlleth, preferably on Wednesday, which is market day.

In the Scottish highlands the scenery is interminable. Climb one mountain and another lies smugly behind it. To motor down the Great Glen is to ramble with a companion who is at first engrossing but finally, by endless repetition, becomes a bore. Welsh scenery has better manners: it knows when to change the subject. Tire of the mountains in Gwynedd and you are offered 291 miles of beach and rocky coastline. Leave the coast and you can wander by forest and farmland. Within the frontiers of the

county is a microcosm of British scenery. Over sixty per cent of
Gwynedd is either a National Park or a designated area of
outstanding beauty. There are ninety miles of heritage coast.

The Snowdonia National Park of 817 square miles is smaller
than the English Lake District but it stretches from the Dyfi
estuary to Conwy and takes in every imaginable landscape. Its
highest mountain peak, yr Wyddfa, Snowdon's summit, is 3,560
feet. It dominates the county. On a clear day you can see as far as
Blackpool Tower in the north, and in the west the Isle of Man and
the Wicklow Hills of Eire. It has been unkindly said that Anglesey
is a platform from which to view the beauty of Merioneth. Living,
as I do, on the edge of the island is like having a private art gallery
– one so greatly appreciated that a proposal to build a toilet in the
village, which some feared might have obscured the view, split
the community; for years living there was like having a walk-on
part in *Clochemerle*.

Happily the view has not been spoiled. You can still sit on a
bench at the foot of the village and watch the mountain landscape
paintings change before your eyes. Wreathed, instantly it
sometimes seems, with mist, the peaks are brushed in ink against
a rice-paper sky in the finest Chinese classical tradition, with the
disembodied crags floating high over the strait; on October
afternoons, flooded with sunset, the strait is bright gold, and
Caernarfon Castle becomes an illumination from a Book of
Hours. In spring, in the gem light of May, the mountains seem so
near that you could reach out and touch them; you can make out
the line of the stone walls and the brush dots of sheep, the thin
smoke signal of the Snowdon Railway running across the
mountain's high shoulder. Pure David Cox. Every day the
mountains maintain the truth of Oscar Wilde's maxim that nature
mirrors art. Even in the winter the mountain towns, their black
slate roofs shiny with rain, might have been painted in the night
by Utrillo.

Drive from the Conwy Valley, the fish-filled frontier of
Gwynedd, down the A55, with the mountains to your left and a
wild sea on your right, to Penrhyn Castle and then up Telford's
other mighty road, the A5, which strikes like a dagger into the
heart of the mountains. Past Ogwen Lake, between the jagged
rocks of Tryfan and Carnedd Dafydd, and down the Nant
Ffrancon pass to Capel Curig with the Llugwy river singing at
your feet. At Capel Curig leave the A5 to make its way to
Betws-y-Coed and take the quieter road to Beddgelert. At the side
of the road is a viewing-platform from which you can pay your
respects to the old gods of Snowdonia and then look down on the

This ornate eighteenth-century garden house, once a pin-mill, is now part of the National Trust Bodnant Gardens

Twilight at Mynydd Mawr from the banks of Llyn Cwellyn, Nant-y-Betws

Part of the mysterious land of Ardudwy: the Roman steps cross a tributary of the River Artro before crossing the mountains from Harlech to Bala. Roman, medieval or eighteenth century – you take your climbing pick and choose

panorama of lake and ancient woodlands which surround the 'Town of the Hound'. In summer Beddgelert is a noisy crossing of roads and shouting water but it contains some of the best salmon- and trout-fishing in Wales. Beyond it again more woods and water and hidden mountain walks. Your companion now is the River Glaslyn, which chatters at your side until abruptly the mountains end and you are in another country of rich pasture and a horizon of salt flats.

From Porthmadog, cross Madocks' toll road, skirt the flat morfa to Harlech. The sea used to wash the foot of the crag on which the castle stands like a stag at bay, for me the most dramatic castle in the world. Llywelyn's banqueting hall was brought here and rebuilt, Owain Glyndwr ruled here in his power. Even now it reeks of war, though it guards only the Snowdon National Park. From Harlech the road goes down the coast to Barmouth.

Bala is gently, satisfyingly Welsh. For many farming families in the hills around it is still a metropolis. Pride of place glows in the faces of the helpful staff in the Tourist Information centre. Unusually for Wales, it is a town of statues and plaques, though not always welcomed with reverence. When the statue of Thomas Edward Ellis, Victorian MP for Merioneth, was erected after his death in 1899 a shopkeeper commented: 'Dunno why he's getting a statue. Does all his shopping in Liverpool.' Much of the land is owned by the Duke of Westminster, of whom a farmer said to me in the bar of the White Lion Royal: 'Rich? Got his own bank, man.'

A second statue commemorates Thomas Charles, the founder of the Sunday School Movement in Wales and of the British and Foreign Bible Society. There is a plaque on the birthplace of John Puleston Jones, a blind evangelist; another recalls the thirty-mile walk to buy a Bible made by Mary Jones of Llanfihangel.

As we have seen, Bala men have founded lasting institutions. The South American colony of Patagonia; Sunday schools in Wales, the Foreign Bible Society and the first Baptist college owe their inception to Bala ministers; the first-ever sheepdog trials were held nearby. Since the World Slalom and Wild Water Racing Championships were held there in 1981, the town has become a venue for many international events. On the site where the slalom championships were held is now a National White Water Centre which controls access to a mile and a quarter of Tryweryn river. Eleven days a year, when there is a release of water from the dam of Lake Celyn, the stretch is reserved for competitive canoeing. On those occasions it is a blood-curdling

sight to watch the Tryweryn change in minutes from a
meandering stream to a raging torrent of white water navigable
only by the most skilful canoeists. For ordinary mortals there are
another 180 days a year when smaller releases of water make less
dramatic canoeing possible.

In the days before the Industrial Revolution, Bala, which is said
to produce the prettiest women in Wales, was the centre of the
Welsh woollen industry. The nineteenth-century rake Lord
Lyttleton described the pleasure he had watching the Bala girls
knitting in the sunshine on the slopes of the Bala Tump, the motte
of the castle that has long disappeared. Tourism is the main
industry now.

A drive over the Berwyns to Llanraedr-ym-Mochnant, the
birthplace of the Bible-translator Bishop Morgan, brings you to
one of the seven wonders of Wales, the 150-foot Pistyll Rhaeadr,
the highest waterfall in Wales. You can view Llyn Tegid (the
correct name for Lake Bala) from the railway which runs along
the route of the old Great Western Railway from Llanuwchllyn to
Bala. Or you may fish the lakes and rivers for trout and coarse fish
and, if you are very lucky, find the *gwyniad*, a blind, white game
fish which is found only here. For the more active there is sailing,
cycling, swimming and mountain walking, especially rewarding
in early summer when the white frog orchid abounds on the
hillsides.

Above all, Bala is water. The town stands on the shores of Llyn
Tegid, $4\frac{1}{2}$ miles long and reflecting in its waters the peaks of three
mountain groups – Berwyn to the south-east, Aran to the west
and Arennig to the north.

The militant Nationalists of the sixties committed the first acts
of violence and civil disobedience in Bala when the Tryweryn
valley was flooded, drowning the village of Capel Celyn to supply
Liverpool with water. At the time it was difficult to find many in
the valley who were not delighted to be leaving their insanitary
cottages for the new houses provided for them on the slopes, but
there was enormous local and national feeling against the
reservoir, largely due to Liverpool Corporation, which behaved
with a crassness that, even by the standards of Merseyside, was
epic, to the extent of having a spectacular opening ceremony and
a sumptuous banquet for the Liverpool councillors and their
wives. Predictably tempers rose and the opening ceremony was
wrecked by angry crowds.

The welcome is much warmer now to visitors. At Parc, near
Bala, is Cyffdy Farm, a delightfully informal place where visitors
can milk a cow, feed the pigs, ride a horse, fish for a guaranteed

catch of trout, watch chickens being hatched and handle, gently, of course, the young chicks. The views over the mountain ranges that encircle the farm are magnificent; the tea in the farmhouse kitchen is delicious. There were farmers at Cyffdy centuries before the Romans built their fort of Caer Gai and the wayside shrine to Hercules on the lakeside. The farm itself is mentioned in the Domesday Book, and the present building dates back to the sixteenth century.

It was hard for the families who farmed there. Cyffdy was a typical Gwynedd mountain holding, subsistence farming at its very toughest, for most of its life. It has 140 acres of enclosed fields with common grazing rights for ninety ewes, and open mountain rights, two miles from the farm two thousand feet up Arennig, for about 210 more. In winter the snowfall is well above average, and there are fifty-five inches of rain annually. Life is so hard there that lambs, selected every year as flock replacements, have to spend the first year of their life away from Cyffdy in the lowland. They need the time to make extra growth to withstand the harsh conditions of mountain grazing.

Bala is an ideal headquarters for a visit to Harlech and the tiny community of Llangelynin, hard against the shore in the foothills of Cader Idris, the gentle woodland of the Mawddach estuary, where a $4\frac{1}{2}$ miles nature trail follows the track of the the disused railway, and the five villages of Arthog, Fairbourne, Friog, Llwyngwril and Rhosleain.

Three miles north of Machynlleth, at Pantperthos, is the Centre for Alternative Technology, where a small group of committed people live and produce their own food and energy using natural resources. The exhibition is fascinating. Displays include thirty different ways of using solar energy, including solar electric cells and tracking parabolic reflectors, and a dozen varieties of high- and low-speed windmills, generating electricity. There is a cottage heated by solar energy, and a solar workshop. A thousand-foot solar roof warms a twenty-thousand-gallon interseasonal-heat stove in the exhibition hall. More electricity is generated from plants and trees using a wood-gas generator and a steam engine. For the less technically sophisticated conservationist, the Centre has an organic vegetable garden with interesting displays of composting, crop-rotation and growing food without any artificial aids.

Machynlleth persists in the claim that it has Owain Glyndwr's parliament house. It is true that Glyndwr's parliament was held in the town but the house which is shown and has recently been restored by the Wales Tourist Board was not built until a century after the death of the last native Prince of Wales.

David Llwyd, the poet and prophet, lived at Mathafarn, Llanwryn, in the hills above the town in the fifteenth century. Henry Tudor, Earl of Richmond, stayed with Llwyd on his way to the Battle of Bosworth where he defeated Richard III. David, who walked everywhere with a tame seagull on his shoulder which whispered prophecies, was asked by Henry to tell him the outcome of the battle. David was reluctant. 'Tell him he's going to win,' his wife advised. 'If he does, your fortune is made. If he loses, you will never see him again.' When the battle was over, Llwyd wrote a triumphal poem:

King Henry hath fought and bravely done.
Our friend the Golden Circle hath won.
The bards re-echo the gladsome strain
For the good of the world crooked R is slain.

In the years which followed Bosworth, the countryside round Llwyd's home was infested by a gang of outlaws, mostly ex-soldiers and their children. They were called 'the red-haired bandits of Mawddwy'. Most of the gang was captured on Christmas Eve 1554 by Lewis Owen, Sheriff of Merioneth, who hanged eighty on the spot. In the same place, a year later on All Hallows Eve, Owen was ambushed as he was returning from Montgomery Assizes and was killed by the surviving bandits, who washed their hands in his blood as he lay dying from thirty wounds.

This was always a wild country. The church of Llan-y-Mawddwy was founded by St Tydecho who lived on a very short fuse. When Prince Cynan of Powys kidnapped his sister, Tydecho struck him blind. Yet no girl was safe on Tydecho's lands, the only district exempt from the law of Hywel Dda that ravishers of young girls must pay a heavy fine.

Nowadays this part of Gwynedd is more famous as a prime place for game fishing. The Dyfi is legendary, but there are smaller rivers like the Dysynni and hundreds of tiny mountain streams which are the home of delicious brook trout, and Barmouth is becoming more popular every year with sea anglers.

Bill Tillman, the founder of the Three Peaks Race, lived in Barmouth. Every year in June yachts from all over the country, indeed from all over the world, assemble in this small seaside town for a sailing, running and climbing race that makes heavy demands on skills and fitness. The yachts sail from Barmouth up to Caernarfon, where runners, picked from the crews, race, usually in the middle of the night, through the streets of the town, up and down Snowdon, back to the yachts, then on to Cumbria to run up and down Scafell Pike and finally to Scotland to do the same on Ben Nevis. Amazingly it takes them only two or three days to complete the course, and prizes are modest. In the true spirit of its founder, it is still a race where sportsmanship is paramount, though these days the teams are getting more and more professional. Tillman envisaged an ordinary member of the crew taking on the running but nowadays there are strict demarcations between 'runners' and 'yachtsmen'. But then Tillman was an exceptional man. He did not take up sailing until he reached his fifties. He disappeared on a long voyage to the Arctic, some think deliberately.

Cader Idris gets its name from Idris the Giant who was celebrated as the bard who invented the harp. It is said that anyone who spends a night in his stone chair, a cleft rock on the peak, will next morning be either a poet or a madman. Daniel Defoe said that because of the impassable mountains there was a saying that the devil lives in the middle of Wales.

No wonder some prefer quiet contemplation by Tal-y-Llyn, the lovely lake at the mountain's foot. Others are more active. The poet Samuel Coleridge climbed Cader Idris in 1794. His companion, Joseph Hucks, wrote: 'Six hundred feet of steep rock, covered, indeed, with short grass, but so slippery as to render the footing very insecure. As we approached the top, the ascent became more abrupt, whilst the scene below us, of craggy rocks, perpendicular precipices and an unfathomable lake did not operate to lessen the alarm that a person, unaccustomed to so dangerous a situation naturally feels ...' Their guide was unconcerned. Wrote Hucks: 'He decanted on the beauties of Cader Idris, the excellence of its mutton and the delicacy of its trout as if he had still been in the public house in which we found him.' But it was all worthwhile. The poets reached the peak, where '... the vast unbounded prospect lay beneath us, unobscured by cloud, vapour or any other interruption to the astonished and delighted eye.'

The Conwy valley is a feast for the heart, from the magnificence of the castle at Conwy to the delightful Inigo Jones bridge and the Gothic chapel of the Wynnes at Llanwrst. Among the happiest of holiday occupations is watching other people at work, a miller grinding corn at Llansantffraid, Glan Conwy, or weavers at work in the woollen mill in the former spa village of Trefriw.

These, then, are the jewels in the crown of Gwynedd, and there is none more glittering than Bodnant Gardens, at the mouth of the Conwy Valley, only a few miles from the town itself and signposted by the National Trust with understandable enthusiasm. The gardens were created in a happy moment by a Victorian builder, Henry Pochin, who bought the house and estate in 1875. His gardening plans were modest, though he created one feature of surpassing beauty. It is the long tunnel of golden laburnum which in early June draws visitors from all over the world. His grandson, the second Lord Aberconway, had more ambitious schemes. He and his descendants extended the gardens to the present eighty acres and created a magnificent series of terraced gardens below the house with, in one, a lily pond and, in another, an open-air stage with yews clipped *en brosse* to represent the wings and backcloth. At the other end of this terrace is the pin mill. Built in the eighteenth century as an Italianate garden house and later used as a factory for making pins, it once stood in Gloucestershire. The second Lord Aberconway bought it and rebuilt it at Bodnant.

The gardens are also a tribute to two remarkable gardeners, F.C. Puddle, who became the head gardener in 1920, and his son Charles, who succeeded him. The gardens they made with three generations of the Aberconway family are open from March, when flowering cherries, crabs and magnolias bloom over a carpet of daffodils, until October, when the mountain ash erupts. It is the heart of Gwynedd.

From the rose terrace, framed by trees, there is a view over the River Conwy to the mountains, Carnedd Llewelyn, Foel Fras, the Drum and Tal-y-Fan. From the pin mill a path, lined with flowering shrubs gathered from all over the world, goes down to the valley floor and the River Heraethlyn. There is a waterfall, in fact a Tudor millrace, and above it the millpond. Halfway across the bridge which passes over the falls is a seat. To rest there a while and repeat the *englyn* by the nineteenth-century poet Gwilym Cowlyd, 'The calm green lakes are sleeping in the mountain shadow, and on the water's canvas bright sunshine paints the picture of the day', is to brush the soul of Gwynedd.

• POSTSCRIPT •

The wildest and loveliest place in Gwynedd is a mountain pass called Drws Ardudwy, 'The Door of Ardudwy'. It is reached by climbing a stairway of massive slates and roughly levelled boulders called the Roman Steps which are cut in the side of a hill in the Rhinog range. The steps are not Roman but in the misty, fabulous land of Ardudwy which lies behind Harlech Castle nothing is quite what it seems.

There are many doors in Ardudwy and each one opens onto marvels. In Harlech an itinerant harpist, Barry Edwards, plays in the forecourt of the castle; Owen Glynne Davies tours cafés with his travelling marionette theatre; on the quay at Barmouth a tree surgeon turned fisherman, Frank Cocksey, carves sea monsters and mythic princesses from driftwood and yarns about Barmouth's own sea monsters.

Robert Graves, who lived there, wrote a poem 'Welsh Incident' about the Barmouth Sea Monster. But his 'un-Welsh, other worldly things' do exist. In 1974 a party of schoolgirls watched one saucer-shaped monster walking down the beach; fishermen in 1984 saw another in the sea just off Barmouth. From the description the schoolgirls gave, Cocksey carved an identikit monster. As a result he believes they are giant leather-backed turtles, strayed from the Gulf Stream which passes the Gwynedd coast. The tornadoes are another matter. In October 1985 a tornado came in off the sea, hit a Barmouth caravan park and lifted caravans a hundred feet in the air. The Meteorological Office said the tornado was part of Hurricane Gloria which devastated parts of the eastern coast of the USA before crossing the Atlantic. A year earlier there had been earthquakes in Gwynedd. But mostly it is a quiet and peaceful county and nowhere more so than in Cwm Bychan which lies at the foot of the Roman Steps and holds between the cupped crags of Ddrwg and Saeth a lake ringed by mountains, hedged by oaks, its shallows a green mist of reeds; a lake so Arthurian that any moment you expect Excalibur to break its surface.

Above all, this part of Wales is a place of walks. Outside Dolgellau is the Torrent Walk along the banks of the River Edog, two miles of tumbling, laughing water, rushing down a ravine cut into woodland filled with birds. The Precipice Walks, New and Old, and the Panorama Walk above the Mawddach Estuary look out over the estuary on the one side to Cader Idris; on the other to the Arans and Snowdonia.

For those who prefer walking in the hills to Hill Walking, a much more rigorous affair, there is a delightful riverside walk from Llanbedr to Nantcol. The mountain roads beyond the river are exhilarating without being precipitous, buzzards wheel over your head and if you cross a field as like as not you will put up partridge. The roads are little travelled, sheep-gated, with grass sprouting through the tarmac.

The problem of this magic land is not finding it, but leaving it. When I planned this book my wife and I decided to tour Gwynedd, researching as we went. We locked up our cottage on Anglesey and drove towards Harlech. After forty motoring miles we reached Talsarnau and a fourteenth-century manor house, Maes y Neuadd, once a stately home, now a comfortable hotel where the Kennedys stayed when they came for the funeral earlier in the year of their friend Lord Harlech. Ideal, we told each other, for an early dinner before we put some more miles beneath our wheels. The hotel is run by an architect, an accountant, a nurse and an engineer, June and Michael Slatter and Olive and Malcolm Horsfall. It stands in a park of fine, rolling lawns and behind it there is a wood made for wandering through. We were still wandering through it a week later. We had walked through one of the hidden doors of Ardudwy. Every morning we drove out to a different wonder, the cliff-hugging road to Aberdyfi, as un-Welsh as any of the Graves' sea monsters, with pretty painted houses and a local accent that owes more to western England than to Wales; we wandered round the castle at Harlech, took afternoon tea in a splendid Victorian conservatory in a cliff-edged garden overlooking the Harlech morfa; admired the miles of dry-stone walling that lies on the hills' breast like necklaces. We explored Barmouth, unpromising to pass through but a delight to wander in. We found the house where Darwin wrote the *Descent of Man* when he wasn't being tempted by the view of Cader. The small round house that served as the Barmouth lock-up for men who had descended further than the law allows. A perfect circle of a house built by some unknown local craftsman from the stones he had found in the fields and on the long seashore.

And in the golden October evening we drove back up the hidden valley by a riverside, past a tumble of white water that crashed down the mountainside to Maes y Neuadd where we dined sumptuously, slept soundly, and dreamed of sea monsters and itinerant harpists and all the glories of Gwynedd.

• BIBLIOGRAPHY •

Gwynedd

Clive Betts, *Cardiff and the Eisteddfod* (Dafydd Cyf Ltd, 1978)

Emrys Hughes and Aled Eames, *Porthmadog Ships* (Gwynedd Archives, 1975)

Ivor Wynne Jones, *Llandudno, Queen of Welsh Resorts* (John Jones, Cardiff, 1975)

Ivor Wynne Jones, *Llechwedd Slate Caverns* (Llechwedd Slate Quarry, 1980)

John Rowlands, *Copper Mountain* (Anglesey Antiquarian Society, 1966)

Ian Skidmore, *Anglesey and Lleyn Shipwrecks* (Christopher Davies, 1979)

Dorothy Sylvester, *Portrait of Gwynedd* (Philimore, 1983)

Margaret Williams, *Ghosts of Conwy* (E.T.W. Dennis, 1981)

North Wales

Arthur G. Bradley, *Highways and By-ways of North Wales* (Macmillan, 1898)

S. Baring Gould, *A Book of North Wales* (Methuen, 1903)

J. Hucks, ed. Alun R. Jones and William Tydeman, *A Pedestrian Tour of North Wales* (University of Wales Press, 1979)

William T. Palmer, *Odd Corners in North Wales* (Skeffington, 1943)

Thomas Roscoe, *Wanderings and Excursions in North Wales* (Charles Tilt & Bimpton, 1838)

C.J. Williams, *Metal Mines of North Wales* (Charter Press, 1980)

Wales

George Borrow's Wild Wales (John Murray, 1865)

Askew Roberts, *Gossiping Guide to Wales* (Hodder & Stoughton, 1885)

Gwyn A. Williams, *When was Wales* (Pelican, 1985)

Kings Works in Wales (HMSO, 1974)

Biography

S. Baring Gould and John Fisher, *Lives of the British Saints* (Hon. Society of Cymrodorion, 1907)

L.T.C. Rolt, *Thomas Telford* (Longmans, 1958)

Ian Skidmore, *Owain Glyndwr* (Christopher Davies, 1978)

Gwyn A. Williams, *Madoc, the Making of a Myth* (Eyre Methuen, 1978)

Sir John Wynne, *History of the Gwydir Family* (University of Wales Press, 1927)

General

Hilaire *The Historical Works of Giraldus Cambrensis* (George Bell & Sons, 1905)

The Chronicle of Jean Creton (British Museum mss)

Ed. I.H. Ellis, *Original Letters Illustrative of English History*, Volume I (1827)

Iolo MSS (National Library of Wales, Aberystwyth)

Barbara Tuchman, *A Distant Mirror* (Penguin, 1979)

M. Ellis Williams, *Packet to Ireland* (Gwynedd Archives, Caernarfon, 1984)

George and Bernard Winchcombe, *Shakespeare's Ghost Writer(s)* (Thab, 1982)

• INDEX •